Erin Kaipainen
May '08.

Students as Colleagues

EXPANDING THE CIRCLE OF SERVICE-LEARNING LEADERSHIP

Students as Colleagues

Edited by:

Edward Zlotkowski

Nicholas V. Longo

James R. Williams

Campus Compact

Contents

Foreword ix

Acknowledgments xi

About the Authors xiii

Introduction 1

part one
Identifying Student Leaders   13

Community Service Scholarships at DePaul: Meeting Students
Where They Are, *Laurie Worrall, Devin Novgorodoff,
and Joseph Stehlin* 15

Bentley's Service-Learning Scholarship Program: Finding and
Nurturing Student Scholars, *Franklyn P. Salimbene and
Stephen R. Kennedy* 25

Indiana University-Purdue University Indianapolis: Supporting
Student Involvement through Service-based Scholarships,
*Julie A. Hatcher, Robert G. Bringle, Lorrie A. Brown, and
David A. Fleischhacker* 35

Community Service-Learning at the University of San Diego:
Recruiting and Building a Team, *Elaine Elliott and Lisa Garcia* 49

More from Antioch College & Defiance College on
Identifying Student Leaders 61

part two

Training Students 65

(sl)^2 at CSUMB: Training Students for Leadership in Service-Learning,
*Tania D. Mitchell, Karly Edwards, M. Crystal Macias-Diaz, and
Olivia Weatherbee* 67

Advancing Engagement at NC State: Reflection Leader
Training and Support, *Patti Clayton and Julie McClure* 77

NCCU's Student Training Model: Preparing Student Leaders for Success,
Rosa S. Anderson, Emmanuel O. Oritsejafor, and James. S. Guseh 89

Service-Learning Advocates at Azusa Pacific: Students Training Students,
Judy Hutchinson, Kristin Gurrola, Debra Fetterly, and Vanessa Fontes 101

More from Mars Hill College, the University of Michigan–Ann Arbor, &
Saint Anselm College on Training Students 111

part three

Students as Staff 119

Providence College: The Community Assistant Model,
Angela E. Kelly and Hugh F. Lena 121

Marquette University: The Student Coordinator Model,
Bobbi Timberlake and Shelley Frank 135

Miami Dade College: The Student Ambassador Model,
*Katia Archer, Yleinia Galeano, Ossie Hanauer, Nicolle Hickey,
Michelle Lasanta, and Josh Young* 147

More from Boise State University on Students as Staff 157

part four

Student-Faculty Partnerships 159

The APPLES Program at UNC: Merging Students, Faculty,
Community, and University, *Dac Cannon, Emily Cupito, Janaka Lagoo,
Kasey Q. Maggard, Leslie Parkins, and Beth Payne* 161

Allegheny's Service-Learning Challenge: Capitalizing on Student and
Faculty Strengths, *Andy Bennett, Michelle Ferry, Karen Hoerst,
Rebecca Milbert, and David Roncolato* 171

Student Leadership Models at Portland State: Partnering with Faculty
and Community, *Dilafruz Williams, Kevin Kecskes, Christopher Carey,
Adam Smith, Candyce Reynolds, and Ronnie Craddock* 181

Penn's West Philadelphia Partnerships: Developing Students as Catalysts
and Colleagues, *Jennifer Bunn, Mei Elansary, and Cory Bowman* 193

More from the University of Richmond & the Jane Addams School
of Democracy on Student-Faculty Partnerships 207

part five

Students as Academic Entrepreneurs   211

Students as Engaged Partners at Duke: A Continuum of
Engagement, *Betsy Alden and Julie Norman* 213

Grassroots Community Development at UMass Amherst:
The Professorless Classroom, *Danyel Addes and Arthur Keene* 227

The University of Utah's SPACE Program: Service-Politics and
Civic Engagement, *William Chatwin, Shannon Gillespie,
Anne Looser, and Marshall Welch* 241

Social Action at Miami University: Lessons from Building
Service-Learning, *Ross Meyer* 255

More from Bates College, Macalester College, Georgetown University, and
Princeton University on Students as Academic Entrepreneurs 265

Conclusion: Beyond Tactical Service-Learning 273

Foreword

OR A SOCIETY THAT OFTEN SEEMS DETERMINED to label our newest citizens as Generation X, Y, "millenials," or "apathetic, self-centered, Net-savvy consumers," *Students as Colleagues* may come as a bit of a surprise. Here we see today's students accepting responsibility for making connections between classrooms and communities, challenging their own status as privileged members of society, and questioning the role and structure of higher education as an institution preparing youth for citizenship in a democracy.

The title, appropriately suggesting that students can be colleagues, proposes that today's students have questions that need answering, a desire for community, a willingness to learn, and a need for respect. As this book illustrates, with appropriate mentoring and structure there is little they cannot do—and the more they do, the more they come to expect of themselves.

As an educator, I find the insights offered in these chapters (most of which were co-authored by a student and a faculty or staff member) about the challenges of reconceptualizing the teaching-learning paradigm to be truly engaging. When Campus Compact Swearer Student Humanitarian Award winner Ross Meyer of Miami University writes, "Volunteer work is important and unfortunately necessary, but its impact is limited in the long term if not coordinated with approaches that address the underlying structures of oppression and inequality," he might as easily have been critiquing an educational process that authors Danyel Addes and Arthur Keene of the University of Massachusetts Amherst portray as "a 'banking' model of education that views teachers as experts depositing information into students."

Such critiques are not the naïve fantasies of anti-authority youth. Rather, they are the informed feelings of students who have worked to institute processes that challenge the academy to remake education so that it fosters what Meyer terms "collaboration, consciousness, and rigor." This book points to an approach to education in which students have responsibilities that far exceed their current charge of jumping through proscribed hoops. *Students as Colleagues* asks that students be viewed with the assets they bring to the table and participate as equals within communities of collegial learners.

RICHARD E. CONE
Executive Director (retired)
Joint Educational Program (JEP)
University of Southern California

Acknowledgments

THE EDITORS WISH TO EXTEND THEIR SINCERE THANKS to Tobi Walker and The Pew Charitable Trusts for making this text possible; to Karen Partridge, Communications and Publications Manager at Campus Compact, who in many ways has served as a fourth co-editor in preparing this manuscript for publication; to Stephen Smith, who preceded James Williams as Student Engaged Scholar on this project; to Abby Kiesa, Dick Cone, and Rick Battistoni, who each have made student leadership a national priority; to Jane Gebhart and Philissa Cramer, who were critically important editorial resources; to John Saltmarsh of the New England Resource Center for Higher Education, who has a keen sense of student politics; to Raise Your Voice State Coordinators Chris Bolin, Piyali Dalal, Jennifer Geren, Chris Hempfling, Sarah Seames, Stephanie Soule, and Allison Treppa; to the Campus Compact National Student Fellows, Tara Germond, Ellen Love, Liz Moran, Sherita Moses, Stephanie Raill; and to Elizabeth Hollander, Campus Compact's Executive Director, whose leadership and support of this project has served as a foundation for our efforts.

About the Authors

Volume Editors

EDWARD ZLOTKOWSKI is a professor of English at Bentley College and Senior Faculty Fellow at Campus Compact. From 1995 to 2004, he served as general editor of the American Association for Higher Education's 20-volume series on service-learning in the academic disciplines. He has designed and facilitated professional development opportunities in service-learning for provosts and deans as well as a series of summer institutes for engaged academic departments. He has written and spoken extensively on a range of service-learning topics, and regularly uses service-learning in his own teaching. He is editor of *Service-Learning and the First-Year Experience: Preparing Students for Personal Success and Civic Responsibility* (National Resource Center for the First-Year Experience and Students in Transition, 2002) and lead author of *The Community's College: Indicators of Engagement at Two-Year Institutions* (Campus Compact, 2004) and *One with the Community: Indicators of Engagement at Minority-Serving Institutions* (Campus Compact, 2005).

NICHOLAS V. LONGO is a program officer at the Kettering Foundation working on issues of civic education, public scholarship in higher education, and international civil society. He received his Ph.D. in education from the University of Minnesota, where he studied the role of community in civic education. Prior to joining the Kettering Foundation, he directed Campus Compact's Raise Your Voice initiative, a multiyear campaign to increase college student participation in public life that involved hundreds of thousands of students at institutions across the nation. Longo has been a special lecturer at Providence College teaching in the public service and global studies programs and is the lead author of *Colleges with a Conscience: 81 Great Schools with Outstanding*

Community Involvement (The Princeton Review, 2005). He is currently working on a research project on political participation among college students.

JAMES R. WILLIAMS is a senior at Princeton University, majoring in the Woodrow Wilson School of Public and International Affairs. A 2005 Harry S. Truman Scholar, he is also an Engaged Student Scholar with Campus Compact and serves on the Compact's student advisory board. At Princeton, Williams chairs the Student Volunteers Council, the largest student organization on campus, with more than 700 active volunteers. He also serves on the Community-Based Learning Initiative, student government, and Religious Life Council, an interfaith group he helps lead. In 2006 he received Princeton's highest undergraduate distinction, the Pyne Honor Prize for scholarship, character, and leadership. Previously Williams served as student member of the Portland (Ore.) School Board and later founded Students for Oregon's Schools, an organization dedicated to adequate and stable public school funding.

Contributors

DANYEL ADDES graduated from the University of Massachusetts Amherst in 2004 with a degree in social thought and political economy. While at UMass she was a member of the UACT curriculum committee and an alternative break co-leader. She received the UMass Chancellor's Award for Distinguished Student Community Service in 2004. She has completed a postgraduate internship in marine ecology and is currently applying to graduate programs in environmental anthropology and marine ecology.

BETSY ALDEN is service-learning coordinator at Duke University's Kenan Institute for Ethics. A United Methodist clergywoman, she created and disseminated a service-learning model for campus ministries, The Praxis Project. In 2006, Alden received the inaugural Robert L. Sigmon Award for service-learning from North Carolina Campus Compact. She holds an M.A. from Indiana University and M.Div. and D.Min. degrees from Perkins School of Theology at Southern Methodist University.

ROSA S. ANDERSON is director of the Academic Community Service Learning Program at North Carolina Central University. She has a master's in human sciences and the family and a master's in career counseling. In addition to her love for people and their spiritual development, Anderson is passionate about women's and children's issues. Under her leadership, with a supportive staff, NCCU designed and implemented the student ambassador model, the research service-learning model, and many other engaged models and programs.

KATIA ARCHER earned an associate degree in business administration with high honors from Miami Dade College. As student coordinator in the Center for Community

Involvement, she served 2,000 students and 40 faculty members. She immigrated to the United States from Haiti after studying in the Dominican Republic. She is pursuing her bachelor's degree in accounting at Florida International University, where she is treasurer of Beta Alpha Psi Accounting Honor Society.

ANDY BENNETT graduated from Allegheny College in 2004 with a major in environmental studies and a minor in values, ethics, and social action (VESA). In addition to being an AmeriCorps Bonner Leader and a co-coordinator in the Service-Learning Challenge, he was involved in myriad campus and community service programs. He is currently working on an organic farm in the Northeast.

CORY BOWMAN has been working for the University of Pennsylvania's Program for Public Service since 1991 and for Penn's Center for Community Partnerships since its inception in 1992. As Associate Director, he supports local implementation and national adaptation efforts of academically based community service courses and university-assisted community school programs.

ROBERT G. BRINGLE is Chancellor's Professor of Psychology and Philanthropic Studies and director of the Center for Service and Learning at IUPUI. His programmatic and research interests include developing ways to implement and institutionalize service-learning and civic engagement. His Ph.D. is from the University of Massachusetts.

LORRIE A. BROWN is coordinator of community service, Center for Service and Learning, at IUPUI, in a position shared between Academic Affairs and Student Affairs. She has served as a community service director fellow for Indiana Campus Compact. She has an M.A. in student personnel from Bowling Green State University.

JENNIFER BUNN is a senior at the University of Pennsylvania in the College of Arts & Sciences, where she is majoring in political science, and in the Wharton School, where she is concentrating in finance/business and public policy. In fall 2005, she co-facilitated an academically based community service honors seminar on the history of African-American education in Philadelphia.

DAC CANNON is a student at the University of North Carolina at Chapel Hill. Originally from Raleigh, Cannon became involved with the APPLES Service-Learning Program during his first year at UNC. He is also involved in his fraternity and spent the summer of 2005 teaching English to children in Ecuador.

CHRISTOPHER CAREY is a former deputy district attorney and assistant professor at Portland State University. His pedagogy and research focus on the "lived experience," engaging students in service-learning with an ethnographic perspective. He is currently engaged in action-based research regarding human trafficking in South Asia and serves as Executive Director of The Daywalka Foundation, an international non-governmental organization dedicated to combating human trafficking around the globe.

WILLIAM CHATWIN is a self-designed major in the bachelor's of university studies program at the University of Utah. He has benefited from the examples of five siblings and gives special recognition to his parents for providing for him at home while he pursues his education.

PATTI CLAYTON is coordinator of the Service-Learning Program at North Carolina State University. She co-developed the Service-Learning Program's reflection model, assessment strategy, student leadership roles, and faculty development processes. Clayton integrates service-learning into all of her own courses, seeking to support the development of undergraduates through reflective practice, leadership, and mentoring.

RONNIE CRADDOCK graduated from Portland State University in 2004 with a major in communications studies. He played a key student leadership role in the university's "Walk in the Woods" project. He continues to work with capstone students in service-learning, leading and teaching hike leaders in the Mt. Hood National Forest.

EMILY CUPITO is in the class of 2006 at the University of North Carolina at Chapel Hill. She has a double major in economics and public policy analysis, with a concentration in health policy. She plans to attend graduate school in public policy.

KARLY EDWARDS graduated from California State University Monterey Bay in 2005 with a degree in global studies. She served as a Service Learning Student Leader for two years in HIV education and prevention, where she trained and supervised more than 50 service-learning students. She is currently a Lead Worksite Organizer for SEIU 715 in San Jose, CA, representing public service workers.

MEI ELANSARY graduated from the University of Pennsylvania's School of Arts and Sciences in 2004 with a double major in the biological basis of behavior and environmental studies. She received Campus Compact's Howard R. Swearer Student Humanitarian Award in 2003 for her work in advancing academically based community service courses. She is currently at Oxford pursuing a degree in medical anthropology.

ELAINE ELLIOTT is director of the University of San Diego's Center for Community Service-Learning. She spent 15 years engaged in community development work in Guatemala and translated the novel of indigenous Mayan author Gaspar Pedro Gonzales: *A Mayan Life*. She began work with community service-learning in 1995 and earned an M.A. in history in 1999.

MICHELLE FERRY graduated magna cum laude from Allegheny College in 2004 with a double major in neuroscience and psychology. She played leadership roles in the Crawford County Mental Health Awareness Program, the Service-Learning Challenge, and Amnesty International, among other groups. She was an Alden Scholar her freshman and sophomore years and a Distinguished Alden Scholar her junior year.

DEBRA FETTERLY is service-learning coordinator for research and development at Azusa Pacific University. She received her M.A. and B.A. in human development from Pacific Oaks College. She has worked for many years in education and provided leadership in social programs serving children and families. Her current academic interests center on action research and effective community-based activities.

DAVID A. FLEISCHHACKER is pursuing an M.P.A. in nonprofit management and an M.A. in applied communication at IUPUI. Fleischhacker is a former community service scholar and current community service associate, recognized as the 2003 Top Male Outstanding IUPUI Student for his combination of academic achievement, campus involvement, and community service.

VANESSA FONTES is currently working as a behavioral therapist for children with autism. She served for three years as a service-learning advocate at Azusa Pacific University, where she earned a B.A. in psychology and a B.A. in Spanish. She is currently pursuing a doctorate in clinical psychology.

MICHELLE (SHELLEY) FRANK is a 2005 graduate of Marquette University, with a major in psychology and minors in Spanish and family studies. Frank worked at Marquette's Service Learning Program for more than three years, serving as a student coordinator, a staff manager, and an assistant to the program administrators. Frank will soon begin graduate work at the Chicago School of Professional Psychology.

YLEINIA GALEANO is a psychology major at Miami Dade College, working at the Center for Community Involvement, where she has helped hundreds of students and faculty members with their service-learning assignments. Born and raised in Miami, Galeano is the youngest of three children whose mother is from Nicaragua and father from Belize.

LISA GARCIA received her M.A. in college counseling and student affairs from the University of San Diego in 2005. Garcia is a graduate assistant in the Center for Community Service and Learning. She is also a member of the Center for Student Awareness Initiatives.

SHANNON GILLESPIE has served as the service-learning coordinator for the University of Utah's Lowell Bennion Community Service Center since 2002. She challenges students to look critically at community social and environmental issues, addressing those issues systemically. Gillespie received a B.A. in psychology and social work from Miami University of Ohio.

KRISTIN GURROLA is associate director for programs, Center for Academic Service-Learning and Research, at Azusa Pacific University. She earned an M.Ed. in college student affairs from Azusa Pacific University and a B.A. in sociology from Pepperdine University. She has overall responsibility for organizing service-learning projects at APU and provides training and supervision for 40 undergraduate interns a year.

JAMES S. GUSEH is a professor in the Department of Public Administration at North Carolina Central University. He has a B.S. and M.S. in economics, a joint J.D.-M.P.A. in law and public administration, and an M.A. and Ph.D. in political economy. His teaching and research interests include the political economy of development, public sector economics, public administration, volunteers, and law and public policy.

OSSIE HANAUER is the campus director for the service-learning and America Reads programs of two campuses at Miami Dade College, involving more than 1,000 students and 40 faculty members. Hanauer has more than 30 years experience in the business world. Involved extensively in community service projects, she has a B.Ed. from the University of Miami.

JULIE A. HATCHER is associate director of the Center for Service and Learning at IUPUI and adjunct faculty in philanthropic studies. Her programmatic and research interests include service-learning, the philosophical work of John Dewey and its implications for undergraduate education, and the role of higher education in a democracy. She has a M.S. from Indiana University.

NICOLLE HICKEY earned an associate in arts degree in biology at Miami Dade College in 2004 and a bachelor's degree in liberal studies at Florida International University in 2006. At Miami Dade, she was a student ambassador for the Center for Community Involvement for two years before being promoted to campus coordinator. She now supervises and manages five student ambassadors.

KAREN HOERST graduated cum laude from Allegheny College in 2004 with a major in values, ethics, and social action (VESA). She received Campus Compact's Howard R. Swearer Student Humanitarian Award in 2003. While at Allegheny, she was a participant and team leader for a wide variety of campus service projects and programs and was an AmeriCorps Bonner Leader and an Alden Scholar.

JUDY HUTCHINSON is director of the Center for Academic Service-Learning and Research at Azusa Pacific University. She received her Ph.D. in urban planning at

UCLA and has served as a consultant to cities across Southern California. Her current research focuses on the measurement and building of social capital in the immigrant inner city and on the connection between faith traditions and service-learning practice and outcomes.

KEVIN KECSKES is director for Community-University Partnerships in the Center for Academic Excellence at Portland State University. He has been involved in community-based work and K-12 and higher education for 25 years. His recent publications focus on partnership development theory, faculty and institutional development for civic engagement, and ethics and community-based research. He recently edited *Engaging Departments: Moving Faculty Culture from Private to Public, Individual to Collective Focus for the Common Good* (Anker Publishing, 2006).

ARTHUR KEENE is The Terrence Murray Professor in Commonwealth College and Professor of Anthropology at the University of Massachusetts Amherst, where he has taught since 1979. He is founder and faculty adviser to the UMass Alliance for Community Transformation (UACT), as well as co-founder and co-director of the UMass Citizen Scholars Program. He was awarded the UMass Chancellor's and the UMass President's awards for Distinguished Faculty Community Service in 2002.

ANGELA E. KELLY graduated from Providence College in 2004 with a major in public and community service studies and a minor in women's studies. In addition to her community service experiences in the United States, she has also done service in Peru and Equador.

STEPHEN R. KENNEDY is a member of the class of 2007 at Bentley College, majoring in information design and corporate communication with a concentration in public relations. As a service-learning student scholar, he co-directs the school computer lab program and the America Clicks! technology tutoring program in collaboration with the Waltham (MA) Public Schools. He also is a member of the Bentley service-learning Steering Committee.

JANAKA LAGOO is an anthropology and economics major at the University of North Carolina at Chapel Hill, with aspirations in medicine and public health. She has been involved with the APPLES Service-Learning Program since her first year and is an active participant in other public service groups on campus and in issues of international women's health.

MICHELLE LASANTA is a history major and student ambassador for the Center for Community Involvement at Miami Dade College, where she enrolled as a single mother. On graduation, Lasanta will pursue a master's in history at Florida State University.

HUGH F. LENA is vice president of academic affairs and professor of sociology at Providence College. Previously he served as associate director of the college's Feinstein Institute for Public Service, where he was a member of the research and development team that created the institute's major and minor in public and community service studies.

ANNE LOOSER, a political science major at the University of Utah, began her involvement in the Lowell Bennion Community Service Center in 200–2001 as a service-learning scholar. Looser is passionate about ending hunger and homelessness. She was a service politics and civic engagement coordinator for the 2004–2005 school year.

M. CRYSTAL MACIAS-DIAZ is a 2005 graduate of California State University Monterey Bay. As a Service Learning Student Leader, she supported three courses and 33 students at the Community Partnership for Youth. Now a community outreach education specialist for MACSA (Mexican-American Community Service Agency), she is also pursuing a master's in education with a concentration in equity and social justice at San Francisco State University.

KASEY Q. MAGGARD graduated from the University of North Carolina at Chapel Hill in 2004 with degrees in Spanish and economics. At UNC she served on the courses and reflections committees and founded Las Guapitas, an organization that mentors Latina girls. Maggard currently resides in Atlanta, where she serves as a consultant.

JULIE McCLURE served as a senior reflection leader with the Service-Learning Program at North Carolina State University. She co-developed the current vision for Reflection Leader training at NC State and served as a research associate for the program. McClure graduated in 2005 with a B.S. in biological sciences, concentrating in nutrition, and is now pursuing a master's in public health at UNC-Chapel Hill.

ROSS MEYER'S passion for social justice and activism is rooted in involvement with Cincinnati's impoverished Over-the-Rhine community. At Miami University of Ohio, he worked with the Office of Service Learning & Civic Leadership, developing the Social Action Center to encourage social and political involvement. A Truman Scholar, member of the *USA Today* All-USA Academic First Team, and winner of Campus Compact's Swearer Student Humanitarian Award, Meyer plans to pursue a master's in public policy.

REBECCA MILBERT graduated from Allegheny College with an English degree in 2006. She received the Lew Davies Award for Outstanding Community Service in 2006 for her work at Active Aging Incorporated. For three years she was the student leader of the Service-Learning Challenge. In addition, she was the student organizer for Allegheny's annual Senior Citizen Recognition Day, and was extensively involved with a range of other projects.

TANIA D. MITCHELL is assistant professor and coordinator for service-learning leadership at California State University Monterey Bay. In this role, she coordinates the Service Learning Leadership minor and the Student Leadership in Service Learning Program. She received her doctorate in social justice education from the University of Massachusetts Amherst. Her teaching and research interests emphasize connections between leadership, service, and social justice.

JULIE NORMAN graduated from Duke University in 2002 with a self-designed degree in media, education, and social activism. At Duke, she was a LEAPS coordinator and facilitator. Following graduation, Norman worked for a year in Cairo through a fellowship. She is now a graduate student in international peace and conflict resolution at American University.

DEVIN NOVGORODOFF is a sociology major and community service studies minor at DePaul University. Novgorodoff served in City Year Chicago before coming to DePaul and is currently a community service scholar through the Steans Center. He has worked with myriad community-based organizations and on political activities.

EMMANUEL O. ORITSEJAFOR is an assistant professor in the Department of Political Science at North Carolina Central University. He has a B.S., an M.A., and a Ph.D. in political science. His teaching and research interests include the political economy of Sub-Saharan Africa, international relations, comparative politics, and nonprofit management.

LESLIE PARKINS is the associate director of the APPLES Service-Learning Program at the University of North Carolina at Chapel Hill. She graduated from the University of South Florida with a communications degree and from Bowling Green State University with a degree in college student personnel. Parkins has been with the APPLES program since 2003.

BETH PAYNE is a psychology and English major at the University of North Carolina at Chapel Hill. She has been involved with the APPLES Service-Learning Program in various capacities since her sophomore year. During the 2004–2005 academic year, she served as the service-learning course chair.

CANDYCE REYNOLDS is associate professor and director of mentor programs in University Studies at Portland State University. Her work focuses on mentors and her scholarship on the development of reflective practices. She holds a Ph.D. in counseling psychology from the University of Oregon.

DAVID RONCOLATO is director of community service and service-learning at Allegheny College and a founding staff member of the Allegheny College Center for Experiential Learning (ACCEL). He has taught courses in theology, spirituality, and Allegheny's Values, Ethics and Social Action minor. He holds a Ph.D. in philosophy from Duquesne University. For two decades he was employed as a lay minister in the Roman Catholic Church. He continues to do work in adult spirituality with his spouse, the Reverend Sarah D. Roncolato.

FRANKLYN P. SALIMBENE is director of the Bentley College Service-Learning Center. Since assuming the position in 2001, he has concentrated on building programming to help faculty develop and implement academic service-learning. As a visiting professor at University College Dublin in 2005, he helped the Quinn School of Business develop a service-learning program. His most recent co-authored publication, "Service-Learning and Management Education: The Bentley Experience," appeared in *The Academy of Management Learning and Education*. He holds J.D. and L.L.M. degrees.

ADAM SMITH is a student leader in the Student Leaders for Service Program at Portland State University. He has been a peer mentor for the University Studies freshman inquiry courses and a PSU student ambassador. Smith was an invited student participant at the Campus Compact National Summit.

JOSEPH STEHLIN is a psychology major and community service studies minor at DePaul University. Stehlin is part of a four-year community service scholarship program through the Steans Center for Community-based Service Learning and has volunteered with the food distribution program at St. Vincent de Paul parish since his freshman year.

BOBBI TIMBERLAKE has been the administrator of the Service Learning Program at Marquette University since its inception in 1994. Her publications include a faculty manual on service-learning, several patient education booklets, and articles in the *Journal of School Health* and the *American Journal of Nursing*. She holds M.S. (educational psychology) and B.S.N. degrees.

OLIVIA WEATHERBEE is a social and behavioral sciences student at California State University Monterey Bay. As a Service Learning Student Leader, she has co-taught a course on Service in Multicultural Communities, coordinated recruitment and service for the Student Leadership in Service Learning Program, and coached the Independent Living Program, which serves teens in the foster care system. She was recently honored by the California Child Abuse Prevention Council for her service.

MARSHALL WELCH has been the director of the Lowell Bennion Community Service Center at the University of Utah since 2001. Prior to becoming director, he was a faculty member and chair in the Department of Special Education. Welch continues to teach service-learning courses and courses on the pedagogy of service-learning, and to conduct research on civic engagement. He earned his Ph.D. at Southern Illinois University in Carbondale.

DILAFRUZ WILLIAMS is professor and chair of Educational Policy, Foundations, and Administrative Studies in the Graduate School of Education at Portland State University. She cofounded the Environmental Middle School in the Portland Public School District and was elected to a four-year term on the Portland School Board. She is a recipient of Campus Compact's national Thomas Ehrlich Faculty Award for Service-Learning.

LAURIE WORRALL is the founding director of the Steans Center for Community-based Service Learning at DePaul, an endowed center that focuses on developing courses and community partnerships that link students and faculty to community-based projects. She has spent 10 years working in the area of university-community partnerships and holds a doctorate in higher education management from the University of Pennsylvania.

JOSH YOUNG is director of Miami Dade College's Center for Community Involvement, overseeing all service-learning and America Reads activities and many other campus-community partnerships. Young has a bachelor's degree in sociology from the University of Virginia and master's degrees in social work and public administration from Florida State University.

Introduction

B
Y ALMOST ANY MEASURE, the adoption of service-learning as a legitimate teaching and learning strategy in American higher education has been a remarkable success story. During the 1990s, we saw the founding and flourishing of the federal Corporation for National Service (now the Corporation for National and Community Service) as well as the Community Outreach Partnerships Centers (COPC) program from the U.S. Department of Housing and Urban Development. We witnessed the phenomenal growth of Campus Compact from a few hundred members to more than 950 institutions and the founding of affiliated state Compact offices in more than 30 states.

The 20 volumes in the American Association for Higher Education's series on service-learning in the academic disciplines (Zlotkowski, 1997–2004) have prepared the way for many other discipline-specific publications and initiatives. The disciplinary associations themselves have begun to take on the work of engagement, from major initiatives at the National Communication Association to more limited but significant developments in the sciences and the humanities. Associations organized by institutional type—such as the American Association of Community Colleges, the Council of Independent Colleges, the National Association of State Universities and Land-Grant Colleges, and private historically Black colleges and universities working through the United Negro College Fund—all have begun efforts to redefine higher education's role in promoting the public good.

We might conclude that the cyclical pattern of rising and falling interest in campus-based service that Arthur Levine referred to in 1994 may finally have been transcended: "The historical reality is that student volunteer movements tend to be a passing phenomenon in higher education, rising and falling on campuses roughly every 30 years" (p. 4). The author specifies "student volunteer movements"; the fact that service-learning is not a volunteer activity but instead a required or optional academic assignment goes a long way toward accounting for its extended (and still growing) appeal. Levine himself explicitly recognizes the fundamental importance of making faculty a central feature of any campus service movement that hopes to sustain itself.

Yet, despite its obvious success in enlisting faculty in service initiatives and thus moving service closer to the core work of academic institutions, service-learning still has not completely fulfilled its promise. While the data suggest that currently perhaps 10-15% of all faculty members use service-learning in their courses,[1] that number must at least double before this approach will be able to transform academic programming. Furthermore, we still have not succeeded in regularly creating the kind of continuity and critical mass of service projects that will bring about measurable, substantive community results.

In organizing and editing this book, we contend that service-learning's full academic and social impact will not be achieved until the circle of service-learning leadership is further extended to include students themselves. This contention may seem paradoxical. Wasn't it the shift from student-led to faculty-led initiatives that made possible today's level of success? Doesn't genuine institution-wide acceptance of the practice demand that service be linked to the curriculum, and doesn't the curriculum imply faculty ownership? Why focus on students when we still need to achieve deeper, broader faculty commitment?

To address these questions, it is critically important to understand that what we here propose and document does not in any way imply a retreat from service-learning as a fully legitimate academic undertaking. To deepen its academic and social impact and to further the process of its institutionalization, we suggest that we revisit the roles students can and should play in making service-learning an essential feature of American higher education. To understand why, we turn briefly to the movement's history.

The National Service Movement

In the mid-1990s, Goodwin Liu, a fellow in residence at Providence College's Feinstein Institute for Public Service, reviewed the rise of the contemporary service movement on American campuses and identified its constituent phases and emphases. In Liu's analysis (1996), the movement owed its origin to the attempt to counter a pervasive stereotype:

> Our story begins with the generational stereotype of college students in the 1980s. The "me generation" label is especially familiar to those of us who came to social consciousness during this period.... It was against this backdrop that students of a different sort made their mark. (pp. 25–26)

---

1. Campus Compact annual member surveys, http://www.compact.org/stats/2004.

According to Liu, the Campus Opportunity Outreach League (COOL) in particular succeeded in focusing "national attention on students who belied the 'me generation' stereotype, and stories of a new wave of student volunteerism began to appear in the press" (p. 26). Thus, in a very literal sense, it was students who "catalyzed the contemporary service movement in higher education" (p. 26).

For Liu, this student-led period lasted from the early 1980s to the early 1990s and began to be complemented—and ultimately supplanted—by two other developments: first, the mobilization of institutional resources to support student interest in service, and second, the spread of academic service-learning. The first of these developments gave rise to Campus Compact and the Corporation for National and Community Service. The latter development allowed for faculty participation and conferred academic legitimacy on the movement. Liu speculated that in the second half of the 1990s, additional steps such as increased attention to service-learning on the part of disciplines and departments, revised promotion and tenure criteria, and evidence of service-learning's "cognitive impact" might "put service squarely within the academic mainstream." Every one of these predictions has been realized.

We contend that service-learning's full academic and social impact will not be achieved until the circle of service-learning leadership is further extended to include students.

Why the Need for Student Leadership?

Because both institutionalization and academic legitimization have proceeded so well during the past 10 years, we suggest that the time has come to expand the circle of service-learning leadership. While much remains to be done to advance both agendas through faculty, administrators, and professional staff, to focus exclusively on these campus constituencies now might be counterproductive. Just as the service movement once needed resources that students alone could *not* supply, so the movement has now reached a point where it needs resources that students alone *can* supply. In the following pages, we explore three different rationales for rethinking and expanding the role of student leadership in academic service-learning.

Students as Enablers

The first rationale can be dubbed *instrumental*. One by-product of the rapid growth of service-learning in higher education has been that the need for "enabling mechanisms" (Walshok, 1995) to support community-based learning has in many instances out-stripped available resources. Because service-learning requires faculty members not only to reconceptualize the way in which they approach the teaching/learning process but also to factor new community-based considerations into their thinking and plan-ning, it is often seen initially as very time consuming. Even when faculty members have become comfortable with service-learning's conceptual demands, they still must find ways to deal with a host of new logistical issues.

For this reason, service-learning rarely achieves any broad currency at an institution unwilling to invest in supportive infrastructure, such as an office that facilitates cam-pus-community connections; addresses transportation needs; assists with student ori-entation, reflection, and evaluation; and provides printed or Web-based forms, guide-lines, and models. These resources can be generic, but only to a certain extent. Ultimately, every campus-community collaboration must be individual and distinct if it is to have the intended educational and social impact. Such personalization, of course, is difficult with a limited staff and a finite budget. Thus we arrive at a kind of Catch-22: the kinds of results that lead administrators to invest in service-learning are them-selves dependent on the willingness of those same administrators to invest in service-learning up front.

Students who can play a substantive role in linking academic learning with real-world problem solving represent in many ways an ideal.

Fortunately, professional staff people are not the only reliable source of practical facul-ty assistance. As many of the programs included in this book make clear, carefully selected, well-trained undergraduates can play decisive roles in making academic-com-munity collaborations powerful, successful experiences. There is no single model for how to find and train students willing and able to play such key facilitating roles, but there is an entire spectrum of faculty-student relationships, from relatively simple help with logistics to full teaching assistantships. A willingness to step outside the box (or circle) of seeing the student role in service-learning as primarily reactive and depend-ent on faculty control is essential.

However, it is not just the academic side of service-learning initiatives that skilled stu-dents can support. Often, students are more familiar with community issues and local organizations than their faculty counterparts. Such students can bring their knowledge and experience to bear to ensure that service-learning projects help advance the interests of community partners. By serving as site supervisors, students can focus and coordinate the contributions of different courses and various disciplines to advance a single project or organization. In this way, students can function as the community's eyes and ears on campus while serving as the campus's representative at a particular community site.

Finally, the willingness and ability of undergraduates to assume substantive service-learning responsibilities both in the classroom and in the community represent an excellent opportunity to align student affairs and faculty affairs. For some time, top administrators at many institutions have recognized that treating student academic work and general student development as largely discrete areas is neither economical nor effective. Many schools have already addressed this problem by administratively linking student and faculty affairs—placing the former under a provost or academic dean, decentralizing student development programs, and creating positions that effectively bridge the two divisions.

Service-learning is tailor-made to support such an organizational rationalization. Because service-learning projects promote the development of the "whole person"— requiring students to link academic, interpersonal, and affective skills to achieve multidimensional results—they relate as much to the concerns of student affairs professionals as they do to those of faculty. Students who can play a substantive role in linking academic learning with real-world problem solving represent in many ways an ideal. What they have learned in non-curricular programs like "Emerging Leaders" is as important as what they have learned in and through their academic assignments.

The Promise of Democratic Participation

Once we begin to explore the importance of holistic student development, we transcend an essentially instrumental rationale for student service-learning leadership. Our second rationale addresses student empowerment directly.

Students have been demanding that higher education take seriously its public mission to support student civic engagement and not simply focus on professional skills and workforce preparation. In 2003, student leaders from colleges and universities across Oklahoma issued a public statement to the governor, state legislators, college and university presidents, and other civic leaders throughout the state:

> We declare that it is our responsibility to become an engaged generation with the support of our political leaders, education institutions, and society.... The mission of our state higher education institutions should be to educate future citizens about their civic as well as professional duties. We urge our institutions to prioritize and implement civic education in the classroom, in research, and in service to the community. (*Oklahoma Students' Civic Resolution*, 2003, p. 2)

The Oklahoma resolution was developed in the context of Campus Compact's efforts to understand better the civic experiences of college students by listening directly to their concerns and giving them the tools and resources to tackle public issues on their campuses and in their communities. This generation of college students cares deeply about community issues and sees service-learning as an important avenue for civic participation. Civic engagement requires not only that students implement faculty and community partner agendas, but also that they have a substantive opportunity to shape those agendas. Students must be partners in service-learning in order for it to realize its full civic and academic potential.

Achieving such creative power supplied the rationale for two related civic initiatives instituted by Campus Compact: the drafting of *The New Student Politics: The Wingspread Statement on Student Civic Engagement* (Long, 2002) and the founding of the "Raise Your Voice" campaign. Both efforts began with a March 2001 conversation among 33 student leaders from around the country gathered at the Wingspread conference center in Racine, Wisconsin.

This meeting, which lasted several days, laid the foundation for *The New Student Politics,* an important, student-written publication in which students discuss their perspectives on democracy and the role of student voice in higher education, arguing that service-learning is an essential mechanism for democratic participation. Sarah Long, the lead student author, sums up what service-learning educators have long recognized—namely, that the nature of one's education changes "immeasurably through a community-based perspective" (p. 7). The Wingspread students conclude that students see service-learning "as a primary vehicle for connecting service and broader social and political dimensions" (p. 9).

The Wingspread document includes several recommendations for making service-learning more substantive. Students do not want one-time programs; rather, they prefer the opportunity to build and maintain strong relationships with the community through ongoing service-learning experiences. Students want their professors to commit to working with the community and to "know the community and community-based organizations well enough to facilitate deep reflection in the course material" (p. 7). They also propose that professors co-teach courses, when appropriate, with community partners.

Finally, a major theme of the Wingspread gathering was creating platforms for student voice. Students at Wingspread were critically aware that they are often treated like "fine china" brought out to impress trustees and honored guests. Yet they also assert that to be more effective, empowered citizens, they need to better understand power on campus, admitting that it takes time to learn how to navigate institutions of higher education:

Many of us who try to navigate the bureaucracy often lack access to the institutional system and find progress to be painstakingly slow and difficult. We often don't understand the inner workings of our institution until we are well into our college careers; by then it is often too late to put this knowledge to work in attempting to make changes on campus. (pp. 11–12)

To address this problem, students suggest that colleges and universities build engaged campuses in which service-learning can play an important role. They also note that their institutions "can encourage engagement by providing space, resources, recognition, information, transportation, and other forms of support" (p. 9). Among their many recommendations is the development of community service scholarships, which are featured in the first section of this book.

In the fall of 2002, using the results of the Wingspread gathering as a starting point, Campus Compact launched Raise Your Voice, a national campaign funded by The Pew Charitable Trusts to increase college student participation in public life. During the following three years, students from more than 400 college and university campuses made civic contributions by participating in statewide student leadership teams, mapping opportunities for civic engagement on their campuses, leading public dialogues, writing public issue statements, and meeting with elected officials.

All this activity has led to many insights into practices that promote student voice on campus and the structures necessary to connect service-learning with substantive civic engagement. Two central lessons have guided the development of this book:

- Creating safe, respectful, and democratic spaces allows students to develop, use, and own their voices on a host of public issues, including reforming higher education.

- Training, mentoring, and supporting students in their civic development using proven interventions (peer-to-peer persuasion, hubs for civic engagement on campus, collaboration among different civic engagement approaches, and connection with the curriculum) lead to deep levels of involvement that go beyond simplistic notions of volunteerism and allow young people to become engaged and responsible civic actors.

Clearly one of the most difficult hurdles for students in becoming both academically and civically empowered is the more or less exclusive control that faculty members have over the curriculum. Hence, much student activism on campus has been co-curricular, and in this space, students can develop their leadership capacities. But the curriculum remains decisive in determining what ultimately "counts" on campus: regardless of the quality of student co-curricular work, degrees are awarded on the basis of credit-bearing academic units. Thus, it is notable that, in the chapters that follow, we find numerous instances in which students exercising leadership as part of the curriculum is not only possible but is institutionally supported and encouraged. Contributing authors describe well-designed programs that allow students, faculty, staff, administrators, and community partners to work together as genuine colleagues. By doing so, they both inspire and encourage us to rethink the role of students in higher education.

A New Generation

Our third rationale addresses the potential of the current generation of students and identifies why *now* is the time to expand the circle of service-learning leadership. Each generation of students is unique, reflecting the paradigms and culture of its age and defined by intergenerational relationships with parents and grandparents. Each generation is also shaped by events. This generation has come to maturity at the same time as the national service-learning movement.

While the tone and nature of campus activism has changed since their parents' time, today's students roam freely with an awareness of their parents' era of student activism and empowerment. Today's students still possess a desire, drive, and passion for meaningful participation in community concerns. According to researchers at UCLA's Higher Education Research Institute (HERI, 2005),

> Two out of three entering freshmen (66.3%) believe it is essential or very important to help others who are in difficulty, the highest this figure has been in the past 25 years. Further, an all-time high of 83.2% volunteered at least occasionally during their high school senior year. The survey also reported a record high of 67.3% who planned to continue volunteering in college. Students are not interested only in helping others through service; they believe it is important to take action on different levels. One in four (25.6%) feels it is important to participate in community action programs, the highest figure since 1996; 33.9% regard becoming a community leader as important; and 41.3% believe it is important to influence social values.

In some respects these figures are not surprising. Many of today's college students have been exposed to service-learning and student engagement since they were quite young. Nationwide, service-learning efforts are cropping up in high schools and middle schools, being integrated into graduation requirements, senior projects, coursework, and internships, and becoming part of major school-reform efforts (Furco, 2002). In many instances, students play a role in developing as well as participating in these programs. In the public schools in Portland, Oregon, for example, students have won passage of policies that mandate their participation in budget and curriculum development, in hiring, and in other academic decisions. Thus, many students are arriving on college campuses expecting to play a leadership role in shaping their own learning. Their rich skills, experiences, perspectives, and energy are the kinds of strengths behind the successful examples described in this book.

One of the volume's co-editors, James Williams, a student at Princeton University, had middle and high school experiences rich in service-learning as an integral part of the curriculum. In addition, he pushed for greater student voice and involvement in his school's decision-making processes. Hence, when he arrived at Princeton, he was immediately drawn to service and leadership opportunities on campus. As a freshman, he became part of the executive board of the Student Volunteers Council, a community service clearinghouse with 700 volunteers active in 47 weekly projects. Later that same year, he was elected to the university's Policy and Governance Council, joining the Priorities Committee, which sets Princeton's operating budget. He also joined the student government, various service committees, and the Community-Based Learning Initiative (CBLI), Princeton's service-learning office.

Through his position on the advisory board of CBLI and as board chairman of the Student Volunteers Council, Williams played a leadership role in helping students expand, integrate, and enrich academic service-learning opportunities. Largely because of student demand, particularly with regard to the immensely popular service-learning writing seminars, Princeton has seen growing interest in and sustained involvement with service-learning projects. The deliberation, participation, and involvement of students is pushing the institution to change.

Although many colleges and universities have been slow to change and reluctant to grant students meaningful participation in shaping the curriculum, there is one area in which students have already been able to demonstrate academic leadership, responding to faculty guidance rather than formal prescriptions: original community-based student research. At Princeton and many other institutions, senior theses, term projects, and major reports allow students to engage in meaningful, original research that makes a public contribution and helps to create new community assets. The vast variety, creativity, and intellectual depth of these efforts testify to the power of involving students more deeply in the fabric of the academy: in its scholarship and research. Rather than posing a threat to faculty, students engaged in research can connect the community, the faculty, and the university in a powerful, productive alliance. The final section of our book includes some examples of this kind of work.

As we have already noted, it is not just through their scholarship that students can contribute to a more creative linking of the academy and the community. In the chapters that follow, we find students serving as staff members and site coordinators, handling those logistical and practical responsibilities that facilitate the implementation of quality service-learning projects. We find students training students, empowering their peers to succeed both in the classroom and in the community. We also find students working closely with faculty to design, implement, and assess course-based community work—and even playing a primary role in defining course-based work. All these roles constitute ways students can be viewed and treated as colleagues, respected and valued for their unique and vital contributions to the service-learning movement.

rather than posing a threat to faculty, students engaged in research can connect the community, the faculty, and the university in a powerful, productive alliance.

In summary, the current generation of students—practicing their own service politics, engaging in important issues, embedded in their communities—represents an ideal group with which faculty, staff, and administrators can renew both service-learning and the structures of the academy. If, as John Dewey (1899) has said, "Democracy has to be born anew every generation, and education is its midwife," the time could not be more opportune. Our country needs to recommit to its democratic ideals, and the academy needs to redefine and clarify its special contribution to our democracy. We hope that this book, by bringing together some of the finest examples of how student leadership is helping to create new and renewed academy-community alliances, may itself contribute to the renewal of both the academy and our democracy. By serving as a springboard for further action, we hope it will add to and deepen what it means to educate students for citizenship.

About This Book

We have organized *Students as Colleagues* into five broad, clearly overlapping sections. Each section focuses on practices or programs that help expand the circle of leadership in service-learning. To find exemplary models, we surveyed more than 100 colleges and universities to review their approaches to service-learning student leadership. We uncovered more models than we could accommodate. For this reason, we chose to include in each section several short vignettes that suggest additional approaches to student empowerment. Some exemplary programs are not included here for reasons that have no bearing on their quality. To showcase a wide range of approaches from a diverse group of institutions, we selected programs that had relatively little overlap with each other. Thus we sometimes had to pass over a school solely because we had already identified a similar model.

Part One of this volume looks at student recruitment, focusing especially on scholarship programs that bring to campus students who have already distinguished themselves as leaders. Part Two presents models for training students to facilitate academy-community collaborations. Each of the remaining three sections centers on a particular type of student role. Part Three offers examples of students in key administrative or support positions. Part Four turns to students who partner with faculty to design and implement new community-based curricular units. Part Five surveys a range of entrepreneurial initiatives in which students create academy-community bridges: engaged research, student-led curricular initiatives, and political or policy action. We conclude by identifying some of the more important lessons we have learned from all of the examples presented.

References

Dewey, J. (1899). *The school and society.* Chicago: University of Chicago Press.

Furco, A. (2002). Is service-learning really better than community service? A study of high school service. In A. Furco & S. H. Billig (Eds.), *Advances in service-learning research: Vol.1. Service-learning: The essence of the pedagogy* (pp. 23–50). Greenwich, CT: Information Age Publishers.

Higher Education Research Institute. (2005). *The American Freshman: National norms for fall 2005.* Los Angeles: University of California.

Levine, A. (1994, July/August). Service on campus. *Change, 26,* 4–5.

Liu, G. (1996). Origins, evolution, and progress: Reflections on a movement. *Metropolitan Universities: An International Forum, 7*(1), 25–38.

Long, S.E. (2002). *The new student politics: The wingspread statement on student civic engagement.* Providence, RI: Campus Compact.

Oklahoma Students' Civic Resolution (2003). Retrieved November 30, 2005, from http://www.actionforchange.org/getinformed/student_ink/ student_ink-OK.html.

Walshok, M. (1995). *Knowledge without boundaries: What America's research universities can do for the economy, the workplace, and the community.* San Francisco: Jossey-Bass.

Zlotkowski, E. (Series ed.). (1997–2004). *Service-learning in the disciplines* (a series of 20 monographs). Washington, DC: American Association for Higher Education.

Identifying Student Leaders

ONE OF THE MOST EXCITING and promising developments in service-learning in recent years has to do with student recruitment. Since the early 1990s, more and more institutions have been using scholarship funds to bring to campus students who have already demonstrated leadership in community service. Once on campus, these students become key components of the school's service-learning infrastructure. Given the logic of such a move, it is surprising that such scholarships are not ubiquitous. After all, colleges and universities have had no trouble justifying athletic scholarships, even in minor sports.

Community service has long been a feature of the college application process, especially over the past two decades, and many colleges profess to pay special attention to service-related accomplishments. However, in most cases, such accomplishments have played a secondary role in the admissions process—insufficiently important to determine its outcome, let alone to serve as justification for significant financial aid. Furthermore, even when service has been central to an award, that award has rarely been designed to deepen and develop skills and strengths related to service. More often, students are simply required to complete a certain number of service hours over a certain period of time.

In the first three chapters in this section, we see a different kind of scenario unfold. At DePaul University in Chicago, service scholarships are the gateway to a wide variety of developmental service-related activities. In 2001, DePaul launched the community service scholars program through its newly endowed Steans Center for Community-based Service Learning. Offering a variety of service-based scholarships, the program helps students work their way up a "ladder" of social and civic engagement, designed to reflect growth in the institution's core commitment to social justice and community outreach. Service leadership and community activism are goals, not byproducts of the scholarship process.

While the scholarships offered through the Steans Center are relatively new, the Bentley Service-Learning Center (BSLC) at Bentley College has administered a service scholarship program for more than 10 years. Students in the program not only receive training and participate in a variety of service-related activities, but also assume major responsibility for the functioning of the BSLC, overseeing projects and programs in many different areas. One of the scholarship's requirements is that each recipient either launch a new program or significantly strengthen an existing one. Since Bentley is a business-oriented institution, such an entrepreneurial emphasis is very much in keeping with its mission.

Chapter three shows what can be done at a very different type of institution. While DePaul and Bentley are private institutions, Indiana University-Purdue University Indianapolis (IUPUI) is public and therefore is able to raise scholarship money through a statewide license-plate program. In other respects, however, the IUPUI program resembles the other two. Most notably, like the others, it deliberately seeks to cultivate in its service scholars qualities that reflect the school's mission. Especially interesting in IUPUI's approach to student service development is its utilization of three different service tracks—direct service, project programming, and social advocacy. Each is meant to appeal to a different kind of student service orientation.

The last chapter in this section describes a process for identifying and developing student service leaders that does not depend on scholarships. Using work-study funds and academic credit to generate and recognize student engagement, the University of San Diego's Center for Community Service-Learning creates a leadership corps consisting of two kinds of positions: course-specific facilitators and community-based site coordinators. San Diego's program grew directly out of research that documented the impact of service on student leadership development. Hence, this chapter includes many powerful student voices.

Part One concludes with vignettes from Antioch College and Defiance College that provide additional insight into the student recruitment process.

Meeting Students Where They Are

Laurie Worrall, Devin Novgorodoff,
and Joseph Stehlin

D E PAUL UNIVERSITY IS AN URBAN, Catholic institution enrolling nearly 24,000 undergraduate and graduate students largely from Chicago and the surrounding suburbs. DePaul defines itself as a teaching institution that values scholarship, especially as it applies to the resolution of critical societal problems, and the use of public service to apply the talents and expertise of faculty, students, and staff to "contribute to the social, economic, cultural, and ethical quality of life in the metropolitan area and beyond." The university derives its name and mission from St. Vincent de Paul, the founder of a religious community—the Congregation of the Mission—whose members, Vincentians, established DePaul. In 1991, DePaul's Board of Trustees approved the following mission statement, which captures the role that community service plays at the school:

> As an urban university, DePaul is deeply involved in the life of a community which is rapidly becoming global, and is interconnected with it. DePaul both draws from the cultural and professional riches of this community and responds to its needs through educational and public service programs, by providing leadership in various professions, the performing arts, and civic endeavors and in assisting the community in finding solutions to its problems.

DePaul has a deep institutional commitment to support students both financially and programmatically and demonstrates that commitment by making available a variety of scholarship and funding programs.

Community Service Scholarships at the Steans Center

DePaul launched its Community Service Scholars program in 2001, shortly after its service-learning program became an endowed center. The scholarship programs at the Steans Center for Community-based Service Learning represent the school's first attempt to integrate community service scholarships into students' curricular and co-curricular experiences. The Steans Center oversees two scholarship programs and an endowed community internship program:

- The DePaul Community Service Scholarship (DCSS) program was established in 2001 as a joint venture between Enrollment Management—traditional enroll-ment services, the university's communications offices, and alumni relations—and the Steans Center.

- The Joan and Richard Meister Community Service Scholarship program solicits nominations annually from DePaul faculty and staff of students with exemplary commitment to community engagement. Scholarships—$1,000 each—are avail-able for traditional and nontraditional undergraduate and graduate students in community-oriented academic programs.

- The McCormick-Tribune Community Internship program funds internships with community organizations that students select. Students can apply to the program or faculty can nominate students to receive funding. Priority is given to applicants who have established a relationship with a community organization and intend to complete a project for which the organization has a need. Internship awards range from $1,200 to $3,600 each.

For DCSS, Enrollment Management envisioned a mission-related scholarship program that would provide institutional financial aid to bright incoming freshmen who did not qualify for academic merit aid, but who came from families with household incomes too high to qualify for significant financial need-based aid. The Steans Center saw an opportunity to help develop a student constituency for its interdisciplinary community service studies program and to provide co-curricular programming that would expand a culture of service and activism among DePaul students.

DCSS offers a $5,000 scholarship to incoming first-year students who have demon-strated a commitment to community service that they intend to maintain. The mission of the program is to reward students who have an exceptional record of community service, provide mentoring during the four years of the scholarship, connect commu-nity service with academic programs through a minor in community service studies, and involve students in service within the DePaul and Chicago communities. The scholarship is renewable for up to four years or for a total of up to $20,000 per student. When the program is fully rolled out, DePaul anticipates funding up to $500,000 for these scholarships annually. Applicants must be admitted to a DePaul University undergraduate program, demonstrate a significant commitment to community serv-ice, declare a community service studies minor, and complete 30 hours of community service per academic quarter for a total of 12 quarters. The Steans Center administers the program and oversees the process that awards 20 to 25 scholarships per year.

In its short history, DCSS has attracted committed undergraduate students who have supported legislation to protect immigrant rights, become involved in the anti-war movement, and conducted voter registration drives. Some have made a long-term commitment to one organization; some are still seeking the one organization or cause that inspires them. Students explore a variety of community service opportunities because each challenges them to wrestle with situations and issues about which they often have preconceived notions.

Community service scholars sit on a student advisory board, recently renamed the DePaul Service and Justice Coalition. While the impetus for the organization came from staff of the Steans Center and University Ministry, the students have been encouraged to take leadership roles. The coalition is responsible for organizing fall and spring summits that bring together students from service and activist groups across the university to learn about service, organizing, and activist activities and to celebrate end-of-the-year achievements.

DePaul also offers a variety of other funding sources to support community service (see the Sidebar on p. 18).

The Ladder of Social and Civic Engagement

DePaul community service scholars are integrated into DePaul's "ladder of social and civic engagement," a conceptual rubric that integrates three areas of experience—curricular, co-curricular, and professional development. The purpose is to provide a framework for students, faculty, and staff to understand how all three experiential elements can work together to encourage students to become increasingly engaged in community work. The ladder consists of five rungs that are each loosely subdivided into the three areas of experience (see Figure 1).

Students can circulate through these areas on each rung or be on different rungs. For example, a student may have advanced to the third rung in curricular experience but be on the first or second rung of professional or employment experience. Although a ladder

When the program is fully rolled out, DePaul anticipates funding up to $500,000 for community service scholarships annually.

Additional Sources of Community Service Funding at DePaul

INSTITUTIONAL COMMUNITY SERVICE SCHOLARSHIPS AND FUNDS

Mayor's Leadership Scholarships are awarded to 10 incoming first-year DePaul students who are residents of Chicago, have an exceptional record of community service and civic activity, and also exhibit financial need. The annual value of this renewable award is $5,000. The scholarship offers various opportunities for internships and other involvement within the Office of the Mayor of the City of Chicago.

The Monsignor John J. Egan Hope Scholars initiative reflects Monsignor Egan's vision for community empowerment, DePaul's identity as an urban institution, and the Vincentian commitment to providing the urban community with access to higher education. The Office of Multicultural Student Affairs provides ongoing comprehensive support for the Egan Hope Scholars until they graduate from DePaul. Five $10,000 scholarships are awarded annually to incoming DePaul students who are residents of the Chicago and have an exceptional record of community service and civic activity and exhibit financial need.

The Vincentian Endowment Fund (VEF) is privately funded by members of the Congregation of the Mission. The grants support student and faculty-student initiatives that have a direct community service or social justice objective.

For example, the VEF funded a project known as "A Land Called Copapayo," in which two DePaul students worked in a Salvadoran village compiling the oral histories of people who survived the brutal civil war in El Salvador. In the past fiscal year, VEF dispersed more than $32,000 in grant funding for such projects.

UNIVERSITY MINISTRY COMMUNITY SERVICE SCHOLARSHIPS

The DePaul Community Service Association provides 33 service and justice scholarships of between $1,000 and $1,200 each to student leaders who coordinate a group of regular volunteers at a service site, lead reflection, communicate with the people at the site, and attend weekly Vincentians in Action leadership training, various retreats, and leadership gatherings. Each coordinator commits to eight hours of community service per week.

Amate House Scholarships provide $19,000 in needs-based scholarships for undergraduate students who have been accepted to live in Amate House-DePaul during the academic year. Modeled after a Catholic Worker House, Amate House is an on-campus residence hall that is organized around a commitment to community service, simple living, and spiritual growth. Each year, 10 DePaul students are Amate House volunteers.

---

implies a linear model of progression, these experiences are interconnected but discrete and staged, rather than sequential. During the past five years, some students have ascended the ladder in all areas. Most, however, are strongest in one area and developing in others. A student might start the climb in one area—organized community service, for example—and emerge at the top of the ladder through curricular experience, such as completing the community service studies minor. The design is meant to remain as flexible as possible.

FIGURE 1: **Depaul University's Undergraduate Ladder of Civic & Social Engagement**

HIGHEST RUNG

McCormick Internship or Meister Community Service Scholarship
Faculty Mentor
Co-Curricular Programming

FOURTH RUNG

Employment	Academic	Service
Steans Center: Community Coordinator Federal Work-Study Community Placement	Community Service Studies Community Internship Community Service Scholars (co-curricular, senior year)	DCSA Senior Coordinator Service Trip Coordinator Amate House Community Member Service Day Coordinator

THIRD RUNG

Employment	Academic	Service
Steans Center: Service-Learning Coordinator Federal Work-Study Community Placement	Community Service Studies Continued Community Service Scholars (co-curricular, junior year) Multiple Community-based Service-Learning Courses	DCSA Coordinator Service Trip Co-Coordinator

SECOND RUNG

Employment	Academic	Service
Steans Center Assistant Service-Learning Coordinator Federal Work-Study Community Placement	Community Service Studies Foundations Course Community Service Scholars (co-curricular, sophomore year) Multiple Community-based Service-Learning Courses	DePaul Comunity Service Association (DCSA) Co-Coordinator Service Trip Participant

ENTRY RUNG

Employment	Academic	Service
	Community Service Scholars (co-curricular, freshman year) Community-based Service-Learning Course	New Student Service Day Vincentian Service Day Service Volunteer

The Community Service Studies Minor

The community service scholars are integrated into the ladder through their service work, but the Community Service Studies minor connects the scholars to the ladder even more substantively. Community Service Studies is an interdisciplinary academic program that offers a six-course minor. The faculty director is appointed by the dean of liberal arts and sciences, who provides a two-course reduction in the director's teaching load. The Steans Center provides the director's annual stipend and funds a half-time program coordinator who provides programmatic support.

Core and Elective Courses

Three foundational service-learning courses create the spine of the program:

- Perspectives on Community Service—This course provides students with an understanding of the role of community service in U.S. history, the history of the social reform movements in the late nineteenth and early twentieth centuries, and contemporary debates about the roles of government and citizen action versus private philanthropy and individual service in the resolution of societal inequity.

- Introduction to Nonprofit Management—This course exposes students to the organizational structures responsible for social services delivery in the United States.

- Community Internship—This course provides experience in projects with community partner organizations with which the Steans Center has had long-term relationships.

In addition, three elective courses are chosen from a variety of courses in various disciplines. Several academic departments have begun developing course sequences that complement the core courses. The departmental initiatives expose students to the community relevance of the disciplines. In addition, an interdisciplinary initiative to develop community-based research courses is under way that will be linked to the Community Service Studies minor.

One section of the introductory course to the community service studies program is scheduled exclusively for first-year scholars in the winter or spring quarter. Enrollment in the course provides a unique opportunity for students to bond with their cohort of scholars. It also helps to focus the students' service work and encourages them to think critically about their own community service; the role that service plays in American society; the connections among community service, advocacy, political and community engagement; and their sense of themselves as agents of social action and change.

Stehlin believes that if it weren't for the scholarship, he would be attending a different school.

The Community Service Studies minor is based on experience and serves as a practice-based minor that enhances more theoretical major courses of study. It helps students find common ground. Some arrive on campus with a substantial history of community involvement and activism through involvement in high school or church activities. Some have had little or no exposure to community service. The three examples below are merely a sample of their experiences.

Students' Experiences

Devin Novgorodoff, one of the authors of this chapter, entered DePaul as a community service scholar in the fall of 2002. Previously he had spent one year working for City Year in Chicago's North Lawndale neighborhood and experienced firsthand the challenges that low-income, urban youth face in large, underfunded public education systems. Novgorodoff expects his university experience to help him hone his skills as an agent of change. He believes that a holistic undergraduate learning experience that combines service, academic study, and employment is the most effective way to experience civic and social engagement.

Novgorodoff sees a link between service-learning and citizen action and the role that service-learning programs can play in developing an ethos of civic engagement on campuses:

> Universities have developed service-learning programs that go beyond typical volunteerism because students become personally invested in a learning experience. Instruction alone doesn't increase social awareness and develop personal convictions. It is experience combined with instruction that broadens the capacity to learn.... The very survival of democracy relies on civically engaged citizens united in associations grounded in a common cause.

DePaul, with two major urban campuses and six suburban campuses, may be too big for some students. The community service scholarship and the Community Service Studies minor have helped Novgorodoff, who has never lived on campus, develop many connections. The scholarship program connected him to the Steans Center, where he was hired as a service-learning coordinator at the beginning of his sophomore year. It enabled him to connect to the university community, to various Chicago communities, and to nonprofit organizations that work with the center. He credits these connections with giving him the motivation to apply for DePaul's sophomore leadership class program, an initiative that provides opportunities for academic enhancement, scholarships, leadership development, and networking to exceptional undergraduates. He also applied for the Vincentian heritage tour to France, which is part of DePaul's Vincentian leadership program. The heritage tour takes students enrolled in a course about St. Vincent DePaul to Paris to understand the historical significance of DePaul's response to the social problems in the seventeenth century.

Joe Stehlin, also one of this chapter's authors, brings a different perspective to the program. Stehlin came to DePaul right from high school and first encountered the issues surrounding urban poverty through the scholarship program, even though he grew up in the Chicago area. Stehlin sees the community service scholarship as providing what most traditional students don't get—a chance to experience social problems firsthand and understand their causes and consequences. Stehlin thinks his courses have broadened his understanding of social problems, such as poverty and illiteracy:

> The courses are designed to show you how severe problems are and make you think about what causes and perpetuates the problems. The community service aspect of the scholarship allows us to do our part to help the situation. I have seen and learned things that I probably never would have experienced without the scholarship incentive.

Stehlin believes that if it weren't for the scholarship, he would be attending a different school. Beyond the financial advantages, this particular scholarship offers students the unique opportunity to develop camaraderie both among scholars entering the same year and among cohorts of different years through curricular and co-curricular experiences. Stehlin believes that the opportunity to meet people with different backgrounds but common interests during the freshman year jumpstarts the feeling of connectedness among scholars.

Kyiesha Baldwin, a scholar in the first cohort, received a McCormick Student Fellows Grant through Illinois Campus Compact to work with Erie Neighborhood House on an experiential learning project that provides Spanish-speaking students with real-world opportunities to practice newly acquired English-language skills. When scholars like Kyiesha Baldwin find the opportunity to develop their Spanish-language skills in a community organization that serves Latino clients, they also confront the challenging circumstances in which many immigrants find themselves. When they are entrepreneurial, as Baldwin is, they take advantage of funding opportunities to design programs with community partners that add value to the organization's current work.

Service-learning practitioners at DePaul believe that the ladder of social and civic engagement facilitates students' development into more engaged citizenship. The community service scholarship program has been integral to fully developing the ladder and the community service studies program, providing a group of students interested in discovering more meaningful, responsible ways to get involved with community service work. DePaul's investment in this program has led to a range of programs and initiatives that have had a major impact both on students and on the quality of community life. Ultimately, then, the success of the Steans Center for Community-based Service Learning comes from DePaul's commitment to its mission.

Finding and Nurturing Student Scholars

Franklyn P. Salimbene and Stephen R. Kennedy

B ENTLEY COLLEGE, FOUNDED IN 1917 as a school of accounting in Boston, developed into a business university with a liberal arts presence that both serves the business disciplines and stands on its own. Bentley offers several nationally ranked business degree programs that draw on the liberal arts, innovative pedagogy, and technologically accented education.

Bentley established its service-learning program in 1990. Since that time, the program has achieved prominence as a national model: *U.S. News & World Report* ranked it among the top 20 service-learning programs in the United States, and it was recently featured in *Colleges with a Conscience: 81 Great Schools with Outstanding Community Involvement* (Campus Compact and The Princeton Review, 2005).

The service-learning scholarship program is key to the success of service-learning at Bentley. Since its inception in 1992, the scholarship program has served many functions, but three stand out as central. First, the program has attracted students who have demonstrated a consistent, mature commitment to service and civic engagement. Second, it has nurtured that commitment by providing scholarship students with leadership roles within the Bentley Service-Learning Center (BSLC). Third, it has promoted BSLC's mission on campus by giving student voice to the goals and objectives of service-learning.

The Program's Beginnings

In an attempt to attract high school students with a demonstrated commitment to community involvement, Bentley College initially used a portion of its financial aid budget to create five $5,000 service-learning scholarships for incoming freshmen. The number of scholarships has steadily risen, and in the 2003–2004 academic year, 18 students had scholarships sustained by a college expenditure of $90,000. That number is set to continue rising, and in 2005 the scholarship amount increased to $7,500 each.

Reflecting on the importance of service-learning student scholars in the development of service-learning at Bentley, Edward Zlotkowski (1998), the founder of what was then called the Bentley Service-Learning Project, wrote:

> It would not be an exaggeration to say that it was the scholarship program around which and upon which BSLP was built. Because students who are accepted into the program have already developed considerable leadership skills, they are capable of assuming responsibilities that would be difficult for other students of their age. (pp. 72–73)

The objective of establishing the scholarship program was to ensure that the service-learning program would have a core group of student leaders dedicated to developing an expertise and experience base that would allow them to become resources for both faculty and fellow students engaged in service-learning. The program met this objective as it matured in the late 1990s. Scholarship students were given increased responsibility in the promotion and management of the program. Working with BSLC staff, they assumed responsibilities as project directors and managers. Working with faculty, they became course coordinators and liaisons both with the students performing the service and with the community partners served. In addition to these broad management responsibilities, these student scholars became the student voice of service-learning across the campus, meeting with faculty both in large-group sessions and in individual departments, mentoring students new to service-learning and developing their own service initiatives.

Student scholars can create and implement a new program, or they can improve and expand an established program.

Students' Responsibilities

The scholarship students' management responsibilities range from the grand to the mundane. In the grand scheme, student scholars assist in program and faculty development, service student placement, site orientations, selecting and mentoring new student scholars, and event coordination. They also serve generally in an advisory role for BSLC staff. On a more mundane level, they often staff the reception desk, answer student inquiries, prepare materials for classroom presentations, and assist in the office. Of all of these responsibilities, three of the most important are class visits, program enhancement, and the service internship.

Class Visits

Class visits are vital to recruiting the general student population for service-learning. Working closely with BSLC's coordinator of academic programs, Jennifer Webster, scholarship students visit classes at the beginning of each semester to explain the various service projects available through the center. To assist the scholars in these visits, Webster meets with them in advance and provides a checklist of points that the scholars should cover in their presentations. The checklist includes several major elements: the distinction between service-learning as an academic activity and volunteerism, a profile of BSLC's community partners, examples of available service projects, logistical issues, and the procedure for application and registration.

Before these visits, individual faculty members would have already agreed to sponsor service projects related to their course curricula. For example, in 2003, one instructor who teaches an introductory course in computer information systems wanted to involve his students in a service-learning project in the local public schools. Because several technology projects had already been arranged with local school principals, this request was an easy fit. Webster assigned several scholarship students to visit the instructor's classes to explain these projects and enlist students. One scholarship student, Dominic Basile, a senior majoring in computer information systems, was selected because of his leadership role as the project director for several BSLC computer programs in local elementary schools.

To prepare for the visit, Basile acquainted himself with the instructor's objective in offering a service-learning project. After introducing himself to the class, he discussed service-learning with the students, asking if they knew what it was and if any of them had already participated in service projects. He stressed the need for them to be truly interested in doing a service-learning project, so they understood they were making a commitment that required follow-through. After his presentation, he asked the instructor to explain the academic requirements for the service-learning project. During that same semester, 10 other service-learning scholars made visits to 39 other classes.

Program Enhancement

A second important responsibility for scholarship students is to develop enhancements to the Bentley service-learning program. These enhancements, which are then left as legacies after the scholars graduate, take one of two forms. Scholars can create and implement a new program, or they can improve and expand an established program. When the scholar is awarded a scholarship, the importance of enhancing a service-learning program is underscored. As a condition of the award, scholars are asked to sign a scholarship agreement, which requires that by the end of their sophomore year, they will have either developed and implemented a new program or enhanced an already existing one (see the Sidebar, below).

Sophomor scholar Scott Morency, an accounting major, created and implemented the "2 + 2 = 5" teamwork project in 2003. The project, as described by Morency, helps fourth- and fifth-grade students "to become better team players, to enhance and build leadership skills ... to enrich interpersonal relations, to understand conflict resolution ... to build trust." The project enriches BSLC's long-term partnership with the neighboring elementary schools in Waltham, Massachusetts. It also allows Morency to men-

---

Bentley's Service-Learning Scholarship Agreement Form

The four-year renewable Service-Learning Scholarship will provide you with $5,000 each year for a total of $10,000 during your freshman and sophomore years. Your scholarship will be renewed in the same amounts for your junior and senior years only upon the following conditions:

1. By second semester sophomore year, you must have either developed and implemented a new service-learning program for the Bentley Service-Learning Center (BSLC) or assumed responsibility for an already existing service-learning program and enhanced it. Enhancement could include adding new features to a program or increasing the program's community outreach.

2. You must maintain a 3.0 GPA as calculated annually.

3. You must commit to at least 10 hours of community service each week.

4. You must attend and participate in the annual September BSLC retreat.

5. You must generally assume a leadership role in BSLC.

In addition, you will be expected to attend and participate in the monthly BSLC student meeting, which will be held from 5:00 to 6:15 p.m. on Thursdays. These meetings often plan BSLC service and civic engagement activities or engage in service-related topics presented by guest speakers. In scheduling your classes, please remember not to schedule classes on Thursdays at 5:00 p.m.

We have read and understand the terms of the award.

SCHOLARSHIP STUDENT	PARENT OR LEGAL GUARDIAN
Print name	Print name
Signature	Signature
Date	Date

tor other Bentley students who assist in the project. Teachers and students at the elementary schools have responded enthusiastically to the "2 + 2 = 5" program.

Service Internship

A third responsibility of student scholars is a 180-hour, three-credit service internship project undertaken during their junior or senior year. The internship—a graduation requirement for scholarship students—is administered by BSLC in collaboration with the relevant academic department. A student scholar presents a written internship proposal to the BSLC's director. The scholar usually prepares the proposal after consulting with the intended community partner and determining what issues to address. After approval by the director, the scholar and the director together identify the academic discipline within which the project falls and seek an instructor within that discipline to supervise the internship. Once an instructor has agreed to supervise the internship, the instructor and the scholar together work out the academic expectations.

In her student scholar internship project, Nicole Macey, a junior accounting major, worked with the City of Boston's Earned Income Tax Credit (EITC) initiative in 2002. Macey collaborated with the citywide EITC coordinator to establish a site office in Boston's Roslindale section, a mixed-income, racially diverse neighborhood on the city's southwest side. The office, a drop-in center, helped residents file their income tax returns. Her responsibilities included marketing the initiative, staffing the office, and helping residents. Macey was thrilled to be able to recover thousands of dollars for residents who might not otherwise have known about the earned income tax credit.

Selecting Scholarship Students

The success of individual projects like Macey's and of the service-learning scholarship program in general depends on the caliber of BSLC's student scholars. Recruiting the right individuals to be service-learning student scholars is key. Because of this, the award of the scholarship is based on the strength of the application rather than on need.

The BSLC has developed a close working relationship with the college's undergraduate admissions office, where the names and profiles of potential service-learning student scholars surface. Each year, the admissions office sends out several thousand application packets to students interested in attending Bentley. Included in the packet is a service-learning brochure that explains BSLC's program. Putting service-learning front and center in the admissions process underscores the college's commitment. It also encourages applicants to inform the college of any service activities that they undertook during high school. Many applicants write about such service in their application essays. Once the admissions office reviews the application and accompanying essay, it forwards to BSLC those that indicate an applicant's personal commitment to service and civic engagement. In any one year, BSLC may receive as many as 50 applications.

Putting service-learning front and center in the admissions process underscores the college's commitment.

The BSLC review team, which consists of five or six current service-learning student scholars and BSLC assistant director Jeannette MacInnes, reviews and evaluates the applications. The review team identifies the 20 or 25 strongest applicants based on the materials provided by the admissions office. MacInnes calls each of the applicants to inform them of their candidacy as service-learning student scholars, explain the selection process, answer preliminary questions, and arrange a telephone interview with the review team. The 30-minute interview by current student scholars is the heart of the selection process.

Based on their own experience as scholars, the review team looks for characteristics that signal a qualified applicant. The usual practice has been to create a checklist of characteristics that the ideal student scholar should have, such as personal dedication, individual initiative, and advanced communication skills. The team then evaluates the application, the essay, and the telephone interview with these criteria in mind. Amber Gradziel, a student scholar who graduated in 2002, reflected, "The objective was always to find a well-rounded person, someone not only who had a history of service, but also who could inspire others and lead. To select the right people took many conversations among the team."

Another student scholar graduate, Amanda Baker, in considering the checklist, always came back to what was for her the key question: "Does this person have a passion?" In seeking an answer, Baker focused on what inspired the prospective student to undertake service, what aspects of leadership he or she had shown during service, and how persistent he or she had been in performing service.

After interviewing and evaluating, the team members select those they think best exhibit the characteristics of the BSLC student scholar. The number of scholars selected varies each year, based on the size and the quality of the original pool of scholar candidates, but usually 12 are selected. The names of those selected, along with the team's evaluations, are given to the director, who makes the final cut if more candidates are selected than can be given scholarships. The director considers the team's evaluations in the context of overall program needs and initiatives. Once the director has completed a review of those selected, the names are sent to the admissions office, which notifies applicants of both acceptance into the college and the award of the scholarship. The award is made only when candidates sign the scholarship agreement.

The 12 scholarships awarded by the BSLC in any one year amount to more than Bentley has to distribute. As with the admissions process in general, not every student admitted to Bentley College will accept the invitation to attend. On average, approximately half the number awarded a service-learning scholarship will actually decide to come to Bentley. Some years, eight or nine will accept, and other years, only three or four will accept. Because of this variability, the Bentley financial aid office, which oversees the distribution of scholarship funds, has arranged service-learning scholarship funding so that it can be flexibly applied from year to year.

During the final stage in the selection process, the director sends each of the selected students a formal award letter and an accompanying scholarship agreement form. The form identifies the scholarship as a conditional award of $5,000 during both the scholar's freshman and sophomore years, renewable at the same amount for the scholar's junior and senior years. Renewal depends on the scholar meeting certain standards as an underclassman (outlined in the Sidebar). In addition, as upperclassmen, scholars must complete the three-credit service-learning internship.

The Scholarship's Impact
By offering $120,000 annually in scholarships, Bentley College opens its doors in a unique way. Many institutions of higher education offer grants and loans to help students and their families afford the high costs of a college education. Many schools attract top athletes and scholars with the enticement of easing the financial burden, often to improve an athletic or academic program. Offering service-learning scholarships produces a similar attraction, but instead of drawing only top athletes and scholars, the BSLC scholarship attracts community-oriented leaders. With their strong commitment to community and service to others exhibited in their high school experiences, these students can deepen their engagement while studying at Bentley. The student scholar experience nurtures their established skills, enhances their classroom education, and allows them to pass their experience on to others.

For freshman Ben Currier, the scholarship made Bentley a more attractive college option: "The fact that Bentley has such a well-established community service initiative made my college selection decision that much easier," he notes. Extensively involved in various community outreach programs during high school, Currier sought to continue his dedication to community in college, and the scholarship made this possible. "My family is not very wealthy. I probably would not have been able to attend Bentley had I not received the scholarship," he explains. The scholarship allows Bentley to make it possible for students, like Currier, who have a proven track record of service in their hometowns to continue to develop as civic leaders while attending college.

Yet the impact of the service-learning scholarship runs much deeper than the obvious financial benefits. It has a meaningful effect on the personal and academic growth of the student scholar. While all students involved in BSLC programs learn to apply text-book knowledge to real-world situations, scholarship students develop a greater depth of understanding of themselves and their studies. Implementing or expanding a BSLC program carries not only great responsibility, but great educational value as well. As project managers and directors, scholarship students must work closely with peers and community partners. For many, this is the first time they have been assigned the task of managing other students with clear service and academic objectives.

Student scholar Dominic Basile acts as the project director of four Waltham elemen-tary school computer labs. Every day, he works with four separate school administra-tions, eight Bentley project managers, two educational technology specialists, and dozens of teachers. Working in such close proximity with groups of professionals and peers has nurtured in Basile his own sense of self and his commitment to civic engage-ment. Drawing on his experience as a student scholar, he has reflected,

> With service-learning, I have learned that you have to be engaged with the communi-ty in order to bring about any change. I have also learned about my level of patience; my technological and communication skills; my role as a mentor, manager, and medi-ator; and simply what I want to do with my life. Had I not been able to work with many amazing teachers and students, I know that I would never be entering the field of education. The scholarship I received certainly helped to act as a catalyst to this process. As I begin to make post-graduation plans, I know that the experiences and relationships I have made at the BSLC will last a lifetime.

This work ethic—one that is nurtured in all BSLC student scholars—is sparked by the scholarship. The scholarship ignites the fire and makes it grow. Senior scholarship stu-dent Kelly Rondeau, a computer information systems major, has spent countless hours leading various BSLC programs. She has directed the America Reads program and has developed and implemented the Massachusetts Comprehensive Assessment System Test Prep program at area elementary schools. Rondeau notes, "One of the greatest strengths of being a scholarship student is having the ability to select a project and take it under your wing to make it your own; to be able to dedicate your service hours to something you believe in and can learn from."

BSLC community partner Alice Shull, principal of the Fitzgerald Elementary School in Waltham, echoes Rondeau's sentiments. Referring to Basile and Noah Gunn, a student scholar and finance major serving as co-director of the Fitzgerald technology project, Shull says, "The scholarship students consistently go above and beyond anything that is expected of them." She appreciates these students' willingness to be fully engaged at Fitzgerald School by attending the annual open house and discussing the computer lab with interested parents and friends of the school. In addition, she notes how they had committed hours of their own time to organize a dedication ceremony for a former Fitzgerald teacher and coworker who had died of cancer: "The ceremony would not have been the same without all their work. I could not have done it without them."

As for the effectiveness of the BSLC computer program at Fitzgerald, Shull comments, "We are seeing increased achievement and confidence exhibited by our students. I have parents coming up to me constantly telling me that their children are learning so much more." BSLC's student scholars are having a true impact on the community and its people.

Conclusion

Since 1992, more than 50 Bentley College students have served as student scholars. The scholarship program has been an important part of their academic, professional, and personal development. It has also attracted students to Bentley who have manifested a consistent, mature commitment to service. It has nurtured their commitment by giving them leadership roles within the college and in the wider community. As a business university committed to funding and promoting service-learning through the scholarship program, Bentley has played a central role in advancing the goals and objectives of service-learning pedagogy and service-learning student scholars.

References

Campus Compact and The Princeton Review. (2005). *Colleges with a conscience: 81 great schools with outstanding community involvement.* New York: Random House.

Zlotkowski, E. (1998). The Bentley service-learning project. In E. Zlotkowski (Ed.), *Successful service-learning programs* (pp. 59–80). Bolton, MA: Anker Publishing Company.

Acknowledgments

The authors gratefully acknowledge Jeannette MacInnes and Jennifer Webster for providing helpful background information for this chapter.

Supporting Student Involvement through Service-based Scholarships

Julie A. Hatcher, Robert G. Bringle,
Lorrie A. Brown, and David A. Fleischhacker

METROPOLITAN UNIVERSITY LOCATED in the Indiana's state capital, Indiana University-Purdue University Indianapolis (IUPUI) takes seriously its responsibility to be an active citizen in the local community (Bringle, Games, & Malloy, 1999). This commuter campus, with 22 academic units, provides highly diversified certificate and degree programs to more than 29,000 full- and part-time students, with an emphasis on professional education in business, dentistry, education, engineering, law, medicine, and nursing.

Since 1993, the Center for Service and Learning (CSL) at IUPUI has been a catalyst for campus engagement for a broad civic agenda through service-learning courses, volunteer programs, and strategic campus-community partnerships. The Sam H. Jones Community Service Scholarship program ($340,000 annually), administered through CSL, is an important campus initiative to involve students in the community as an integrated aspect of their college experience.

The center and the scholarship program have evolved over time. In 1994, CSL began to coordinate the License to Learn Scholarship, which was funded by revenues generated from the sale of IUPUI license plates. The state of Indiana allows nonprofit organizations, including colleges and universities, to create license plates with logos of the organization as a form of fundraising; the nonprofit organization receives $25 in revenue from each license plate sold. In 1998, a decision was made to more closely align the use of scholarship funds with campus mission, including civic engagement. The community service scholarship program was expanded to recognize service as merit in awards and to recruit and retain students with a demonstrated commitment to civic involvement (Hatcher, Bringle, & Muthiah, 2002).

In 1999–2000, an allocation of $120,000 in campus-based funds was made to support five types of service-based awards: the freshman service scholarship, the community service scholarship, the community service associate scholarship, the America Reads/America Counts team leader scholarship, and the service-learning assistant scholarship (see Figure 1).

In 2003, the service scholarship program was named in honor of Sam H. Jones, a dedicated public servant who provided dynamic leadership as the chief executive officer of the Indianapolis Urban League. Jones served on the IUPUI Chancellor's Board of Directors and Diversity Cabinet. The scholarship program has strengthened the campus partnership with the Indianapolis Urban League and focused on urban issues and social advocacy. In 2004–2005, $248,000 was awarded to 115 service scholars who contributed 15,150 hours of service to more than 75 community organizations.

The Center's Mission

The Center for Service and Learning, a centralized campus unit that reports to the executive vice chancellor and dean of faculties, supports civic engagement across all academic units. Its mission, to involve students, faculty, and staff in service activities that mutually benefit the campus and community, is achieved through five program goals:

1) To support the development and implementation of service-learning classes,

2) To increase campus participation in community service activities,

3) To strengthen campus-community partnerships,

4) To advance the scholarship of service and civic engagement, and

5) To promote service-learning, professional service, and civic engagement in higher education locally, nationally, and internationally.

The vision of CSL is to make service a distinctive aspect of the educational culture at IUPUI. CSL has been recognized nationally and internationally for the quality of its programs and scholarly contributions to the field of service learning and civic engagement in higher education (see http://csl.iupui.edu).

Implementing the Mission

Because civic engagement is a valued component of IUPUI's mission, CSL has developed a number of programs over the past decade to support the involvement of students in the Indianapolis community. Consistent with national norms, approximately 70% of undergraduates come to IUPUI with previous experience in voluntary service or service-learning in high school (Sax & Astin, 1997; Bringle, Hatcher, & McIntosh,

FIGURE 1: Overview of the Sam H. Jones Community Service Scholarship Program

NAME AND PURPOSE OF SCHOLARSHIP	CRITERIA FOR APPLICANTS	ANNUAL SCHOLARSHIP AWARDS	EXPECTATIONS OF SERVICE SCHOLARS	CHARACTERISTICS OF SERVICE INVOLVEMENT
Freshman Service Scholarship (FSS): To recognize entering students who have successfully demonstrated a commitment to community service and to facilitate their involvement in service and service-learning	CORE 40, Honors Diploma, or Regular Admission status at IUPUI Merit in service to high school or community Essay Two letters of recommendation from those familiar with service contributions Personal interview	15 scholarships @ $2,500 each; $37,500 awarded annually	Enroll in Introduction to Psychology service learning course Contribute 3 hours of service each week at George Washington Community School in fall and site of choice in spring Participate in at least one campus-wide service event with FSS team per semester Attend monthly leadership seminars in spring	Direct service All FSS students work at the same community partnership site during fall FSS students have option to select new partnership site during spring
Community Service Scholarship (CSS): To recognize continuing students who have demonstrated ongoing service to the campus or community, and to facilitate their continued involvement in service and service-learning at selected community partnership sites	2.75 GPA 15 credit hours at IUPUI Merit in campus or community service Essay	15 scholarships @ $3,500 each; $52,500 awarded annually	Enroll in Community Service Seminar, Philanthropic Studies service-learning course Participate in United Way Day of Caring with CSS team Contribute 4 hours of service per week at partnership site of choice during academic year	Direct service and programming CSS students select community partnership site CSS students typically not with other scholars at site

NAME AND PURPOSE OF SCHOLARSHIP	CRITERIA FOR APPLICANTS	ANNUAL SCHOLARSHIP AWARDS	EXPECTATIONS OF SERVICE SCHOLARS	CHARACTERISTICS OF SERVICE INVOLVEMENT
	Two letters of recommendation from those familiar with service contributions Personal interview		Work with CSS and CSL staff to plan Dr. Martin Luther King, Jr., "Day-On" of Service Attend monthly leadership seminars in spring	CSS students organize "Day-On" of Service, a campus-wide service event, in January
Community Service Associate (CSA): To recognize previous freshman service scholars, community service scholars, or outstanding student service leaders who have demonstrated exemplary leadership abilities through their commitment to community service in the Indianapolis community	2.75 GPA 30 credit hours at IUPUI Selected as FSS or CSS, or demonstrated outstanding leadership in civic engagement Application Two letters of recommendation from those familiar with service contributions Personal interview	6–12 scholarships @ $3,500 each; $21,000–$42,000 awarded annually	Contribute 10 hours per week during the academic year to coordinate campus-community events Provide informal mentoring to freshman service scholars Assist with monthly leadership seminars in spring Advocate for student participation in service and social advocacy through student organizations	Direct service, programming, and social advocacy CSA students select social issue to advocate for through campus programming CSA students select community partnership site that aligns with social issue CSA students work with CSL staff on program implementation

NAME AND PURPOSE OF SCHOLARSHIP	CRITERIA FOR APPLICANTS	ANNUAL SCHOLARSHIP AWARDS	EXPECTATIONS OF SERVICE SCHOLARS	CHARACTERISTICS OF SERVICE INVOLVEMENT
Service Learning Assistant (SLA): To recognize students who have successfully completed a service learning class and who are skilled and motivated to assist in implementing a service learning class	2.75 GPA 12 credit hours at IUPUI Successful completion of a service-learning course Recruited, interviewed, and selected by service-learning instructor	100–120 scholarships @ $750–$2,250 each; $170,000–$190,000 awarded annually	Assist service-learning instructor 5-10 hours per week on implementing, monitoring, or assessing service-learning course Participate in training sessions offered by CSL Complete final report for CSL	Direct service and programming Activities vary depending upon goals of service-learning instructor
America Reads/America Counts Team Leader: To recognize exemplary America Reads/America Counts tutors and to facilitate their involvement as site leaders at tutoring locations	2.75 GPA 30 credit hours at IUPUI One year as a tutor with demonstrated merit Recommendation of site supervisor Personal interview	12–16 scholarships @ $2,500 each; $30,000–$40,000 awarded annually	Serve as site leader for 5 hours per week Maintain accurate records for tutors and program Attend monthly leadership sessions Assist CSL staff with tutor training sessions	Direct service and programming Maintain effective communication with teachers, staff, and parents of youth Design service projects with other tutors and youth at tutoring site

1999). CSL fosters their continued participation through various programs, including America Reads/America Counts work-study tutoring programs, service-learning courses, campus-wide days of service, alternative break service trips, and student service organizations.

The Sam H. Jones Community Service Scholarship program advances the campus mission of civic engagement by recruiting and retaining undergraduates who demonstrate a strong commitment to civic involvement. The program recognizes students for previous service contributions to their high school, campus, or community and supports their personal development, academic achievement, and civic commitment. Program components support the leadership development of scholarship recipients so that they actively increase the participation of other IUPUI students, faculty, and staff. Thus, the scholarship program is meant not only to recognize previous service but also to cultivate an ongoing commitment to civic engagement. As one service scholar stated, "The scholarship gives you an opportunity to better serve the community and at the same time helps with your tuition.... It is a win-win situation for all parties involved."

Program Goals

The following goals form a framework for program activities and are the basis for developing a service-based scholarship program:

GOAL 1. *Recruit and retain students who demonstrate commitment to community service and civic involvement.*

- Promote service as an integrated aspect of the students' higher education experience.
- Articulate campus commitment to civic engagement in recruitment materials.
- Provide opportunities for meaningful interaction with faculty, staff, and peers.
- Create a strong peer network of service-minded students.

GOAL 2. *Support the personal development, academic achievement, and civic commitment of service scholars.*

- Provide educationally meaningful service and service-learning experiences.
- Provide opportunities for formal and informal reflection.
- Support leadership development of service scholars through training and feedback.
- Offer pre-professional experiences that develop personal, academic, and civic skills.

GOAL 3. *Involve service scholars to increase the participation of IUPUI students, faculty, and staff in civic engagement.*

- Design leadership opportunities for service scholars to organize service activities.
- Coordinate campus-wide group service projects.
- Provide resources to support service project implementation.
- Recognize campus and community contributions of service scholars.

GOAL 4. *Strengthen campus-community partnerships through the ongoing involvement of IUPUI students, faculty, and staff in community organizations.*

- Promote community-service experiences through a variety of roles.
- Increase service scholars' understanding of social issues, community assets, and nonprofit organizations.
- Build campus-community partnerships that support and recognize service scholars.
- Assess outcomes of service scholars' involvement in community organizations.

Program Design

Diverse Service Models

The design of the scholarship program has been shaped by principles of best practice in service-learning (Howard, 1993; Eyler & Giles, 1999) and Morton's three models of service: charity or direct service, project programming, and advocacy for social change (Morton, 1995). Some students may feel most comfortable providing direct service by picking up trash during an environmental cleanup, serving meals at a homeless shelter, or tutoring youth in an after-school program, for example. Others may prefer projects that involve implementing plans to address problems in partnership with others, designing programs, recruiting volunteers, and writing grant proposals. Some students may prefer to advocate for changes in social policy, educate others on social issues, and mobilize communities, which are dependent on long-term relationships with others to improve social conditions.

Most students who come to IUPUI prefer to be involved in direct service (44.4%) or project programming (36.4%). Only a small number (12.2%) have indicated a preference for social advocacy (Bringle, Hatcher, & McIntosh, 1999). The scholarship program is designed to invite students to explore all types of service. Service scholars reflect on their experiences in meaningful ways through service-learning course assignments, training and leadership seminars, monthly log sheets, final reports, and both formal and informal conversations with CSL staff. The emphasis on reflection is consistent with good practice in service-learning (Hatcher & Bringle, 1997; Bringle & Hatcher, 1999).

Scholarship Focus

The focus of each of the scholarship programs emphasizes one or more of the three types of service: direct service, programming, and advocacy.

The primary focus of the *Freshman Service Scholarship* is direct service. During an orientation session in August, first-year students are introduced to program goals and to CSL staff. Freshman service scholars are required to enroll in a service-learning course, "Introduction to Psychology," during the fall semester, usually taught by the CSL director. As part of the course, the scholars provide three hours of tutoring and homework assistance each week to students at George Washington Community School, a multi-faceted partnership site close to campus. During the second semester, they may choose to remain at the same school or select another site for their three-hour-per-week commitment. They also participate as a group in campus-wide service days (for example, Service First, United Way Day of Caring, and the Dr. Martin Luther King, Jr., "Day On" of Service).

The *Community Service Scholarship* program focuses on direct service and programming. Community service scholars are required to enroll in "Community Service Seminar," a course about philanthropy in American culture, volunteer motives, and civic engagement in higher education, which is offered each fall and usually is taught by CSL's associate director. The scholars are required to work with a community agency for four hours each week during the entire academic year. Readings and structured reflection activities link the service experience to the learning objectives of the course and the scholarship program.

During an orientation session in May, community service scholars learn more about program expectations and begin the important process of selecting a community organization. Students receive a list of preferred partnership sites, listen to past scholars speak about their service experience, take a self-assessment inventory to determine their preferences, and consult with CSL staff on site selection. Students are encouraged to select an organization that will give them an opportunity for both direct service and programming, and will introduce them to new service experiences. Students identify two or three community organizations of interest, set up interviews with agency staff, and discuss activities for the coming year. Community agencies value the participation of community service scholars because they are dedicated, mature students with experience in direct service and an interest in assuming greater project responsibilities.

Service scholars develop leadership and problem-solving skills so they can involve others in service, work effectively with others from diverse backgrounds, and reach consensus through dialogue.

America Reads/America Counts team leaders and service-learning assistants participate in direct service and programming. Team leaders work with other tutors at America Reads/ America Counts tutoring sites, organize special events for children and families, and host campus teams for one-day service events at their community sites. Service-learning assistants help faculty implement service-learning courses. As faculty assistants, they may facilitate community placements, monitor student participation, collect evaluation data, or support program development with the community partner.

Community Service Associates are involved in direct service, programming, and advocacy for issues of social justice and civic engagement on campus and within the community. They select a social issue and community organization to focus on during the year, both for direct service and for programming campus and community events. For example, an associate may volunteer with Gleaners Food Bank and organize an Oxfam Hunger Banquet on campus, volunteer with Habitat for Humanity and sponsor a Shantytown Sleep-out to raise awareness of homelessness, or work with the Westside Cooperative Organization to organize community events and identify new campus-community partnerships. Further program development is expanding the role of associates to work directly with campus staff to increase political participation and social advocacy through the activities of the American Democracy Project.

Student Development and Leadership Skills

The scholarship program intends to cultivate in service scholars a commitment to be active citizens, the confidence to make a difference in local communities, and a respect toward others from diverse backgrounds. It increases students' knowledge of the non-profit sector and the role of volunteers in the community, of community assets and challenges within Indianapolis, of their role in the community through their professional work and volunteering, and of their educational and career goals. The program promotes more frequent interaction with peers, faculty, and staff; increased voluntary participation in campus and community organizations; and follow-through on commitments to others.

Service scholars develop leadership and problem-solving skills so they can involve others in service, work effectively with others from diverse backgrounds, and reach consensus through dialogue. Freshman service scholars tutor youth and work as a team on group service projects. Community service scholars assist in administrative tasks such as program supervision, publicity and marketing, and grant writing. They also work with CSL staff to coordinate the Dr. Martin Luther King, Jr., "Day On" of Service. They collaborate with community organizations, produce publicity and marketing materials, recruit approximately 400 volunteers annually, and plan the breakfast and program speakers.

Service scholars attend monthly leadership seminars during the second semester that focus on a wide range of topics, including personal development, organizational skills, and community development. In 2003–2004, they conducted a campus asset-mapping activity during which they identified issues, interviewed stakeholders, and created an action plan detailing how IUPUI could use its resources to improve the campus. As part of this assessment, they investigated issues such as the way campus police treat the homeless and the feasibility of campus food services purchasing free-trade coffee. This asset-mapping activity encouraged students to take an active role in the campus community by making them aware of their dual roles as campus members and service scholars.

the retention rate of service scholars is significantly higher than that for undergraduates as a whole at IUPUI.

More accomplished leaders are the community service associates, who act as role models to freshman service scholars, community service scholars, and peers. In addition to their service experiences in programming and social advocacy, they informally mentor freshman service scholars and help lead orientation and leadership sessions for the scholarship program. The associates also volunteer as student office staff for CSL, recruit for service programs and activities, and contribute to quality programming (see the Sidebar on p. 45 for an example).

Recruitment and Selection

Recruitment for the Sam H. Jones Community Service Scholarship program varies, depending on the type of award. The program seeks applicants with a wide range of

Students as Campus and Community Leaders at IUPUI

Students like Juana Watson exemplify the goals of the Sam H. Jones Community Service Scholarship program. When Watson entered IUPUI, she was strongly committed to improving the lives of others through community service. For years, Watson had been a classroom volunteer in her children's schools. She also organized service trips for high school students and church members to her native town of Calnali, Mexico, a rural village in the Sierra Madre Mountains.

Watson was a community service scholar for two years as an undergraduate at IUPUI. She tutored youth at Crispus Attucks Middle School and became convinced that service opportunities can change lives for college students and recipients alike. As a community service associate, she worked with CSL staff to arrange meetings with faculty across campus to identify ways that IUPUI students could contribute to the work in Calnali. As a result of her leadership, faculty and graduate students from the Indiana University schools of medicine, nursing, and dentistry have made annual service trips to Calnali for the past eight years. Plans are in place for a permanent health clinic to be built in Calnali to continue to improve health care delivery to this rural Mexican village.

IUPUI and the mayor of Calnali signed a formal partnership agreement in November 2004 to further program expansion, marking the first time the campus has signed a formal partnership with any community. Watson has connected IUPUI faculty with their peers at Universidad Autonoma de Hidalgo to create the Calnali Service-Learning Program. Through this program, both American and Mexican college students will be involved in providing health care and direct services to villagers.

Juana Watson recently received the Governor's Award for Excellence in Community Service and Volunteerism and currently serves as Senior Advisor for Latino Affairs for the state.

academic skills, experiences, and service preferences. CSL works closely with the Office of Student Scholarships to provide accurate information on all scholarships for publications and the campus scholarship website (see www.iupui.edu/~scentral). Recruitment for the freshman service scholarship is supported through direct mailings to high school guidance counselors and service organizations such as Key Club and Youth as Resources, high school presentations sponsored by the Enrollment Center, and dissemination of program information during campus visit days with prospective students. Continuing students are recruited for the community service scholarship through the Freshman Service Scholarship program, flyers, announcements to student organizations, notices to faculty who teach service-learning courses, and postings on campus listservs. Faculty and staff recruit America Reads/America Counts team leaders and service-learning assistants. These students have demonstrated dependability and interest in further involvement through their experiences as tutors or students in service-learning classes.

Selection of service scholars is based on a review of scholarship applications; in addition, a selection committee interviews all finalists. The interview provides students with a clear understanding of program expectations and an opportunity to ask questions about the program. A review committee composed of staff from CSL and other campus units selects freshman service scholars and community service scholars. A sponsoring faculty or staff member selects community service associates, America Reads/America Counts team leaders, and service-learning assistants.

Program Evaluation

Each year, CSL compiles an annual report on the scholarship program for the Office of Scholarships and the Financial Aid and Scholarship Program Advisory Committee, which documents the number of scholarships awarded, tracks academic achievement, and covers other aspects of the program. Two dimensions of achievement are particularly important: 1) retention of students overall, and 2) recruitment and retention of minority students. The retention rate of service scholars (87% in 2004–2005) is significantly higher than that for undergraduates as a whole at IUPUI. Additionally, minority student participation in the scholarship program (34% in 2004–2005) is significantly higher than minority student enrollment on campus (19%). The annual report has fostered a high level of confidence in the ability of CSL to coordinate such a large scholarship program for the campus.

The Sam H. Jones Community Service Scholarship program is continually being refined to best meet the goals of supporting student development and leadership, advancing the campus mission of civic engagement, and building strong campus-community partnerships. In some cases, the experiences of service scholars have brought about changes to the program; at other times, the changes have occurred because of a deeper understanding of good practice in cultivating commitment to civic engagement.

Throughout the year, focus groups and end-of-year surveys of service scholars, community-site supervisors, and faculty and staff, as well as informal feedback, provide program evaluation. This feedback provides important information for improving the program. For example, the orientation for community service scholars was moved from August to May to give students additional time to select partnership sites. The number of service hours that community service scholars are expected to contribute was reduced from six to four hours each week in response to recommendations from previous scholars. A training session for service-learning associates was designed in response to feedback from faculty who teach service-learning courses.

A formal evaluation of the program will examine what the service scholars have learned, including knowledge, skills, attitudes, and behaviors. A more structured assessment of the service scholars' community impact will also be conducted. CSL is interested in comparing its program with service-based scholarship programs at other institutions. This research will be important both to IUPUI's program and to service-learning and civic engagement in general.

Formal longitudinal research on what service scholars have learned will provide a better understanding of the scholarship program's effect. Of key interest is the extent to which the required component of a service-based scholarship contributes to a long-term civic commitment of participants. Program components—which can include required service, amount of service, service-learning courses, choice of community agency, group service experience, leadership opportunities, interaction with faculty, and interaction with peers—could be redesigned on the basis of these evaluations. During the next decade, CSL staff will address these issues so that the Sam H. Jones Community Service Scholarship program can contribute to a broader understanding of how to develop civic-minded graduates.

References

Bringle, R.G., Games, R., & Malloy, E.A. (Eds.). (1999). *Colleges and universities as citizens.* Needham Heights, MA: Allyn and Bacon.

Bringle, R.G., & Hatcher, J. A. (1999, Summer). Reflection in service-learning: Making meaning of experience. *Educational Horizons,* 179–185.

Bringle, R.G., Hatcher, J.A., & McIntosh, R. (1999). *Student involvement in service and service learning.* Paper presented at the Association for Research on Nonprofit Organizations and Voluntary Action, Washington, DC.

Eyler, J., & Giles, D.E., Jr. (1999). *Where's the learning in service-learning?* San Francisco: Jossey-Bass.

Hatcher, J.A., & Bringle, R.G. (1997). Reflection: Bridging the gap between service and learning. *Journal of College Teaching, 45,* 153–58.

Hatcher, J. A., Bringle, R.G., & Muthiah, R. (2002). Institutional strategies to involve freshmen in service. In E. Zlotkowski (Ed.), *Service-learning and the first-year experience: Preparing student for personal success and civic responsibility.* Columbia, SC: National Resource Center for the First-Year Experience and Students in Transition.

Howard, J. (1993). Community service-learning in the curriculum. In J. Howard (Ed.), *Praxis I: A faculty casebook on community service-learning*, p. 219–227. Ann Arbor, MI: OCSL Press.

Morton, K. (1995). The irony of service: Charity, project, and social change in service-learning. *Michigan Journal of Community Service Learning, 2*, 19–32.

Sax, L.J., & Astin, A.W. (1997). The benefits of service: Evidence from undergraduates. *Educational Record, 78* (3–4), 25–32.

COMMUNITY SERVICE-LEARNING AT
THE UNIVERSITY OF SAN DIEGO:

Recruiting and Building a Team

Elaine Elliott and Lisa Garcia

THE UNIVERSITY OF SAN DIEGO, like the city in which it is located, is named after San Diego de Alcalá, a Franciscan lay brother from the Spanish town of Alcalá de Henares, near Madrid. The University of Alcalá de Henares served as a physical and philosophical model for USD's founders, guiding both USD's architectural style and its determination to prevail as an educational institution that serves society. USD—a private, nationally ranked, Roman Catholic institution with 678 faculty members and 7,262 undergraduate, graduate, and law students—embraces its Catholic moral and social tradition in its commitment to serve with compassion, foster peace, work for justice, and prepare leaders for ethical conduct and compassionate service. Service-learning, like many co-curricular service opportunities, furthers that mission.

The foundation for the service-learning program was laid by the USD community service staff, faculty, and student teams after they attended California Campus Compact's Summer Institutes in the early 1990s. Faculty members made a commitment to infuse service-learning into their courses, but expressed concern about the additional time required to administer the program. A spring 1994 pilot project strengthened faculty interest and made service-learning seem feasible by identifying some successful strategies for implementation. A team approach of faculty working with student leaders evolved as a way to develop students in new ways and generate collaborative assistance for the faculty.

USD's service-learning program formally began with the support of a Learn and Serve grant from the Corporation for National Service. Since then, more than 150 courses from a broad spectrum of disciplines have included a service-learning component. Two-thirds of these courses are offered on a continuing basis. In some courses, all students are engaged in the same service-learning project, while in others, students can choose among four or five different options.

The mission of the Center for Community Service-Learning reflects the importance of students as leaders in service: "Through service, we engage USD students, faculty, staff, and alumni to learn in partnership with the community, and make life-long commitments to promote social change and justice." Programs to fulfill this mission include co-curricular projects, which were the first thrust of service in 1987; they continue in what is now known as the Center for Awareness, Service and Action (CASA).

anybody can be a leader, particularly in a collaborative model of leadership.

CASA builds awareness via programs throughout the year, connects advocacy issues to the service experience, and facilitates an annual social issues conference that began in 1989 with major speakers. The center offers a one-unit seminar, "Leadership for Social Change," that connects students to advocacy groups. The center also promotes service within residence halls. A large America Reads/America Counts tutoring program is funded by the Federal Work-Study program. Staff and alumni can also participate in various service opportunities. All of these programs depend on student leadership.

In addition to student leaders, two professional staff members spend substantial time working on service-learning courses and attending to community connections, faculty development, and student leadership. The program also has a half-time graduate student who contributes to its success. Still, without a core of 40 to 50 student leaders, the program simply could not manage the 800 students and 40 classes it assists each semester.

Developing Student Leaders

Student leadership is the foundation of USD's community service-learning program. Each semester begins with the important process of identifying students and building them into a working team. Students who choose to become service-learning leaders assess their experiences very positively. "The most beneficial skills I learned in school were through my service-learning leadership experiences," wrote a recent graduate. Another student reflected on important lessons from her initial leadership position:

> The first semester of being a student leader was such a great learning experience. The seminar, "Leadership through Service-Learning," helped me learn a lot about the role of ethics, morals, and faith in service and in my life in general. It helped me view my future career plans, friends, classes, and professors in a different light.

Dr. Judy Rauner, director of the program from 1987 to 2002, found that having the opportunity to be service-learning leaders not only encouraged students to play an integral role in the course-based program but also helped them develop key skills and values. Student leaders in her study, who once had seen leadership in a traditional top-down way, now perceived it as occurring "when an individual engages and influences collaborators in reciprocal learning relationships to develop a mutual purpose and work together toward intended change" (Rauner, 1995). They also reported that the experience developed their communication, problem-solving, and time management skills; expanded their self-perception and awareness of others as they confronted stereotypes; helped them advocate for service and recruit new leadership; and gave them a greater awareness of social issues, the causes of inequities, and the challenges that institutions face in addressing community needs.

Identifying Service-Learning Leaders

The recruitment philosophy for the service-learning program is based on the leadership philosophy of all the programs at USD. Anybody can be a leader, particularly in a collaborative model of leadership; therefore, the program is open to all students who are interested in building a team. Astin and Astin (1996) describe collaborative leadership as being 1) concerned with fostering change, 2) inherently values-based, and 3) a group process that considers all people potential leaders. USD follows this model, which reflects true appreciation of whatever interests and abilities students bring to the team.

USD recruits two groups of student leaders: service-learning leaders and site coordinators. The service-learning leaders are recruited from service-learning classes and collaborate with faculty members in a team approach. These students are available to their peers not only to facilitate reflection on their experiences, but also to address any practical problems their peers may face. They work closely with faculty to ensure that participants have positive service-learning experiences that meet the academic learning goals of the course and serve identified community needs.

Faculty members recruit service-learning leaders from their classes early on. On the first or second day of class, a staff member and a former student leader make presentations about the leadership opportunity. This opportunity includes the option to take a one-unit "Leadership through Service-Learning" seminar offered through the School of Education Leadership program, in addition to helping peers in the classroom. An application form is distributed along with a simple syllabus, so expectations are clear. Recruiters appeal to students' existing commitment to service. As one staff member pointed out, "With a wealth of service-oriented students to draw from, recruiting a student leader in the classroom is just a matter of having them reconnect to their own service experiences."

Most students who apply for leadership positions have had previous service experiences, although their leadership experiences vary widely. Some have an undeveloped social conscience, while others a highly developed social conscience. Students apply because they understand that someone must serve as a leader, they are seeking avenues for personal growth, they see themselves being useful, or a combination of these reasons. Most students value the opportunity to get an additional credit and add something to their resumes that reflects practical skills. Many freshmen and sophomores apply, partly because the service-learning courses are lower division courses, but also because this is an attractive avenue for involvement in a new environment.

A personal service commitment often serves as the motivator for the student leaders. One student explained:

> I knew that one of my goals in college was going to be to dedicate a good portion of my time to volunteering. The huge focus on service was one of the major reasons I came to USD. During the first class of "Social Problems," I was excited when the professor told us that our class was going to have a community service component. I learned they were looking for someone to help organize it and take a one-unit community service-learning class. Immediately, I knew this was perfect for me.

Another student was motivated by curiosity: "I wanted to learn about resources on campus and ended up finding resources on and off campus. The connections I have made this semester truly exceeded my expectations and will help me in future endeavors."

Many students who take this step find a new challenge. One student explained that after three years at USD, she wanted to be more than a student. Another realized she needed new perspectives. Some students apply because they have had strong previous community service experience and long-term goals for service. One student explained:

> I plan to join the Jesuit Volunteer Corps and eventually the Peace Corps and use the knowledge gained to lead a nonprofit NGO working to improve living conditions abroad or domestically. Because of previous, in-depth service experience, I feel as though I have the tools to lead effectively and to learn extensively. An opportunity as a community service-learning student leader would help me to continue to develop the skills necessary to move from empathy to action—the most important turning point in a career for a dedicated activist. I want to share my intense passion for service work and solidarity with those in need of a little help. More importantly, I want to continue to learn from service experiences.

These varying motivations bring a diverse group of students together for the semester as a learning community. Orientation workshops help students build connections to one another and learn about each other's interests and preferences. This friendly foundation makes cooperation to carry out any service-learning task much easier. In the workshops, the center's staff members try to build a common vision for service as a contribution to justice. They share inspiring quotes about service, justice, and leadership, one of which is: "A vision without a task is a dream. A task without a vision is drudgery. A vision with a task is the hope of the world." Ideas like this energize the team to deal with mundane concerns in order to transform thinking, relationships, and society.

Identifying Site Coordinators

A second group of student leaders is assigned to the community sites where the service-learning students work, serving as site coordinators who facilitate their peers' learning experiences. They complement the work of the service-learning leaders by providing continuity and connection to the community organizations and schools with which the students work and building build team relationships.

The majority of these students receive Federal Work-Study (FWS) funds. Thus, the service-learning program's financial aid liaison is a key partner in helping the program recruit this group of leaders. Each summer, FWS applications for community service learning (which are sent to students as part of their financial aid package) begin to flood into the Center for Community Service-Learning. An experienced site coordinator looks for the most promising applications to fill the 80 to 100 positions for America Reads/America Counts tutors. Students are selected on the basis of the written applications and phone interviews, with experienced returning students the obvious first choices. From this pool of enthusiastic tutors who work in the community, some are encouraged by the America Reads/America Counts student leadership to apply to be site coordinators at one of the local schools or at other sites. This kind of screening process—seeing how people work in schools—leads to other leadership positions.

Enthusiastic service-learning students are also encouraged to apply for leadership positions once the semester is over. If they are eligible for work-study, they can step into a coordinating position at a familiar site. If they are not eligible, they can receive a unit of leadership credit for their work. Many, however, choose to work without compensation simply because they have become attached to their site. Having become familiar with the site through their experiences connected to a particular course, they are well prepared to assist new students. One site coordinator explained that she chose a program in which migrant workers are paired with students who teach them English after realizing how much she enjoyed the work. "I found that I had an extreme passion for working with these men and learning more about the issues that caused them to be where they are in life," she wrote.

For some site coordinators, service-learning provides important connections that give them a sense of belonging. One student explained:

> I came from a low-income, working-class family. The main concern of my family was to survive, not to serve. This service provided a process of reciprocity, where I benefited just as much as the community I was providing service for. Before this experience, I felt lost, being a transfer student and coming from a low-income family, when most students at my university were financially privileged.

Site coordinators receive the orientation necessary for their responsibilities and some ongoing coaching from the staff and, when possible, the former site coordinator; however, there is a learning curve. One former site coordinator noted, "When I first started my job as a site coordinator, I had no idea what would be required of me. However, the orientation proved useful, as did the very detailed packet of beginning steps. It helped me get started, and after a while I was able to figure out exactly what needed to be done."

Building Service-Learning Teams

During the second week of the semester, service-learning leaders meet for lunch to become better acquainted, learn more about the program, and meet the site coordinators who will help make community connections. Approximately 20 service-learning leaders join the group of 20 site coordinators and the faculty, where their respective roles are explained. The lunch is organized in three teams, corresponding to the different places where people will be working—one group goes to schools, another to sites serving Spanish speakers, and the third to youth sites, such as a juvenile hall or an alternative school.

Making these connections enables the students to help solve problems for other students when they first have difficulties (usually scheduling conflicts) and, in turn, to help the staff. The students' ability to share the necessary information with one another gives them the power to make arrangements and answer questions, increasing their confidence as leaders. Students soon realize they are making a difference for their peers. One student wrote:

> At the beginning of the semester, when we were first learning about community service learning, there was a lot of confusion in class about what we were supposed to do as tutors. I think that with my communication with the site coordinators, our teacher, and all the countless e-mails to these people and the students, all the confusion has been sorted out. Without communication between these people, I feel like everything would still be up in the air.

Supporting the Teams

A critical part of team building takes place during the ongoing learning workshops provided for students throughout the semester. (Some site coordinators are funded as quarter-time AmeriCorps students, allowing them to devote a portion of their commitment to training.) During the workshops, students learn about reflection, facilitation, and other leadership skills. Some outstanding workshops on diversity training and ethical reflection have taken students to a much more sophisticated level in their understanding of their work in the community. However, the majority of the learning occurs as they facilitate their peers' experiences, solve problems, connect to the center's staff and to site staff, and handle practical matters such as scheduling work, monitoring attendance, and organizing orientations.

For the student leaders recruited from the classroom, the emphasis on leadership includes workshops on communication, reflection, human relations, social change skills, conflict management, and ethical leadership. After an initial Saturday training, a one-unit seminar meets during Thursdays at a time when no classes are held. Students post journal entries on an online message board, and at the end of the semester they create posters about their engagement in the community to display at a celebratory dinner.

The new student leaders soon learn they have concrete responsibilities and play a critical role in keeping the program on track and well organized. One student noted:

> At the beginning of the semester, I honestly thought my role as a student leader was going to be minimal and rather insignificant. However, as the middle of the semester approaches, I believe that I have done a lot and will continue to do a lot in the communication and organization between my class, the professor, and the Community Service-Learning Center. I have sent numerous e-mails and have spoken to the classes to organize the three community service options.

Another student expressed the interpersonal aspects of the position as well as the practical:

> My role consisted of acting as a liaison, and if anyone needed information in my class, I could point them in the right direction. Students could identify and communicate with me in a convenient, comfortable atmosphere. That role suited me perfectly. I enjoyed resolving issues about schedules, talking about their experiences in the field, and especially relating it to the topics we discussed in class. Finding a bridge between all those involved was very fun and rewarding.

Student leaders constantly struggle to make the service experience positive for everyone. While self-reported outcomes at the end of each semester show positive results, students initially are concerned that the service experience will fail in their class and somehow it will be their fault. One student explained:

> I was afraid at first that if I didn't do everything correctly, the service project would never grow into something fruitful. But now the USD students talk about what an interesting, beneficial experience going to the school was for them and for the kids who attend the school.

Creating a Learning Community

The Center for Community Service-Learning's staff attempts to create an atmosphere of enthusiasm and growth for all students. It tries to instill the core values of wisdom, knowledge, and the development of critical thinking skills in analyzing social issues and community solutions. The center's aim is to provide mutually respectful training and support for meaningful community involvement. The center emphasizes diversity—inclusiveness and respect for the dignity of each individual—unity, and continual movement toward a just society. Teamwork builds authentic, lasting relationships through shared experiences. Reciprocal growth and development help staff members and students encourage each other in their work.

> "**b**efore I started working in community service-learning, I was one of those people who didn't have much of a social conscience. Now all of that has changed."

The center has a common-sense approach to taking risks and encourages progress, not perfection. The emphasis on creativity and taking risks means the staff looks for innovation and flexibility and is open to new approaches and ideas. The staff accepts mistakes with equanimity, understanding that they are part of the learning process and required for students to become capable, effective leaders. These efforts create a learning community.

To build personal relationships, the center selects experienced students to mentor those new to the role of site coordinator or service-learning leader. Mentors collaborate with staff to teach the leadership course, preparing workshops and modifying what has been done in the past to continually improve. Thus, they hone their own facilitation and leadership skills by supporting the work of the student leaders. In addition to these mentors, a graduate student also serves as a mentor to all the students. She describes her role as being an adviser to the full student team. Advising includes serving as an information resource, problem-solver, liaison to other departments, and personal role model.

Reflections on the Program

Many students note that their service and leadership experience results in tremendous personal development. One wrote: "My service-learning experiences were the most enlightening and transformative experiences of my life." According to one student leader who looked back on her first year of school, the experience helped her mature: "Through this opportunity, my eyes have been opened. The more that I surround myself with people like those that I have met through experiences like this, the more I feel myself leaving my selfishness behind." Students learn about social responsibility, as another student expressed: "Before I started working in community service-learning, I was one of those people who didn't have much of a social conscience. Now all of that has changed, and I say, 'Put me in the trenches to do the real work to make a difference.'"

Some students who become aware of social issues through this service experience also learn skills for making change through advocacy. One commented, "When I saw the impact that each student can have on serious social issues, I was more empowered than ever to learn more and create positive change in my community. I then decided to take the energy that I was feeling from my service experience and do some independent research." When this student learned of the International Right to Know Campaign, which calls for corporate disclosure on human, environmental, and labor rights abroad, she contacted the campaign coordinators in Washington, DC. She even scheduled a meeting with the congresswoman from her district to support the proposed legislation. Other students have noted the impact of their service work on their future goals (see the Sidebar on the next page).

Faculty say student support makes the tasks associated with service-learning more manageable and enables them to sustain their commitment to this teaching and learning method. Many professors comment that having the support of the center and student leadership makes it possible for them to continue to incorporate service-learning without excessive time or stress. One faculty member explains:

> Student leaders are an integral part of the service-learning courses I teach. They help with planning and coordinating class projects (from arranging car pools to telephoning students), they increase participation by facilitating in-class reflections, and they provide me with an honest appraisal of what is happening in the class. More importantly, student leaders serve as important links between the students and me by providing their insights and perspectives on the course materials and class projects. Our relationship models the importance of collaboration and teamwork that are important aspects of what it means to build community. By working with student leaders, I am more effectively able to create strong bonds with the other students in the class and to create a more student-centered learning environment.

Community partners report that they are able to have more student volunteers at their sites because the site coordinators take the burden of managing them. These partners appreciate the students' leadership styles as well. As one partnering K-12 school staff member noted:

Student Leadership and Career/Lifelong Development

Students' leadership experiences at USD not only help them meet their academic and personal goals while in school but also assist them in developing their career goals. One student explained:

> All this involvement has inspired me to go to graduate school for postsecondary adminis-
> tration and student affairs. My goal is to be an administrator on a college campus so that
> I can interact and work with energetic students, and inspire them to commit themselves
> to service and action for the rest of their lives.

Another student noted:

> I got involved in community service learning in an "Intro to Sociology" class. I have been
> involved for over four years now, and I will continue for the rest of my life. By becoming
> a public defender, I can help those who are in need. Working with the boys and girls at
> juvenile hall helped me to further my interest in justice issues.

Once students have graduated and are able to look back on their college experiences, they are in a better position to evaluate the motivation, interests, and skills they gained in these roles. One graduate who had been out of school for four years wrote:

> As I look back and think about my development in college, I consider my positions with-
> in community service-learning as the most formative for me personally and professional-
> ly. The things I was exposed to, along with the responsibilities I had, encouraged my
> growth and self-confidence. I learned to love and appreciate our neighboring community
> and took pride in supporting it. I learned not to be afraid of differences or "different"
> parts of my community; I saw that there is always something to embrace and be curious
> about and explore. Being exposed to so many community agencies as a site coordinator
> working with other coordinators showed me just how big our world is and how many
> options for community service there are.

> One thing that made the student a great leader was her attention to detail. She took
> charge when needed, but also had the ability to step back and allow students to learn,
> grow, and work together as a team. Her energy and her tenacity were contagious. The
> students love and miss her terribly. She changed their lives.

Site coordinators bring their special skills and strengths to the team. A partner with an after-school program for middle-schoolers describes the site coordinator she worked with as someone who came "with a huge heart, a creative talent, and lots of ideas to get students involved in community service. There was no job to big or too small for her to tackle." Among the projects this volunteer worked on were a four-week unit called "Healthy Lifestyles," an all-day sports camp, and a dance program.

Conclusion

Baxter Magolda (1992) wrote of the development of "contextual knowing" as a type of intellectual development that people rarely achieve while still in college. However, the more leadership responsibility that students assume in the program, the more the characteristics of this stage develop: students compare perspectives, think through problems, and integrate knowledge. They learn from their peers in a reciprocal manner. With the staff, faculty, and community partners, they apply knowledge in context, critique, and receive criticism.

By encouraging students to explore, experiment with, and reflect on leadership, the Center for Community Service-Learning offers them a valuable resource for their futures. Many USD graduates become partners and professional peers in the community, and they know that their service-learning experiences have prepared them for life after graduation. Their conversations reinforce the fact that the center has effectively been "preparing leaders dedicated to ethical conduct and compassionate service," as the USD mission states, and that many have made lifelong commitments to promote social change and justice because of this encouragement.

References

Astin, H. & Astin, A. (1996). *A social change model of leadership development.* Los Angeles: Higher Education Research Institute, UCLA.

Magolda, B. (1992). *Knowing and reasoning in college: Gender-related patterns in students' intellectual development.* San Francisco: Jossey-Bass.

Rauner, J.S. (1995). *The impact of community service-learning on student development, as perceived by student leaders.* Unpublished doctoral dissertation, University of San Diego.

Identifying Student Leaders

Community Learning at Antioch College

In 1992, the Bonner Foundation brought the Bonner Scholarship to Antioch College as part of a national community-service scholarship program. The program seeks to transform the lives of students at 25 colleges and universities, including Antioch, as well as their campuses, local communities, and the nation by providing access to education and opportunities to serve.

To achieve this mission, the Bonner Foundation provides four-year community service scholarships to approximately 1,500 students (Bonner Scholars) annually. The scholarship serves those individuals who have high financial need and a commitment to service. It heightens the scholars' overall education by engaging them in ongoing service work and helping them develop the tools and knowledge necessary to make that work meaningful and lasting.

Every year, the program selects 10 students from Antioch's incoming class to be Bonner Scholars. The 40 Bonner Scholars at Antioch receive a service scholarship that includes $1,050 per semester for academic expenses during study semesters, and a total of $5,500 for up to three off-campus service jobs (co-ops). In addition, the students receive a $1,600 loan reduction if they complete all their requirements. The students perform 140 hours of service (predominantly off-campus) during study semesters and approximately 500 hours during co-op terms. This community service can include work within Antioch and in the Yellow Springs, Dayton, Springfield, and New Carlisle (Ohio) communities. The program also directly supports the Center for Community Learning, which was established in 1997, when the Bonner Scholars recognized a need for a central resource for community service.

The center is a resource for any student, faculty, or staff member interested in community service opportunities, service-learning, and the Bonner Scholars program. Its mission is to provide meaningful civic engagement, which recognizes the powerful intersection between service, learning, empowered communities, and social change. It supplies technical support for service-learning and community service placements, and provides professional development opportunities for students, faculty, staff, and community partners, as well as network opportunities with local, state, regional, and national organizations.

Antioch also administers half-time AmeriCorps service terms through the Bonner Foundation. A student with 900 hours of service over two years is awarded a $2,362.50 Education Award, which can be used to pay higher education tuition or loans.

The Community Responsibility Scholarship was established at Antioch in 1999 to recognize the importance of community service and was expanded in 2001, both in number of scholarships and monies given. Antioch selects Community Responsibility Scholars from the incoming class each year based on their past demonstration of community involvement. In exchange for a $5,000-$10,000 renewable annual tuition reduction, recipients commit to 50 hours per term of active participation in the college's governance system, work-study positions, or other local community agencies.

Defiance College's Service Leadership Awards
Each year, Defiance College offers up to 40 students (10 per class) with established records of service to their school and community a $2,000 renewable scholarship—the Bonner Leader Award. The award allows students to continue their commitment to service throughout their years at Defiance. Students must have a strong record of school and community service in high school and must complete an application form, including an essay and two recommendations.

Recipients participate with a variety of local and national agencies. In addition to weekly volunteering, service leaders join forces in one major project each year. Past projects have included Back Bay Mission in Biloxi, Mississippi, an Oglala Sioux reservation in Pine Ridge, South Dakota, and community agencies in Murfreesboro, North Carolina, as well as international trips to Jamaica, Kenya, and China.

A second schoalrship, Defiance's Citizen Leaders program, awards up to 50 incoming students with an interest in service and/or leadership with a $1,000 renewable scholarship to continue their commitment to civic engagement while at the college.

These scholarhips exemplify Defiance's commitment to finding and supporting civically engaged students. Service-learning at Defiance is coordinated by the Office of

Service Learning and is required in Freshman Seminar and "Life in Society," both general education courses. All Defiance students are involved in service-learning their freshman year. In addition, 19 fall and 17 spring major courses include a service component as part of the class requirement; 14 majors include service-learning as a part of their course curriculum.

Training Students

ALTHOUGH IT IS CLEAR THAT UNDERGRADUATES have the ability to assume major new leadership roles, the success of the programs featured in this book also stems from a keen appreciation of the importance of training. In this section, we look at several different approaches to skill development. Some of the ground covered has already been alluded to in earlier chapters, but here the training process itself is featured in more detail.

One of the most ambitious training programs in the United States is located at California State University Monterey Bay (CSUMB), an institution founded with community service and service-learning at its core. Perhaps this primary institutional commitment to engagement made it possible for CSUMB to consider so demanding a program in the first place. CSUMB's Student Leadership in Service Learning program requires its participants to commit to its four-week Summer of Service Leadership Academy (SoSLA). This training prepares them to co-facilitate classroom discussions, supervise at community sites, and implement co-curricular service experiences.

As North Carolina's land-grant institution, North Carolina State University was founded with service in mind. In order to help faculty in all disciplines reclaim this outreach dimension, the school's service-learning program developed a very special kind of student training focused on facilitating reflection. Utilizing a three-step model, the program teaches student leaders to take primary responsibility for a reflection unit that can be integrated into courses across the curriculum. To become qualified for such work, participating students must themselves enroll in a special seminar.

The third chapter draws on still another service tradition: that of historically Black colleges and universities (HBCUs). At North Carolina Central University (NCCU), as at

several other HBCUs, all students must fulfill a service requirement in order to graduate. In such a context, it is only natural that some students should be groomed as service leaders, facilitating the community involvement of their peers. At NCCU, these student leaders have been dubbed "student ambassadors" and are prepared for their role
through a training process that draws on Paolo Freire's consciousness-raising model,
Conscientizacao. The vehicle for this process is a series of service-learning circles, reflection sessions that include faculty and community partners as well as student leaders.

Most training programs draw deliberately on more experienced students as a resource
to help less experienced students develop their awareness and abilities. So important is
this student-student mentoring process that it deserves a chapter of its own. Azusa
Pacific University's careful investigation of the mentoring process answers this need.
When the university's Center for Service-Learning and Research was about to experience a potentially devastating turnover of service-learning advocates, the program con-
sciously set out to take advantage of the final few months before graduation to have its
outgoing advocates train a new cohort and ensure that the work of the center would
not suffer.

The vignettes included in this section, from Mars Hill College, the University of
Michigan-Ann Arbor, and Saint Anselm College, provide highlights of the training
strategies these institutions use to make student leadership a hallmark of their engagement efforts.

Training Students for Leadership in Service-Learning

Tania D. Mitchell, Karly Edwards,
M. Crystal Macias-Diaz, and Olivia Weatherbee

S ERVICE-LEARNING IS AN INTEGRAL PART of the education that students receive at California State University Monterey Bay (CSUMB), a state university founded in 1994. The emphasis on serving the immediate and surrounding communities, and on preparing students for significant roles in these efforts, is expressly included in the campus vision statement. It is a challenge and commitment that distinguishes CSUMB as a four-year institution.

All students who walk through the doors of CSUMB go though a comprehensive service-learning program in which they identify issues of social justice, oppression, dominance, and marginalization through their experiences with class, gender, race, sexuality, ability, and several other components of social identity. CSUMB requires all its students to successfully complete two service-learning courses. Upon graduation, students will have completed a minimum of 60 hours of service to the community, combined with relevant course material and intense reflection. In addition, approximately half of all students (approximately 1,800) are engaged in service-learning experiences every year.

In the fall of 1996, the Service Learning Institute at CSUMB expanded its infrastructure support for faculty, community partners, and students involved in service-learning by establishing an innovative student leadership program. Student Leadership in Service Learning, or (sl)^2, places students in critical roles where they facilitate the service-learning process among students, faculty, and community members. The program is course-based—Service Learning Student Leaders serve as co-teachers in service-learning classrooms—and community-based—the leaders serve as peer coordinators for service-learning students entering the community. The (sl)^2 program also is responsible for co-curricular service and creates action plans and program events in support of the diverse tri-county community that CSUMB serves.

The $(sl)^2$ program is a resource for campus and community. Service Learning Student Leaders frequently consult with faculty on effective practice from a student perspective, help community members create meaningful service opportunities for students, and work with other students on engaging respectfully with community members. The Service Learning Institute supports the program by providing a faculty coordinator who serves as a resource for students in planning and implementing projects. The coordinator recruits, trains, and supervises the student leaders and manages the program's finances.

Service Learning Student Leaders have diverse responsibilities. Their work may include such activities as organizing a week of events on the issue of homelessness, designing orientations and workshops for first-time service-learning students, leading classroom discussions and activities about race, and working with faculty members to develop a course syllabus. Members of the $(sl)^2$ program must be well trained to manage these roles effectively.

This chapter describes the training that gives CSUMB students the skills and information needed to be part of the Student Leadership in Service Learning program. The training regimen begins with lower-division service-learning courses, followed by a core four-week Summer of Service Leadership Academy. In addition, ongoing training experiences provide continuous opportunities for leadership and skill development for student leaders in service-learning.

The Lower Division Service-Learning Experience

The initial experience with service-learning is one of the most important aspects of training. The lower division service-learning requirement, unique to CSUMB, helps develop students' commitment and action toward social justice. "SL200S: Introduction to Service in Multicultural Communities" is the first opportunity students have to combine their academic experience with community involvement, making connections with the community and expanding their knowledge of systemic injustices. These injustices include sexism, racism, homophobia, and other forms of oppression that infringe on procedural and personal justice through institutional policies.

By challenging students to look at their service experiences in this context, the course builds connections not only between the classroom and the community but also between both of those and students' lives. Students engage with community members for 30 hours during the semester and contribute to a community need through their service. At the same time, in the classroom, they try to understand their relationship to the community and how their membership in various social identity groups affects their experiences with privilege and oppression. As part of this process, the course trains students to articulate injustices they may have felt their entire lives or voice identities previously unrecognized or marginalized. One SL200 student credits his lower division service-learning experience with changing his perspective:

> This [SL200] experience has made me realize so much about myself. I knew that I was lucky growing up as I did, but I never really made that connection to privilege, to realizing that everyone doesn't start from the same place. It seems so obvious now.... I know that because of this class, my conversations with my friends and family are different. The way I look at everything has changed.

The lower division course introduces students to the kinds of material required to facilitate service-learning effectively for other students and to be respectful participants in the community. The idea is that in order to work as service-learning student leaders, students must first understand the roots of oppression, the role service-learning plays in both perpetuating and alleviating inequality, and the way they as individuals fit into society. A current student leader sees the course as the foundation of her work both in the community and in training other students: "I always go back to my SL200 experience. The activities we did in class, readings, videos—I look to these things in thinking about how to best work with my community partners and to best prepare my service learners."

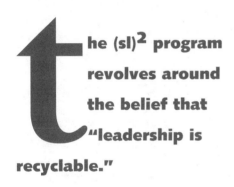

The (sl)^2 program revolves around the belief that "leadership is recyclable."

Another integral part of the training is the opportunities that students have to lead conversations on social justice issues. The curriculum prepares them to speak up during uncomfortable moments to help others understand their role in social justice and systemic oppression. To serve as effective allies, leaders must learn how to stop perpetuating the marginalization of certain identities. The real training is in how to stand up for social justice and create spaces for other voices to be heard.

The Summer of Service Leadership Academy

In addition to teaching specific skills and training students for further learning, the lower division course develops common knowledge and a base of understanding for the Summer of Service Leadership Academy (SoSLA), which is the core of the training experience. The SoSLA is an intensive four-week program that provides students with the skills and experiences necessary to guide their peers in service-learning courses.

Through this program, student leaders build on the skills and knowledge developed during the lower division course and enhance their leadership, communication, planning, and organization skills.

Student leaders at CSUMB serve three critical roles in the service-learning process: co-facilitating classroom discussions, training and supervising students in the community, and developing and implementing co-curricular service experiences. The SoSLA curriculum is designed to meet those diverse training needs. The $(sl)^2$ program revolves around the belief that "leadership is recyclable." The program's success depends on current members encouraging their peers to apply to and participate in SoSLA and sharing their experiences with the new SoSLA cohort.

SoSLA meets five days a week from 9:00 a.m. to 5:00 p.m. each day. Each week of the training emphasizes a particular knowledge area essential to student leadership in service-learning: 1) privilege, oppression, and liberation; 2) facilitation and communication; 3) community knowledge; and 4) taking action. These knowledge areas are consistently supported by an element of team building (collaboration, trust, and collegiality are essential to the program) and guided by the process of reflection.

Week One: Privilege, Oppression, and Liberation

Each summer, SoSLA begins with a retreat. The cohort members and a facilitator travel to a nearby retreat center to begin an intensive three-day exploration into self and others. The program focuses intently on self-discovery, sharing, and social justice; participants stay overnight away from roommates, family, financial responsibilities, and other distractions. Because the retreat is the first activity of SoSLA, participants are able to get to know each other, build rapport, and establish relationships quickly. A former SoSLA student notes, "By the end of the retreat, you really feel like you know the other members of your cohort. You definitely trust them, which makes it easier to participate in some of the conversations and workshops that follow."

While the atmosphere of the retreat is intense, it is not necessarily "heavy." The challenging moments are balanced with other more casual opportunities for bonding and interaction. Along with music, films, outdoor activities, and food, students tackle difficult issues, experiences, and scenarios in ways that are enjoyable as well as educational.

After the retreat and the return to campus, SoSLA participants also attend several workshops on social justice. Learning to identify oppression on internalized, interpersonal, and institutional levels is key. Participants explore various systems of oppression (e.g., capitalism, patriarchy, heteronormativity) and how they become evident (e.g., classism, sexism, heterosexism). Students think of examples of oppression in their own lives, on campus, and in the community, locally, nationally, and globally. They investigate how systemic inequalities and perceived differences have an impact on different people and explore strategies for examining privilege. They also discuss the different ways that service and service-learning might contribute to liberation. In this discussion, the program facilitators emphasize the need to pay attention to root causes of community issues and people's intentions when engaging in service, because these aspects play a major role in determining whether community work might in fact be liberating.

Toward the end of the week, students develop scenarios of experiences they are likely to encounter as Service Learning Student Leaders working with faculty, students, and community members. One student leader remarked, "When you're brainstorming and acting out these scenarios, it can feel a little ridiculous. But two months later, when it comes true, you can't help but laugh and be really grateful that you had that practice during SoSLA!" The scenarios explore ways that different parties in the service-learning experience might invoke privilege, examples of oppression perpetuated in the classroom or agency, and their own levels of comfort with various issues of oppression and identity. The student leaders role-play these scenarios and work with each other to develop responses.

TEAM BUILDING. Many activities during the first week are aimed at building the team. The environment created through opportunities for sharing experiences is effective in developing the cohort. Participants engage in activities in which they strategize and work together. The experience of working together across differences affords an additional opportunity to investigate attitudes and assumptions that have an impact on working relationships. Students explore situations in which they take leadership or defer, interact, and engage, and examine how power, privilege, and oppression might affect those actions.

REFLECTION. Throughout the first week, each day begins and ends with a check-in. Each workshop and activity includes time for debriefing, so that students are able, if ready, to share their thoughts, feelings, and learning about the previous activity. In addition, students participate in guided reflection in which they respond in writing directly to the various activities and accompanying readings of the week. They also write in their journals and have other time throughout the week specifically for reflection.

Week Two: Facilitation and Communication

Activities during the first week of the academy are based on theory; during the second week, they are based on skills. The new cohort of student leaders practices facilitating discussions, developing and leading reflections and other activities, and engaging in respectful conversations with diverse audiences.

The week begins with a multicultural communication workshop in which students assess their own communication styles and learn about the different factors that influence and shape intercultural communication. They consider how identity and power have an impact on one's ability to engage and interact in various situations. They explore the ways in which body language affects communication. The workshop facilitators introduce different scenarios that explore common situations for student leaders in the service-learning process. Participants analyze the experience using a multicultural communication framework to better understand how identity, history, assumptions, power, position, and intentions may have an impact.

A second workshop on public speaking prepares students to research issues, create talking points, and share important information in a clear way. Students learn about the use of visual aids (effective colors, text size, fonts, styles of writing, and appropriate images), tips for opening and closing presentations, and the importance of tone, volume, and eye contact.

Practice in public speaking occurs on two levels. During the workshop, each participant has a topic for which he or she develops a short presentation. Students research the issue, outline their presentation, and create a visual aid before presenting it to their cohort. Afterward, the presenter evaluates him- or herself, and the workshop facilitator and cohort offer feedback. In the second public-speaking experience, at the end of SoSLA, each participant develops a presentation on her or his experience and learning. Using a creative element and incorporating what they have learned from the public-speaking workshop, participants make their presentations before an audience of students, faculty, and community members they have worked with throughout SoSLA.

SoSLA participants also attend a workshop in which they evaluate their listening skills, consider the challenges of being good listeners, and practice active listening. To develop facilitation skills, student leaders receive training from faculty members. They learn how to share experiences effectively and how to develop questions and useful tips for guiding discussion.

A reflection workshop finishes the second week of SoSLA. Current and former members of the Student Leadership in Service Learning program work with SoSLA participants to discuss the importance of reflection. They discuss various ways to reflect (for example, writing in a journal, small group discussions, artwork, round-robins) and the most effective types of reflection activities. Student leaders share different reflection techniques, instructing SoSLA participants in how to facilitate those experiences for others. Finally, participants develop their own reflection activities that they practice during the third week of SoSLA.

TEAM BUILDING. A number of activities serve as "icebreakers" to build team unity. These activities are targeted toward the communication process to help students feel comfortable communicating with each other at a deep level.

REFLECTION. Check-ins before and after each day facilitate reflection. Students write in their journals and reflect on ways in which communication will be important to their role as service-learning student leaders. Socials throughout the week give the SoSLA participants an informal setting in which they can discuss the experience so far.

Week Three: Community Knowledge

The third week of SoSLA focuses on community knowledge. As facilitators of the service-learning process, the students must know and understand the tri-county area from the perspective of community members. SoSLA participants meet with community leaders, visit organizations throughout the area, and engage in service with and for diverse communities in the region.

During each service experience, SoSLA participants research the relevant community to understand better the role and purpose of the agency. Students look for root causes underlying the need they are attempting to address. They spend time in the local community (outside of the agency) to understand the context for service. They meet with community members to build rapport and meet with agency or organization leaders to learn more about logistics and practice. Because community-based students lead orientations and supervise students in their service, knowledge about agency logistics is extremely important to their work. Following the service experience, students study local policy and the work of the agency in depth to understand how they might serve that organization to promote social change and social justice.

TEAM BUILDING. Students working collaboratively in service often build teams. Working at a soup kitchen, SoSLA participants plan the menu, shop for food, cook together, and serve meals. It is an exercise in cooperation and communication that promotes camaraderie and collaborative leadership.

REFLECTION. Throughout the community knowledge week, SoSLA participants are encouraged to write in their journals. Both as part of their practice and to promote reflection on the service experience, students facilitate the reflection activities they developed during the second week. This gives them a chance to develop skills in facilitation and critical reflection and creates another way to receive feedback.

Week Four: Taking Action

The final week of SoSLA focuses on taking action. In a critical aspect of the program, students develop co-curricular service opportunities for the campus. Co-curricular service-learning at CSUMB follows a three-tiered approach to taking action: raising awareness, creating opportunities for dialogue, and engaging in meaningful action. To develop such opportunities, student leaders research community issues and needs by seeking input from community members and focusing on relevant, important events.

SoSLA participants are trained in the CSUMB $(sl)^2$ programming model, which includes researching and assessing needs, establishing outcomes, brainstorming potential interventions, determining a particular strategy, creating a budget, establishing a timeline, delegating tasks, marketing the event, and implementing the project. Training is supplemented with workshop discussions of previous action planning facilitated by the student leaders.

After the workshop, SoSLA participants spend the remainder of the week meeting with community members, current student leaders, and the program coordinator to develop a co-curricular service experience to implement during the fall semester. The SoSLA cohort develops all aspects of the experience (with the exception of project implementation) during this week. At the end of the week, they present their plan to a panel of campus and community leaders for approval. The plan must include a definable issue and a rationale for their focus on that issue, a campaign that raises awareness, an event or experience that creates opportunity for dialogue, and a community experience that engages students and community members in meaningful action. The panel offers feedback on the proposed experience that the students can use to improve their planning before the project implementation.

TEAM BUILDING. The conclusion to the SoSLA training program centers around the team that has been created. Students must reach consensus about an issue on which to focus their project, learn to work together under deadlines, and collaboratively develop a presentation and action plan. This experience tests the strength and unity of team members and frequently motivates and strengthens the team for future action.

REFLECTION. Participants engage in self- and group reflection during this week. Students complete a guided reflection activity in which they consider their commitment to the project and their contributions to the team. Additionally, SoSLA participants routinely check in during the week to understand how people feel about the process, the project, and the overall experience.

The SoSLA experience prepares students for their work as Service Learning Student Leaders. Following this four-week training experience, they begin their official employment as members of the program.

Opportunities for Ongoing Training

Because preparation and training are essential parts of being a successful Service Learning Student Leader, CSUMB provides a systematic program of continuous training throughout the academic year. The lower division course provides the necessary foundation; SoSLA provides specific skills and regular program meetings provide ongoing development to enhance skills and abilities.

The program meetings take the form of skill-development workshops facilitated by students as well as opportunities to develop and plan co-curricular service experiences. The workshops may include advanced practice in facilitation—sharing new reflection or experiential activities—and identity work that allows student leaders to consider their social identity as members of the program. Their facilitation of program meetings allows students to develop further their public speaking and presentation skills. In the meetings, they also work actively to develop three co-curricular service experiences each semester. They are continually challenged to respond effectively to community needs, to engage others in dialogue, and to work collaboratively to accomplish goals. The meetings also give students the opportunity to consult with their peers to solve problems, learn from one another, discuss ways to improve practice, and give peer-to-peer support that strengthens team collaboration and communication.

having a student leader in class shows that service-learning "is not just a bogus requirement."

A current student leader has remarked, "Training isn't actually training until it is put into practice, and until it is implemented, one cannot know its validity." The program meetings allow student leaders to assess the effectiveness of their previous preparation. A former leader explained: "It's a check-in. We get to think about how well we've been prepared to meet the challenges of the job, and when we see gaps, we can use this time to think about what additional training we need and then make it happen."

Conclusion

The lower division course is only a beginning in the education and preparation for student leadership. CSUMB takes that foundation and builds on it during the SoSLA experience. The ongoing training gives new and returning student leaders a chance to share experiences and to continue building their skills. Through their individual placements, student leaders gain a different perspective of the service-learning experience—

that of facilitator. They bring questions and challenges to program meetings and work collectively to evaluate their roles and generate solutions.

Through these many opportunities for training and development, students acquire the skills and experiences that make them effective leaders in the service-learning program. The training is vital to the student leaders, but it is also important to the whole student body, which benefits from peer leadership. One student commented that having a student leader in class "shows that people our age care about social justice." Further, the student noted, it shows that service-learning "is not just a bogus requirement." Student leaders can establish relationships and communicate with their peers in ways that faculty and administrators cannot. They make an indelible contribution to their peers' learning and development, while continuing to develop themselves as active, responsible community members.

Training students for leadership in service-learning requires attention to social justice, skills for facilitation and communication, learning about the community, and planning and organization skills. At CSUMB, the combination of the summer program focusing on these concepts, the preparation students have before entering SoSLA, and the continuous exposure to these concepts they have afterward is key to their success as leaders in the facilitation of service-learning. Student leaders and the skills they develop make innumerable contributions to the service-learning process at CSUMB. For the students themselves, these skills are tools that build a strong foundation for life.

Reflection Leader Training and Support

Patti Clayton and Julie McClure

> You can wait until you graduate and use this opportunity to prepare and prepare and prepare; or you can begin living now, accept this university as "real" and find your own best way to influence this community so that it becomes a better institution to serve those who come after you.
>
> —*Robert Greenleaf (1967)*

THE NORTH CAROLINA STATE UNIVERSITY (NC State) Service-Learning Program has, from its inception, been co-created by students and faculty. It was launched in 1999 by a leadership team of three undergraduates, two instructors, and two professional staff members. The students created and implemented the community liaison and reflection leader positions. Five years later, the range of student leadership roles at the interface of classroom and community has expanded and deepened as the program has grown and become more formalized. The guiding principle of student-faculty co-creation, which remains at the heart of the program, has been largely responsible for the rapid development of materials and processes designed to support quality service-learning.

Many students who have taken leadership roles during the past five years have experienced this work not merely as a job (they generally receive a stipend) but more important as an avenue for leadership development through reflective community engagement. Seeking opportunities to "influence this community so that it becomes a better institution," they have pursued the legacy of former NC State Chancellor John Tyler Caldwell: a vision of maximizing the potential of the undergraduate experience as a unique opportunity for students to grow as servant leaders. Students' work as co-creators of the program has been mutually transformative, shaping their own growth as well as that of the university.

The Service-Learning Program has focused on developing the role of the reflection leader, and it is through this role that much of its development has occurred. This chapter discusses the evolution of the role of reflection leader and its associated training process, culminating with the current vision. As the program has evolved, the objectives for and approach to training and support have improved. This process has been a combination of creating opportunities and responding to challenges, leading to a continuous mode of reflective experimentation. Reflection leaders help to carve out developmental space at the interface of teaching and learning, research, and service, thereby enacting and advancing engagement. Appropriate training and support is crucial both for the students as individuals and for the broader landscape their work helps to shape.

Developing the Reflection Leader Model

During the spring of 1999, juniors Nick Haltom and Gretchen Lindner worked with instructor Patti Clayton (one of this chapter's authors) to develop a summer capstone service-learning project on HIV/AIDS efforts in the Philippines and a corollary reflection framework. The framework included a set of questions to structure reflection in accordance with students' objectives of improving the quality of service over time, growing as leaders, and learning more about themselves and about issues related to AIDS (modified from Kiser, 1998).

The following fall, these students designed and filled the role of reflection leader, each partnering with an instructor to support the reflection component of two field-test service-learning courses. They attended class meetings and completed readings, guided students through discussion of their service experiences using a revised version of their framework in small-group reflection sessions outside of class, and debriefed the service-learning process regularly with the instructors.

Haltom and Lindner thus served as the first two reflection leaders, and their design remains the core of the current model. Their training was in the trenches, however, and they struggled with managing group dynamics and interpersonal conflict, crafting appropriate roles with the students and instructors, and supporting the students' analyses of their experiences. Their summary of important lessons learned included recommendations for a training process for future reflection leaders—a process that has evolved over time.

Learning to Train and Support Reflection Leaders

The training of reflection leaders has gone through several iterations. In the fall semester of the 2000–2001 academic year, Clayton and junior Jason Grissom met with seven trainees, most with no service-learning experience, on an ad hoc basis. The first meeting was a day-long retreat that consisted of a service experience and a reflection session led by Grissom. This immersion into service and reflection continued, with each student successively leading the others in reflection and being videotaped for later critique. The students served as reflection leaders during the spring semester and met a few times as a group to share experiences.

Review at the end of the year generated a vision for more in-depth, academically grounded training and prompted further refinements to the reflection framework. One improvement that has proved crucial in the evolution of the program's understanding of reflection was Grissom's formalization of the "articulating learning" step. This step brings reflection sessions to a close with a four-part structure—"What did I learn?" "How did I learn it?" "Why does it matter?" and "What will I do with it?"—and thus helps focus students on expressing and exploring their most important learning outcomes.

In the fall semester of the 2001–2002 academic year, Grissom and Clayton co-facilitated reflection leader training as a pass/fail special-topics course in the Department of Political Science and Public Administration. Six students—each with experience in service-learning—participated in a range of one-time service experiences and took turns leading reflection sessions, which were again videotaped. Course material focused on reflection, citizenship, diversity, ethics, communication, mentoring, and role crafting. During the spring, the students met occasionally to reflect on their experiences as reflection leaders.

During the 2002–2003 academic year, Clayton taught the special-topics training course for six students, most of whom had taken her leadership seminar and were thus familiar with service-learning and the reflection process. In addition to the material from the previous year, the course involved two rubrics for guiding the feedback on written reflections. The students undertook a semester-long service project rather than a series of one-time activities. Because of the need to support more faculty in service-learning, many of the students were serving as reflection leaders while in training, thus making the training requirement more difficult to balance. Finding time for the periodic support gatherings became difficult.

During the spring of 2003, Clayton's leadership seminar served as the focal class for research on the reflection rubrics. Due to the intensity of reflection, students learned much about leadership and civic engagement as well as reflection and critical thinking. Although all were well suited to become reflection leaders, only one, Julie McClure (the other chapter author here), was able to take a second, similar course during the 2003–2004 academic year. The four trainees served as reflection leaders during the semester of training, so the course returned to using a series of one-time service experiences in order to reduce the problem of schedule overload. Unfortunately, this shift generated a low level of commitment because this service was perceived merely as material for reflection. Problems with accountability arose, and there was a tendency to view the course as a job requirement rather than a learning and leadership-development opportunity. No spring semester support gatherings were held.

A careful review of the training course offered during the fall of 2003—particularly compared with the more successful leadership seminar—suggested the need for substantial revision. By the end of the fifth year, the program team better understood the role of the reflection leader, the process of reflection, and the requirements for successful training and support. The new vision should maximize the potential for student leadership in service-learning and other forms of student engagement. The remainder of this chapter presents the program's understanding of the role of reflection leader and the model for training and support currently envisioned.

Culminating Vision for the Reflection Leader Role

The recommended model for reflection sessions has certain core features, although each reflection leader-instructor pair adapts them as appropriate:

- Students working on the same service-learning project meet in the same reflection session group throughout the semester. The group ranges from two to six students.

- Two-hour reflection sessions are held six times during the semester. The first is an introduction, the last is a concluding review, and the middle four are structured in accordance with the reflection framework.

- A reflection leader supports up to four student groups and holds, at most, two reflection sessions each week.

- The reflection framework is structured according to the program's three-step reflection model, called DEAL: Describe experiences→Examine experiences (from personal, civic, then academic perspectives)→Articulate Learning (in each category—personal, civic, and academic) (Ash & Clayton, 2004). Written articulation of the learning process begins in the reflection sessions but continues after, with the reflection leader and instructor providing feedback.

- As the semester progresses, students become less dependent on the reflection leader, who takes a largely passive role by the fifth session.

- The reflection session is a safe yet critical space. The reflection leader has no role in grading and reports to the instructor only on issues of attendance and participation and on questions about academic material. The reflection leader and students are responsible for maintaining norms of mutual respect and for appropriately challenging one another's assumptions and conclusions.

The model for the partnerships between the reflection leaders and instructors also has certain core elements:

- Reflection leaders should have experience with service-learning and have completed training before undertaking the role. Instructors should have participated in the program's faculty development process before having access to a trained, program-funded reflection leader.

- Instructors can either identify a student from their own classes to take the training course or partner with a student recruited by the program.

- It is helpful, but not required, for the reflection leader to be familiar with the instructor's discipline. Familiarity with the course content is required, which is achieved through regular class attendance, review of readings, and discussion with the instructor.

- To ensure a strong partnership, the instructor and the reflection leader need to share an understanding of their roles, of the most important academic material, and of their primary objectives for service-learning in the course. Regular, open communication is vital, as is their students' awareness of the relationship as a partnership.

- An independent-study arrangement can add an intellectual dimension, giving the partnership substantive, versus simply logistical, content and validating the role as part of the reflection leader's curriculum.

- Generally, neither instructors nor reflection leaders participate in service along with the students, although they are encouraged to attend on-site orientations. Reflection leaders are generally not responsible for managing the logistics of the service-learning projects.

- The instructor and the reflection leader must minimize the potential to introduce an artificial separation between the service-learning component and the rest of the course. Both instructors and reflection leaders need to understand the service-learning process, facilitate reflection, and provide feedback to students.

The most important personal characteristics required for the reflection leaders include responsibility, flexibility, maturity, commitment to their own and others' growth, and sensitivity to trade-offs. Also important are organizational skills, community-building skills, and the ability to see connections, to relate well to peers and adults, to communicate effectively in writing and orally, to multitask, and to be reflective.

helping students to deepen their learning through reflection on experience requires highly developed critical-thinking skills.

To implement this model successfully, several important elements of service-learning–related knowledge and ability are required. Reflection leaders must share with their instructors the conviction that service-learning is a powerful pedagogy and be aware of its strengths and challenges. They must understand that service-learning is different from traditional teaching and learning strategies and service opportunities. Students need to be able to make the "shifts in perspective and practice" that service-learning requires and to support students in making similar adjustments (Clayton & Ash, 2004).[1]

In addition, because reflection is structured to produce outcomes in each primary category of learning objectives—personal, civic, and academic—reflection leaders need to be able to think from each of these perspectives and see connections among them. Helping students to achieve such learning through reflection on experience—particularly by providing meaningful feedback—also requires highly developed critical-thinking skills. Reflection leaders need to internalize the program's reflection rubrics so that standards of reasoning and critical thinking increasingly characterize their own thinking.

A New Vision for Reflection Leader Training and Support
The development of a new vision for training and support was aimed at producing outcomes in accord with best practices and without the shortcomings of the previous training. This vision therefore needed to support student leaders in undertaking complex roles with peers and instructors, in internalizing the reflection model, and in mastering the theoretical foundations of personal, civic, and academic analysis as well as the foundations of leadership development, service-learning in general, and reflection in particular. It had to allow for both preparation and on-the-job learning, while focusing on the development of the student leaders and on the learning of the students they would support. It had to cover substantial content, while also providing intense exposure to and practice with service-learning and reflection. It had to overcome difficul-

---

1. Reflecting on their own experience, students launched the "shifts in perspective" project in 2003. They began to identify and explore the ways in which service-learning requires and fosters perspectives and practices distinctly different from those associated with more traditional teaching. This work has been further developed into reflection activities for students and faculty.

ties of recruitment, accountability, and scheduling and involve veteran as well as new reflection leaders.

The resulting vision has the following elements:

- Broad scope
- Focused recruitment
- Comprehensive training
- Ongoing training and support

Broad Scope

In accordance with its land-grant mission, NC State is increasingly focusing on connecting students systematically with engagement opportunities. The reflection leader role is just one example of how a student well-trained in reflective thinking and community partnering can help to advance engagement. An expanded vision of leadership roles might include working with students to design and reflect on opportunities for studying abroad or completing internships with an engagement dimension, establishing informal reflection mechanisms to enhance learning from extracurricular service, or working to integrate service-learning into honors, scholarship, and leadership programs.

The training model for the reflection leader role could thus serve as a gateway for students into multiple leadership opportunities on campus. Students might take a service-learning course or participate in a service-learning trip during spring break and then serve in one or more leadership capacities (potentially increasing the level of responsibility each semester). Ultimately, they might design their own capstone experience, whether research, travel abroad, or collaboration with faculty on program development or scholarly dissemination. Thus, students would experience engagement—and leadership to advance it—as a deveopmental journey throughout their undergraduate careers.

Focused Recruitment

Sharing this broad vision of the opportunities for student leadership should facilitate recruitment of students into the training program. In addition, it should attract students with a range of interests—service, service-learning, leadership, and research—and make participation especially attractive for students who want to make leadership and service central to their undergraduate careers. Focused recruitment thus involves telling the story of this developmental journey to students. The program could regularly offer information sessions where interested students can talk with current student leaders. It could sponsor opportunities for students to serve in the community, reflect

the vision for training includes a comprehensive, graded course that offers honors credit and fills a general education requirement.

on that experience, and then discuss it as an example of the range of engagement opportunities available to them. Above all, the recruitment process should help students see this work as way to accomplish their academic, service, leadership, research, and employment objectives simultaneously.

Comprehensive Training

The vision for training includes a comprehensive, graded course that offers honors credit and fills a general education requirement. Called "Changing Paradigms of Leadership, Learning, and Service," the course merges the best of the special topics course and the leadership seminar. Ideally taught every semester, the course is enhanced by service-learning and co-facilitated by an experienced reflection leader. Students cannot serve in a leadership role funded by the program until they have completed the course. It is broad enough to accommodate students with or without service-learning experience and open to students interested in its content but not yet committed to leadership roles.

The course offers four credits. It meets twice a week for 1 hour and 15 minutes and includes a weekly 2-hour learning lab during which the six reflection sessions, dinner seminars with guest speakers, and other enrichment activities occur. The ideal registration is 8 to 12 students, with a maximum of 15. The service-learning project requires a minimum of 20 to 25 hours. On average, the students complete one reading for each of 30 class periods. In addition, they keep a guided journal; collaboratively produce a service-learning project proposal, progress report, and final report; produce and peer-review articulated learnings; and give a final public presentation (see the Sidebar on the following page for the structure of this course; this and other service-learning syllabi are available on Campus Compact's website at www.compact.org/syllabi).

The course gives students continuous experience with the program's reflection model and the dynamics of self-directed learning. An activity, followed by reflection, on each of the first few days of class confirms that everything is worthy of reflection and that the DEAL process (**D**escribe→**E**xamine →**A**rticulate Learning) is the primary form of encounter with the service projects and class material. The same three-step model is used throughout the semester in reflection sessions and in class—in discussion of readings and of the service process—to prepare the students for the reflection leader role

Training Course Overview

Part I exposes students to the process of and rationale behind service-learning. It considers the differences between service-learning and traditional learning and the shifts in perspective and practice required for successful implementation. It also explores the dynamics of a learning community, considers engagement as an element of maximizing the undergraduate experience, and establishes the rapid pace of change in the twenty-first century as the analytical context for changing paradigms of leadership, learning, and service.

Part II addresses the changing understandings of leadership, learning, and service through the lens of the evolving worldview of Western civilization. Against the backdrop of Kuhn's work on paradigm shift and Greenleaf's servant lead-

ership theory, Part II examines the tensions at the heart of current theory on civic engagement, citizenship, leadership, and education.

Part III focuses on concepts and processes associated with promoting positive change among individuals and communities. Topics include mentoring, the tension between individual rights and the common good, power, community building, and various perspectives on citizenship.

Part IV reviews the semester and revisits important connections. Students draft a personal plan for their undergraduate years, given what they have learned about themselves and the nature of leadership, learning, and service in the twenty-first century.

and also to teach them to become continuously reflective. Each student facilitates at least one class period, leading discussion on one or two readings in the context of other readings and the service-learning project.

As the semester progresses, the reflection leader shifts virtually all the responsibility for the reflection sessions to the students. This approach highlights the importance and value of guided practice in that students do not facilitate significant learning among their peers until they are reasonably well prepared to do so effectively.

Ongoing Training and Support

Included in the vision of training are a two-and-a-half-day retreat at the beginning of each semester and a biweekly seminar during the semester for all students serving as reflection leaders. The retreat includes participation in and reflection on a morning of service (student leaders and instructors together) and practice in leading reflection and in designing reflection mechanisms for use during the semester. It also includes work with the reflection framework and rubrics and the tutorial *Learning through Critical Reflection*, introduction of new and revised reflection and assessment materials, and time to plan. The retreat is the first opportunity for all the student leaders to be together, so it serves as a planning forum for establishing goals and discussing modifications to the training process.

Within the structure of the biweekly dinner seminar, students explore related topics, with specific content determined by the issues facing student leaders in a given semester. The seminar series includes guest speakers. When appropriate, seminars converge with the learning lab from the training course to assist in scheduling appropriate guests for both groups and to encourage more new students to pursue the reflection leader role. The seminars provide space for reflection leaders to share successes and struggles. They also enhance the learning potential of the reflection leader role through systematic reflection on the experience of leadership. The seminars focus on revising the process and its associated materials and celebrate the accomplishments of student leaders.

It takes time to fully implement this—or any—vision of reflection leader training and support. An approach that is

Reflections on Service-Learning and Leadership Training

If I had not become involved in service-learning as a sophomore, I undoubtedly would have taken on other leadership roles within the university, but nothing that would have had such a profoundly positive impact on my personal life and my future career. In my personal life, as a result of my service-learning experiences, I have learned to resist my initial instinct to overly advise others. I have also learned to see my previous form of leadership—"carrying" the group—as harmful, and now choose to be a leader who removes the barriers that keep others from success. I see living "in the name of the best that is within me" as living up to my own internal standards, based on my own terms and not on what role others think is best or what commands more respect or earns more money.

In terms of my professional development, as a sophomore, I planned to attend medical school and become a practicing physician, but changes in perspective associated with my work as a reflection leader have led me to revise my plans. I have learned that sometimes one can make more of an impact working on the macro level, and I now tend to think in terms of systems of cause and effect and not just single events in isolation. Consequently, while I still see the need to treat illnesses and injuries, I believe more strongly now in the role of prevention. When I served as reflection leader for a life-cycle nutrition class, I developed a strong interest in nutrition and found myself attracted as well to teaching. As a result, I have changed my career plans from medicine to nutrition policy and intervention.

My work as a reflection leader has taken me to ever-higher levels of leadership and learning: co-developing the new training process, conducting research, helping to rework the nutrition class, coauthoring papers, and presenting at conferences. Never before have I felt so in control of my own education or so much a part of the learning and growth of others. It is a high level of responsibility, but my work as a leader in the Service-Learning Program has honed my abilities and given me the confidence to know that I am up to the task.

experimental, reflective, and co-created ensures adaptation for ever-changing opportunities and challenges.

McClure's own reflection (see the Sidebar on p. 86) suggests the impact of student leadership in advancing engagement on student leaders themselves and provides perhaps the strongest rationale for an institution to undertake a similar process of co-creation. Ultimately, students' understanding of themselves as agents of change and as having responsibility for their own learning and growth is among the most important goals of higher education.

Conclusion

Throughout its evolution, the reflection leader training and support process has been strongly influenced by particular aspects of the Service-Learning Program and by particular moments in NC State's institutional history. Engaging in such a process will, therefore, be different on each campus. The value of NC State's story lies in its commitment to student co-creation; in the value placed on reflective experimentation; in the intertwining of leadership, learning, and service; in the synergy between student development and institutional capacity-building; and in the philosophical commitment to the developmental potential of the undergraduate experience when the university is perceived as the "real world."

References

Ash, S.L,. & Clayton, P.H. (2004). The articulated learning: An approach to reflection and assessment. *Innovative Higher Education, 29,* 137–154.

Clayton, P.H., & Ash, S.L. (2004). Shifts in perspective: Capitalizing on the counternormative nature of service-learning. *Michigan Journal of Community Service Learning, 11*(1).

Greenleaf, R. (1967, 1988). *Have you a dream deferred.* Newton Center, MA: The Robert K. Greenleaf Center.

Kiser, P.M. (1998). The integrative processing model: A framework for learning in the field experience. *Human Service Education, 18,* 3–13.

Acknowledgments

The authors wish to acknowledge the many student leaders, faculty, and staff who have contributed to the development of the reflection leader role and training process. We hope we have represented the full range and richness of their perspectives on this work.

Special acknowledgement goes to Nick Haltom, Gretchen Lindner, Jason Grissom, Mary Catherine Brake, Jennifer King, Sarah Ash, Myra Moses, Jim Svara, Maxine Atkinson, the Faculty Center for Teaching and Learning, the Division of Multidisciplinary Studies, the Office of Extension and Engagement, The Caldwell Programs, and the Center for Student Leadership, Ethics, and Public Service. Our sister service-learning programs at Duke University and UNC-Chapel Hill provided helpful models for student leadership in service-learning as our program first began. The authors wish to thank Sarah Ash for her review of earlier drafts of this chapter.

Preparing Student Leaders for Success

Rosa S. Anderson, Emmanuel O. Oritsejafor,
and James. S. Guseh

NORTH CAROLINA CENTRAL UNIVERSITY (NCCU) is one of the 16 constituent institutions of the University of North Carolina System. The university is a historically black institution with a majority of African American students. It was chartered in 1909 as a private institution and opened to students the following year. The university's purpose has been to develop young men and women through the character and sound academic training required for real service to the nation.

Faced with the ongoing challenges of nurturing and developing future civic-minded leaders, the university established the Academic Community Service-Learning Program (ACSLP) to enhance commitment to civic engagement among students, faculty, administrators, and staff. The program seeks to guide campus members in meaningful service-learning and community service experiences. The ACSLP encourages student participation in defined activities designed to benefit the community. Students complete 120 hours of service as one of their undergraduate degree requirements. They are encouraged to develop skills in communication, group process, and cooperation, which can serve them not only in the classroom but also in the greater society through engagement in effective civic responsibilities. The program has been cited in many local and national publications, perhaps because it is one of only a handful university programs in the country that require a set number of community service hours before graduation.

The ACSLP, in partnership with academic and community leaders, is able to identify a wide range of outlets for students to serve and thereby gain broad service-learning experiences. In conjunction with creating these opportunities, the ACSLP is committed to making service-learning experiences as beneficial as possible to all concerned by providing extensive training for students, staff, and faculty before their placement with community partners. With effective training, students and other stakeholders find their collective service-learning experience productive and meaningful.

Overview of Service-Learning Training

Gary Paul (2002) notes that historically Black colleges and universities (HBCUs) were established to serve the community, produce leaders, develop responsible citizens, and strengthen civil and democratic society. At the same time, he suggests that the primary purpose of the academy is to conduct research and disseminate skills and tools essential for economic development and upward mobility—a focus that has contributed little to the social and civic competencies of college students. It was to address this lack that the ACSLP created its service-learning programs and the training necessary for students to succeed within these programs.

Service-learning circles were established deliberately to encourage discipline-specific and interdisciplinary dialogue.

NCCU's training and mentorship approach is based on extensive research on the impact of service and service-learning on college students—including their level of civic engagement (Oritsejafor & Guseh, 2004), "social capital" (Smyth, 2000), intention to vote (Koliba, 2004), and retention (Gallini & Moley, 2003)—as well as on effective practice. In addition to enhancing civic and academic learning, service-learning training is seen as a means of enhancing career preparedness; "to provide training for students focusing on career development through service-learning opportunities" is one of the ACSLP's stated service-learning goals.

In keeping with its service requirement, the ACSLP has mandatory training for students, with a range of sessions offered each term focusing on topics such as volunteer training, setting goals and expectations, team building, money management, and developing successful programs. Service-learning training specifically has three main components:

- Service-learning circles, which promote critical reflection and help students measure outcomes.

- Service-learning ambassadors—experienced students charged with recruiting and monitoring service-learners, disseminating information, and promoting the

ACSLP's mission, as well as coaching other student groups in the skills needed for community work.

- Service-learning fellows, a group of faculty and administrators chosen on the basis of their exemplary service-learning work, who train and mentor students as well as others on campus in incorporating academic community service-learning into the curriculum.

Service-Learning Circles

The ACSLP has found that service-learning circles are the best approach for facilitating student discussions of service-learning. A circle consists of students, service-learning fellows, department chairs, staff, and representatives of community-based organizations. The Service-Learning Coordinator recruits individuals who have active projects at community-based organizations as well as those who want to develop a project.

Service-learning circles were established deliberately to encourage discipline-specific and interdisciplinary dialogue. Participants discuss all aspects of the conceptualization, development, and implementation of programs linking service with academic study. Those with experience, including service-learning ambassadors and service-learning fellows (see descriptions later in this chapter), can share their experiences in effectively incorporating service-learning into the curriculum. All participants have a chance to raise questions and develop their own concepts and theories. The discussions, which often focus on establishing learning objectives that students want to see implemented in their curriculum, are lively.

The Training Model

The training model for effective circle discussions targets faculty fellows and student ambassadors who work with community groups, as well as representatives from community-based organizations. The main goals of the training model are to enhance the social awareness of students and others working in the community and to build direct skills for interacting with youth and other community populations as part of the civic engagement curriculum. Training is based on a two-stage train-the-trainer process that reflects these goals, developed by Dr. P. Masila Mutisya of the Department of Educational Leadership & Professional Studies at NCCU's School of Education.

Stage One of the model is rooted in character education and cultural identity awareness. This stage is based on Paulo Freire's literacy training model, which engages participants in a process known as *Conscientizacao*, an approach designed to engage participants at a degree of consciousness that enables them to see social systems critically. Participants are able to perceive and understand the contradictions that affect their lives arising from educational, economic, social, and political forces—and to generalize those contradictions to others around them. The outcome of the training process is a heightened awareness that leads to self-empowerment. In essence, participants learn to know themselves before engaging and making summary judgments about those from others races, genders, cultures, or economic backgrounds.

Stage Two focuses on implementation, which involves teaching direct skills for interaction with community-based organizations. The background in personal and social awareness training provides a context that enhances training in communication and other skills. All of this preparation makes the service-learning circles themselves more effective venues for generating and discussing ideas.

Training Structure and Schedule

Stage One activities occur in the fall (August–December). During this time student trainers are recruited from the Educational Majors Advisory Council (EMAC) and other programs, with the number of students dependant on the available resources. Other campus personnel and individuals from community-based organizations who may benefit (and benefit from) the training process are also identified.

In August, Stage One activities are laid out and a preliminary meeting is held to schedule the rest of the term's training sessions, typically the second Wednesday of every month. The next meeting, which occurs during NCCU's service-learning awareness week in October, introduces the training model to participating students, faculty members, and community partners. The bulk of the training occurs during the November session. Discussions include the *Conscientizacao* process and integration of character and cultural identity in working with community-based organizations.

In December participants both reflect on the training process and prepare the spring semester activities for Stage Two. As part of the reflection, participants assess their own character and their attitudes toward different cultures and belief systems. This exchange can be very enlightening and is a good note on which to end (or begin, depending on participants' readiness to act on what they've learned).

Stage Two activities are scheduled for the spring (January–April). The second week in January begins with a joint general session for all students, faculty, staff members, administrators, and representatives from community-based organizations. Activities to develop direct skills for interaction with community-based organizations in the joint general session are reinforced in ongoing training from Durham Congregations, Associations, and Neighborhoods (C.A.N.), a grassroots organization. C.A.N.'s primary mission is to teach average citizens how to get and keep political power by building multiracial, interdenominational alliances within their community and tackling large problems by creating one specific solution at a time.

C.A.N. teaches people to take an ongoing problem and turn it into an issue that's specific, immediate, and winnable—and, more important, that has a face to it. This training builds on existing knowledge but focuses on relationship building through several means:

- One-on-one relationship meetings to identify the most active community leaders.

- A house meeting to identify leaders and begin conversations about community problems.

- Organizing to develop concrete strategies for addressing community-identified problems, with a focus on issues citizens need to understand in order to be effective advocates.

- A Walk for Success, where community and NCCU students go into the community in pairs to listen to problems, fears, hopes, and ideas for change.

- A joint evaluation of the walk by NCCU students and community members to identify focus areas and strengthen unity and collaboration.

- An assembly held by C.A.N. two weeks after the walk, inviting public officials to commit to community efforts.

- An ongoing process for finding solutions to each identified issue.

the service-learning ambassadors, mentored by faculty and administrators, lead all student-driven projects.

During the second week in February a general training session is conducted for other stakeholders as roles develop based on grant partnerships and other community-based work. A training session for NCCU faculty and staff on civic engagement awareness and its role in community service wraps up the first-year cycle during the second week in April.

Upon completion of Stages One and Two of the training model, students, faculty, and community representatives are ready to implement their training as leaders in the monthly service-learning circles.

Student Service-Learning Ambassadors

Service-learning ambassadors are a group of juniors and seniors who take on a leadership role in the university's service-learning program, including recruiting, training, and monitoring service-learning students, as well as disseminating information about service-learning and the ACSLP more broadly. Ambassadors often coach other student groups in organizing group sessions, conducting effective meetings, administering surveys, and other skills needed in community work. This structure helps NCCU faculty, students, and community participants to examine social issues and define realistic strategies to implement positive change.

The service-learning ambassadors, mentored by the faculty and administrators who make up the service-learning fellows, lead all student-driven projects. In addition to receiving guidance from the fellows (described in a later section), students can benefit from the university's open communications with community organizations and representatives. By engaging with community as well as campus resources, student ambassadors are able to develop and/or direct projects that address real community issues. They are also well positioned to provide ongoing training to other service-learning students.

Ambassador Selection and Training

The training process for ambassadors begins in the lower grades with the "patron" position. Patrons are freshmen and sophomores who provide support services to NCCU student volunteers and staff members, such as tracking student data and disseminating program information to students and the community. Patrons must apply to participate; application requirements include a GPA of at least 2.5, experience with community involvement, excellent communication and leadership skills, ability to take initiative, and knowledge of basic computer applications. An interoffice committee screens and trains the patron applicants, and the ACSLP director and staff monitor their progress. The position requires an academic-year commitment that includes mandatory in-service training sessions throughout the year.

This experience provides the basis for more advanced work once students reach their third year. Service-learning ambassadors are upperclassmen selected from a pool of patrons and others experienced in service-learning. A committee of ACSLP staff and former ambassadors reviews applications and makes the selections. Qualifications for service-learning ambassadors include community service experience, project knowledge, familiarity with appropriate policies, and communication and leadership skills, as well as a GPA of 2.5 or higher. They are asked for a one-year commitment to mature and develop leadership skills. The ACSLP director and administrative team monitor this process closely.

The specific responsibilities of the ambassadors include providing weekly progress reports to ACSLP staff, monitoring the relationship between NCCU students and community representatives, organizing and participating in projects, recruiting community participants and student volunteers, serving as liaisons between departmental faculty members and community organizations, tracking the impact of services provided on community and student participants, and disseminating information to various stakeholders.

In addition, all service-learning ambassadors must attend in-service training sessions throughout the year. A training module dubbed "Eagles: Preparing to Fly Higher" is provided through a collaborative effort of the ACSLP, Career Services, and NCCU's Leadership Training Programs. It is designed to complement students' professional preparation with additional professional skills building. Training includes specific information on effective practices for community work as well as team-building exercises and training in areas such as communication, time management, leadership and organization styles, budget management, and goal setting.

Training includes several other components as well. Formal reflection sessions, held monthly, focus on topics such as the faces of homelessness, social justice, and community awareness. Leadership training focuses on subjects such as parliamentary procedures, money management, networking, successful program development, grant writing, and entrepreneurship. In addition, Career Services, in partnership with campus units, offers training in motivation and initiative, analytical skills, integrity, interpersonal skills, flexibility and adaptability, work ethic, detail orientation, teamwork skills, and leadership skills.

For both patrons and ambassadors, work begins with a "Ceremonial Induction" that takes place during the first semester. The induction, led by former ambassadors, includes an introduction, lighting of candles, a cake-cutting celebration, and the sharing of personal vision statements. In addition to providing a meaningful introduction to the work ahead, this ceremony allows former ambassadors to pass on some of their knowledge to the next group of student leaders.

Student-Led Projects

Although they continue to receive guidance from service-learning fellows and other faculty members, the service-learning ambassadors have a great deal of responsibility in leading community projects. Following are some examples of student-driven community projects that highlight the role of the student ambassadors as leaders and trainers. (See the Sidebar following these examples for some student reflections on their service and service-learning work.)

INTERNATIONAL OUTREACH TRAINING. Esteria Woods, a student ambassador and sociology student who is a native of Liberia, designed this project in collaboration with students from the Political Science, Criminal Justice, and Public Administration departments as well as the ACSLP. Together students established the Esteria Woods International Outreach Program, which focuses on improving the ability of relief efforts to reach the truly needy in the war-torn countries of Liberia and Sierra Leone. Students were able to forge cross-cultural collaborations with other service organizations, both locally and internationally. Some of the participating students committed to continue this work beyond the initial project after gaining a broad understanding of the crisis in this region following several service-learning circle discussions and presentations.

TECHNOLOGY TRAINING FOR COMMUNITY ORGANIZATIONS. Student ambassadors, in partnership with a community of volunteers, designed and led this comprehensive training project at the behest of the ACSLP, which wanted to add practical experience to students' services in the areas of technology and data management. Before beginning, ambassadors received training in various aspects of project management as well as relevant technology skills, including how to set up a technology hub, organize community sites, test connections, open dialogues with the off-site coordinator, schedule training sessions, and recruit and train tutors. The students had access to a technician, off- and on-site coordinators, and tutors to fully implement this process. The ambassadors also developed a student advisory board that provided support for the overall operation.

DATABASE MANAGEMENT PROJECT. Student ambassadors, in a partnership with Seedco and AmeriCorps/VISTA volunteers as well as a community volunteer, spent a year designing and implementing an automated database management system to register community-based organizations and students working at community sites. The ambassadors shared their project with NCCU students and representatives from community-based organizations and offered database training to help automate the registration process.

THE SERVICE INFORMATION CYBERLAB. NCCU's Service Information Cyberlab is an electronic communications hub, database management process, and research and evaluation component established to monitor the ACSLP's research methods and projects. It also enhances the networking and problem-solving efforts of the ACSLP's partnering volunteer and community service organizations. Student ambassadors who have led a variety of projects across academic areas use the Cyberlab to track and manage data. The Cyberlab also provides a mechanism for evaluation and assessment by documenting student learning, operational aims, and community impact.

Department instructors and unit coordinators guide students' efforts. To strengthen students' learning, unit staff members developed an interdisciplinary partnership with the Undergraduate Research Program, which provides opportunities for undergraduates to conduct scholarly research through one-on-one collaboration with a faculty mentor. Selected student research papers are published in the *Undergraduate Research Journal*.

By providing a powerful research tool, the Cyberlab allows students to combine development of civic leadership with academic and research leadership. The research components (problem analysis, synthesis, methodology, and conclusions) are an integral part of the service provided to the community. Students participate in a structured process of critical evaluation on ethical, intellectual, and civic aspects of their experiences while also producing a tangible research product for their community partner.

The Cyberlab has afforded student ambassadors an additional opportunity to learn and lead by working with unit staff members on the design and maintenance of a service-learning website. The website provides service-learning information for students, faculty members, and community-based organizations. Students use this tool as a means of providing technical assistance, promoting volunteer opportunities, maintaining community connections, and gaining access to national and local service initiatives.

Student Reflections on Service and Service-Learning

The community project that I most benefited from was assisting students in the McDougald Terrace Community Center. I helped students with their homework as well as helping them build their critical thinking and problem-solving skills. I decided to challenge myself with this project in order to learn more about the Durham community and its students. I found that there is a great deal of need for assistance in the urban communities of our county. The students were all eager to get assistance as well as to make friends and have positive role models. The relationship NCCU has established with the surrounding elementary schools plays an essential role in building the foundations of our community.

This particular project made me feel especially important to my community. The students I encountered and worked with were so appreciative of our effort to assist them. The highs of this project were seeing the particular students that I worked with improve their grades, and the low of the project was when it ended and I had to wonder if they would continue to excel. Working with these children was not always a piece of cake. I had to learn a lot of patience because often they were more excited about seeing the tutors then they were about doing their work. I had to learn how to help them learn to appreciate their personal accomplishments rather than appreciate what I could help them do.

continued on next page

I take from this experience a new commitment to my endeavors. It wasn't simply my community service hours on the line if I did not complete my task efficiently; it was the education of the children I was working with. Community service projects are about helping others. In order for projects to be successful it takes dedication and a commitment to excellence, something this school strives for.

I participated in the 36th Annual Liberian Studies Conference under the direction of the ACSLP staff. The conference was deliberating on civic engagement in Liberia while searching for strategies for peace and sustainable development. This was a good experience because you don't hear about Liberia too much compared with other African countries.

I can use what I learned in this project to help promote and educate others on the problems in Liberia and to help raise funds. This experience helped me to become more open-minded about situations that aren't happening in North Carolina. It helped me to see the bigger picture that you have to help others and make sure they are straight before you begin helping yourself. Because if your quality of living is high and others' aren't then it wouldn't be a fair and balanced world.

Through this project I have learned teamwork and humbleness as well as awareness of Liberia's conditions. I believe you need to have good volunteers, sound content in terms of information, and teamwork to make any project work.

On February 19, 2004, I got the chance to attend the Campus Compact Midwest Collaboration's national Teleconference on *The New Student Politics* (Long, 2002).

The service project itself was very good because it was a way for students to get together and share their thoughts about ways to help motivate our peers to become politically involved. I think the service impacted people who were also at the teleconference because they got to see what civic engagement was about. I learned that there are other people who feel the same way I do when it comes to leadership. I was glad that the community got involved to learn what people thought throughout the nation as a whole.

It was useful to see how civic engagement is seen in the eyes of different people. This experience can begin to break down the stereotypes and barriers for people to come together collectively and share different views.

Faculty/Administrator Service-Learning Fellows

The Service-Learning Fellows are faculty and administrators experienced in incorporating academic community service-learning modules into courses or supervising students in the performance of service-learning. These individuals are available to share their experiences with other faculty, administrators, students, and staff interested in service-learning as part of their teaching pedagogy.

Fellows mentor other faculty and administrators who are interested in redesigning curricula to include service-learning components or developing community-related research projects and activities. They also serve as mentors for the student service-learning ambassadors. In addition, they are asked to develop modules for promoting service-learning and civic engagement; present service-learning to faculty, administrators, students, and community agencies at workshops and conferences; and participate in the Faculty/Administrator Service-Learning Exchange Program.

One focus of the mentorship that fellows provide for the ambassadors is to introduce them to the nonprofit sector as a potential career choice. They do this through several routes, including a nonprofit career fair and professional development courses offered by fellows from the School of Business. Training activities include developing the types of skills required to fill staff positions at nonprofit agencies.

Like the ambassadors, the service-learning fellows are appointed through an application process. Applicants must submit a one-page description of a service-learning course they have taught as well as a syllabus. The course description must explain the impact of the course on service-learning and learning in general, its impact on the university and the larger community, and how the work has affected the faculty member or administrator personally. The previous year's cohort of fellows chooses new members. To ensure a full year in the position, the process occurs early, with applications due the first week of September and selections made and notification sent before the end of the month.

Conclusion

North Carolina Central University is the gatekeeper of its community. The Office of the ACSLP coordinates the efforts of students, staff, administrators, and faculty who take this commitment seriously by working to develop and promote service-learning at NCCU. As part of this effort, the ACSLP recognizes that a strong infrastructure that infuses students into the top management of the service-learning model is necessary to sustain high-quality service-learning.

References

Gallini, S.M., & Moley, B.E. (Fall, 2003). Service-learning and engagement: Academic challenge and retention. *Michigan Journal of Community Service Learning, 10*(1), 5–14.

Koliba, C.J. (Spring, 2004). Service-learning and the downsizing of democracy: Learning our way out. *Michigan Journal of Community Service Learning, 10,* 57–68.

Long, S.E. (2002). *The new student politics: The Wingspread statement on student civic engagement.* Providence, RI: Campus Compact.

Oritsejafor, E., & Guseh, J. (2004). Civic engagement among college students: A case study. *Journal of College and Character, 2,* 1–19.

Paul, G.R. (2002, Fall). Democracy in the classroom. *Education, 123,* 205–210.

Smyth, J. (2000). Reclaiming social capital through critical teaching. *The Elementary School Journal, 100,* 491–511.

Acknowledgment

The authors gratefully acknowledge the contributions of Dr. P. Masila Mutisya, Professor, Department of Curriculum Instruction & Professional Studies, School of Education, North Carolina Central University, for his contributions to this chapter.

Students Training Students

Judy Hutchinson, Kristin Gurrola,
Debra Fetterly, and Vanessa Fontes

S USTAINABLE, HIGH-QUALITY SERVICE-LEARNING programs are challenging to establish and maintain. Service-learning departments are subject to several impediments: the mismatch between service-learning practice and tenure or promotion criteria, the ivory tower perception (and often reality) of the town-gown divide, and the changing priorities of university leadership. But each impediment may be at least partially ameliorated by having students promote and facilitate service-learning.

Students are an important, often underutilized resource for running service-learning programs. A core group of undergraduate student leaders passionate about the concept of combining academics with service not only can market service-learning to fellow students and to faculty and administrators, they can also provide vision, organizational design ideas, implementation and evaluation assistance, program strategies, and effective project concepts.

A major drawback to this powerful resource is that it is short-lived; a student population is transient. Besides the ultimate separation—graduation—many other interruptions can occur when opportunities such as study abroad and external internships arise for the bright, concerned students who are most often committed to service-learning. Azusa Pacific University (APU) confronted the need to maintain a high-quality, consistent student-run program despite the natural turnover of student leaders. The challenge was to make up for the losses that naturally result from these personnel changes.

After the initial shock caused by the impending graduation of six of nine service-learning student leaders in one year, the program staff discovered an important principle: embedded in the problem was the solution. As a study in the *Phi Delta Kappan* (Marais et al., 2000) concluded, each student was "valued because he or she contributes unique experiences, resources, skills and perspectives." Each had also accrued the knowledge, developed the skills, established the relationships, and gained the influence that had made the programs strong. They would provide the bridge to ensure not just program survival, but even improvement in the design of an appropriate hand-off process. The staff decided to study whether the strategies for developing self-directed work teams that the director (one of the authors) had created for major oil companies could be redesigned for this transition process.[1] The staff decided on a "pilot test."

Service-Learning at APU

Service is not new to APU, which has a century-long history of community service. Started in 1899 as a training school for Christian workers, APU has maintained service as one of its cornerstones. Every four-year APU undergraduate student must complete 120 hours of community service—30 hours each year—to graduate. Service-learning provides opportunities for students to fulfill this requirement through their academic courses.

The Center for Academic Service-Learning and Research, founded 15 years ago as the Office of Community Service-Learning, is an academic entity and reports to the provost. The center facilitates between 60 and 70 classes involving approximately 1,300 APU undergraduate students each semester. Service-learning courses range from math to physical education, music to art, social work to business, and leadership to journalism. Service sites include local homeless shelters, tutoring centers, Alzheimer's care facilities, food banks, centers for individuals with special needs, and hundreds of classrooms in more than 30 public and private schools.

The center carries out its mission with the support of 14 staff members, including two graduate interns and four professional positions: a director, an associate director, a coordinator for research and development, and an administrative assistant. The bulk of the service-learning programs, however, are facilitated, managed, and evaluated by nine undergraduate Service-Learning Advocates (SLAs).

Role of the SLA

The center is more dependent than any other academic unit on the skill and commitment of undergraduate students, who organize, manage, and ensure the quality of service-learning experiences across the campus. The SLAs, invaluable resources to the

---

1. Dr. Hutchinson designed these processes while working with three major oil companies (Mobil, Chevron, and Pennzoil) creating self-directed work teams on the off-shore oil platforms in the Gulf of Mexico.

service-learning program, are responsible for understanding and upholding the philosophy of service-learning in order to support the goals of the department and those of the students, faculty, and community partners they serve.

In supporting faculty, an SLA helps design and facilitate the service-learning component of various courses. At the beginning of the semester, SLAs meet with their assigned faculty member to review the syllabus and course objectives for service-learning. During this meeting, a timeline is developed for the service-learning experience, along with methods of reflection, accountability, and evaluation.

The SLA leads a classroom orientation for each class, giving the students necessary information about the project, including the requirements and instructions on how to work with a community partner. SLAs also support students as they contact their assigned agency (school-based and/or community-based sites) to begin their service experience. Throughout the semester, students can contact their SLA with any questions or issues.

Each SLA plays a major role in building community, serving as a liaison to faculty, students, and the local community. Depending on the type of service-learning project, an SLA is responsible for contacting schools and agencies to facilitate the connection with a particular class, developing quality partnerships that ease the transition from semester to semester and from year to year. They also build community within the center. Beginning with a fall retreat and weeklong training, all SLAs not only manage their own programs, but also share their strengths and specific skills with all other staff members.

Each year, the center experiences some turnover among the SLAs and must hire new undergraduate interns. Students are usually the best judges of the talent and character of applicants, so it has become a tradition to have the current SLAs assist in recruiting and hiring new SLAs. During the past several years, SLAs have recruited their roommates, friends, classmates, students currently enrolled in service-learning classes, and even siblings to work.

Loss and Potential

Given their past and current role, it was clear that the loss of two-thirds of the SLAs in one year portended, in the best case, management overload for the program's staff, and in the worst case, serious disarray. As co-designers and organizers of the programs they had managed, these student leaders were the major links with professors and other critical on-campus networks. As repositories of both the human and social capital of the center, their understanding of the programs was the most contextual and up-to-date. The relationships they had formed both on and off-campus constituted the strongest working networks for both communication and execution of the mission. The task was to optimize their final months of work to ensure that the center's influence and productivity would not suffer.

The Training Design Process

The center's staff chose an approach of "peer-to-peer training or learning—a type of team learning and team building" (Cusimano, 1996), with the departing SLAs in the role of subject-matter experts. Six committed, experienced students—three with three years of experience at the center—participated in a collaborative design process that would enable them to pass on necessary knowledge and skills to their successors.

The first step was to create a comprehensive competency checklist, which would create the basic guidelines for the training process. The staff and the SLAs brainstormed a task list specific to the various roles. This free flow of ideas provided an opportunity to discuss every task related to the position. It became clear that these students were indeed the most knowledgeable resources—the real experts in facilitation of quality service-learning programs.

The next step—categorization of the job tasks into key competencies—enabled the group to determine which tasks had been left out during the brainstorming process and which competencies needed further clarification. After additions and modifications had been made, the group put together a final competency checklist (see the Sidebar on the next page).

The training for the incoming SLAs was designed to occur during three months, beginning in February. All SLA trainers had to schedule, design, and implement enough training sessions so that their trainees acquired the requisite competencies. During their first session with their trainees, SLA trainers developed plans of action with timelines not only for the training itself, but also for accountability and quality control. At the end of the period, each pair met with the associate director of the Center for Academic Service-Learning and Research to review the completed competency checklist and evaluate the success of the process. At this time, management affirmed and evaluated the work of the trainers and trainees, working with them to determine additional topics for the training week in August, before the start of the next school year.

Benefits of Training

SLAs responded positively to the training process. Those participating as trainers gained significant benefits, as did new students being trained. Students' thoughts about the value of the training program on both personal and professional levels are documented in the next sections.

Incoming Service-Learning Advocate (SLA) Comprehensive Competency Checklist

SLAs: _____   Program: _____

❏ Program overview and review of job description

❏ Course list for program
— Discuss faculty and classes that participate in the program

❏ Working with faculty
— Beginning of the semester faculty meetings—planning for service-learning
— Program description form (course objectives, timeline, choosing agencies)
— Mid-point reflection session/checkpoints

❏ Working with community partners
— Review agencies/schools that work with each program
— Discuss ways of connecting with agencies/schools

❏ Working with students
— Classroom orientation
  • Orientation handout
  • Contract/liability form
  • Student information sheet
  • Orientation folder
  • Azusa Unified School District (AUSD) maps/dress code (if applicable)
  • AUSD volunteer card (if applicable)
  • Service-learning and civic engagement handout
  • Student accountability
  • Mid-point reflection/checkpoints

❏ Filemaker Pro
— Service-learning program data entry (review course call numbers for classes)

— Assigning ministry credit at the end of the semester
— School-based programs only—data entry in Teacher Info file

❏ IDEA evaluation
— Review evaluation forms for students and train on how to administer the evaluation as a component of the IDEA faculty evaluation
— Letter to the professor—allow the new SLA an opportunity to summarize the short answer questions from the evaluation and write the letter to the professor (use letter template)

❏ Office policies and procedures
— Review weekly staff meetings—program reports and leadership training
— Computer files (M drive and L drive)
— Email (personal folders) and phone communication (message carousel)
— Duplicating forms—making copies for orientations
— Review office norms and policies (in handbook under section 1)

❏ Other job responsibilities specific to your program (to be accomplished over the semester)
— Introduce the new SLA to the professors in your program
— Visit an agency/school to see a service-learning project taking place
— Take digital pictures to document your program

Personal Benefits

Students who participated in the training noted benefits ranging from personal satisfaction and feeling valued to gaining confidence in their ability to advance the center's work.

RELATIONSHIP BUILDING. Trainees considered relationship building as crucial to their ability to do the job and build competencies. One SLA trainee commented, "I feel more comfortable and relaxed when I know those I'm working with. I get to know their strengths and vice versa, so it helps me to learn from these people information and skills that I'm lacking." A trainer added, "This experience helped me learn how to make and balance work relationships and social relationships with the same people."

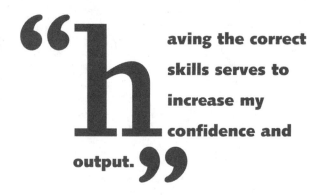

"**h**aving the correct skills serves to increase my confidence and output."

Both student trainers and trainees spoke of a sense of balance and congruence between relationship building and work outflow. One student said, "A staff that is made up of healthy and caring relationships can depend on each other as co-workers and as friends . . . [they] can learn from one another and can really excel and reach their goals."

TEAM MEMBERSHIP. Once relationships were formed, the process of working together as a team became central in importance. "Team membership with those in the office, as well as people I work with outside of the office, makes things run much more smoothly," noted one trainer. And in fact this description highlights one factor necessary for high-quality service-learning—the ability of the service-learning advocate to be a team builder inside and outside the office. An SLA trainee said, "I began to feel a sense of belonging. This greatly increased how valued and comfortable I felt here as well as increasing my dedication to my work."

RESPECT. The respect that flowed between those leaving their positions and those assuming them was clearly paramount to their overall satisfaction. SLA trainers also valued the confidence that supervisors had in them, evidenced by their responsibility for training incoming students. "The respect I get from the department only drives me harder to succeed toward my own personal goals and toward the work that the office does as a whole," said one student.

SKILL BUILDING. The quality of the student leaders has been a great asset to the center. Their primary goal is to be skillful SLAs. One trainer said that passing on his skills provided closure on leaving the advocate position and "helped me feel confident that the programs I had worked hard to improve or maintain would continue to grow."

A trainee noted that the training process "is key to job performance, because the [trainer] finds specific skills that work best for the job that the trainee can build and learn from." There was wide agreement with the sentiment expressed by one SLA that "having the correct skills serves to increase my confidence and output." Both trainers and trainees said they felt a responsibility to see that the teaching and learning process would strengthen job performance and that the transfer of skills would enhance the center's work.

RETAINING THE LEGACY. Both student groups commented that a legacy not only is related to the past, but is also a goal or baseline to catalyze future improvements. "Once I felt valued and I valued the team, retaining the legacy and even improving upon some aspects became much more important to me. It became my way to contribute to the department," one student commented. Another discussed the pressure of the legacy, saying, "I don't want to be worse than the person before me. To be better would be a good thing."

Professional Benefits

One responsibility of an institution of higher education is to help students develop skills and acquire proficiencies that will benefit them in future education and careers. The SLAs are expected to maintain professional working relationships with faculty, university students, community and agency partners, and one another. The training and subsequent transfer of roles, expectations, and skills between students was predicated on their ability to communicate clearly with each other.

TASK ANALYSIS. For some students, the transfer of skills between departing and incoming SLAs measured the degree to which both groups of students understood their roles and responsibilities. One trainer saw the importance of analyzing the role: "I had to think in detail about the things that made my program successful and mistakes I had made that hindered my program."

The trainees were eager to benefit from the experience and knowledge of peer trainers. One student commented, "It is possible to get a clear understanding of the job descriptions from the experience of your trainer."

TRANSFERABLE COMPETENCIES. Trainers reflected on the professional skills that their SLA experience had developed and sharpened. They considered how their time as SLAs contributed to the skills they would take with them. They were often amazed as they recounted the skills they had acquired, especially those related to future possibilities.

> "the competencies I gained in my work in the service-learning office and my training of peers were as significant as my four years of college preparation."

One student remarked, "Some of the transferable skills I gained from my time in service-learning are training, evaluating, program development, communication . . . and computer skills." Another said, "In the application process for a position I just got with a major drug company, I realized that the competencies I gained in my work in the service-learning office and my training of peers were as significant as my four years of college preparation."

RÉSUMÉ BUILDING. Students described how their experiences related to their professional portfolios. A graduating senior stated, "Many employers have found my responsibilities here impressive. They set me apart from other applicants." Another student noted that because the job and subsequent training process were demanding, her future résumé would include acquired skills that "taught me a lot about myself, adaptability, and change."

TRAINING AND EVALUATION SKILLS. The peer-training process was itself a significant development experience for the SLAs. Highlighting the themes of professional assimilation and leadership, one student said, "The peer-training process is important to becoming part of the office and learning the professional demands in a comfortable way." Another student reflected, "It is not only how our training was designed, but how we implemented what we learned from it that helps us to complete programs and be successful." One trainee said he felt more prepared to train the next SLA because he had already undergone intensive training himself.

The training design included sections on monitoring and evaluation. One graduating senior described how being part of the SLA team complemented her future professional ambitions. Knowing how to apply practically the skills she had acquired was a benefit that she could explain to her trainee: "In social work, especially, program evaluation is highly emphasized and very important. I am glad I have had experience in this specific area."

A newly trained student said of monitoring, "Because I am so self-motivated and driven, I don't really need much monitoring. However, evaluation is helpful, because it is always in the back of my mind to do well so I can honestly report back." Yet another noted that the monitoring and evaluation process allowed the students to receive guidance and direction as they practice being community leaders. (See the Sidebar on p. 110 for a student's reflection on the SLA training experience.)

Implications and Conclusions

How do these findings relate to the issues of tenure, town-gown divide, and institutional support for service-learning? This study is limited—a single year's pilot with six students training others. That the findings are positive, however, has important implications for scholars and practitioners of service-learning in higher education. A situation in which students train students offers important benefits to the functioning of the service-learning office, which in turn has a positive impact on the future success of service-learning.

With their own tenure or promotion at stake, many professors are discouraged from getting involved in service-learning. Most of their major fears—the extra time commitment, difficulties finding and coordinating appropriate service opportunities, and fears about student evaluations—can be, in large part, assuaged by partnering with highly trained, professional, and committed SLAs.

The impact of the training described here offers evidence that the quality of the connections that SLAs make between the university and many sectors of the community can help overcome the much-lamented town-gown divide. The SLAs' vision for "serving as a professional and hospitable resource creating an effective, lasting bridge between community and scholarship" provides a framework for quality control, ensures ongoing improvement of the programs that they manage, and, finally, ensures that their legacy will endure both in the community and within the university.

References

Cusimano, J. (1996). Managers as facilitators. *Training and Development, 50,* 31–33.

Marais, J.D., Yang, Y. & Farzanehkia, F. (2000). Service-learning leadership development for youth. *Phi Delta Kappan, 81,* 678–680.

Student Reflection on the SLA Training Experience

As an SLA, I have seen the dramatic improvements that have resulted from the peer-training program. The trainees reported that an important aspect was skill building, learning from the best. Those who go before you usually have a pool of knowledge that trainees can absorb.

I did not have the benefit of this experience when I came into the program three years ago. During my first weeks as a SLA in the center, I felt insecure and unorganized. My lack of skills and prior knowledge of tasks made me uncomfortable and gave me a sense of incompetence that made my work and time in the office difficult. I expected to be able to organize my time to work comfortably within set schedules and approach my responsibilities with organization and a plan. As I began my role as an SLA, I realized that I did not know all that was expected. This made it very difficult for me to organize my work with confidence and made me wonder whether I was leaving important work incomplete.

I began to question whether I was the right person for the job. I was now in charge of a program and knew that I was expected to communicate program goals and progress reports regularly, but I did not fully understand how I was to interact with faculty members on a professional level. I felt the same insecurity when I needed to contact the teachers and principals in the Azusa Unified School District.

Although I was warmly welcomed in the service-learning office, it took some time to feel comfortable with my co-workers. The formal preparation for my position began with a weekend retreat followed by a weeklong training session. This training period was necessary and very informative, but I remained anxious. For the first couple of weeks, I did not feel comfortable with the office staff or the graduate student interns who were working in the office, and I felt intimidated by the more experienced SLAs. It was not until several weeks later, when I began to settle in as part of the team, that I began to feel more assured of my position and comfortable with everyone in the office.

Team membership, I have found, is based on relationship building. The trainees in the center's new program have demonstrated the vital role of relationships in building confidence and allowing all team members to maximize their ability to do their job effectively and build required competencies. It is important to feel comfortable with co-workers and with your role on the team.

It is easier to transition smoothly in your position in the context of established relationships. In my experience, relationship building took about a month. Many of us had different office hours and work schedules. We would see one another at staff meetings, but it took time to get to know everyone. Now, after three years in the same office, I feel strongly connected to each member of the staff. Although we may relate differently with one another, there is a definite team spirit.

It took a long time before I clearly understood my tasks and could create reasonable goals, but with patient guidance from my supervisor and much practical experience, learning through successes as well as mistakes, I eventually gained the skills to perform my duties as an SLA with competence. As I prepare to graduate, I am beginning the process of training my replacement. I am amazed at her abilities and the potential she brings to carry on and improve on my legacy and contribute to the team I leave behind in the center.

Training Students

LifeWorks at Mars Hill College

The LifeWorks Learning Partnership at Mars Hill College aims to help students determine their calling and maximize the impact they can have in whatever field they choose. Through the partnership and general education courses, students climb a staircase of leadership consisting of *knowledge, skills, values,* and *experiences* for lifelong civic engagement in a wide range of fields.

The LifeWorks program consists of weekly one-hour leadership meetings each semester that focus on specific knowledge bases, skill sets, value themes, and experiences in the community. The learning objectives and activities are connected to the Commons, the core general education courses that all students take (see the Sidebar on p. 112 for an outline of the LifeWorks themes and the courses they connect with).

In the weekly meetings, students spend five weeks on the knowledge base, five weeks on the skill set, and five weeks on the value theme. This process involves multiple learning styles. Interactive exercises, writing in journals, film, music, and group discussion reinforce the leadership themes for each week. Community partners are invited to workshops where they connect the texts students are reading in the Commons courses with their work in the community.

For example, in the first-semester Challenges course, students read Martin Luther King Jr.'s "Letter from Birmingham Jail." Twelve community partners also read the piece and participate in a workshop with faculty to discuss how each of them can use the text to understand the service experience in the classroom and in the community. In the LifeWorks meetings that follow, the text generates discussion of issues such as timing and time management, springing from King's discussion of the timing of the Civil

LifeWorks Themes and Courses

STAGE ONE: FIRST YEAR

- *Knowledge base:* The role of service in society (connected to the Challenges course)
- *Skill set:* Time management
- *Values theme:* Wonder

STAGE TWO: FIRST YEAR

- *Knowledge base:* The role of the individual in community (connected to the Character course)
- *Skill set:* Active listening
- *Values theme:* Courage

STAGE THREE: SECOND YEAR

- *Knowledge base:* The role of interest groups in community (connected to the Civic Life course)
- *Skill set:* Facilitation
- *Values theme:* Respect

STAGE FOUR: SECOND YEAR

- *Knowledge base:* The role of faith and reason in community (connected to the Critique course)

- *Skill set:* Civil discourse
- *Values theme:* Integrity

STAGE FIVE: THIRD YEAR

- *Knowledge base:* The role of careers in community (connected to the Creativity course)
- *Skill set:* Resource development
- *Values theme:* Motivation

STAGE SIX: FOURTH YEAR

- *Knowledge base:* Synthesizing the roles of individuals, interest groups, faith and reason, and careers in serving the community (connected to the Capstone course)
- *Skill set:* Evaluation
- *Values theme:* Confidence

STAGE SEVEN: POST-GRADUATION

- *Knowledge base:* Making a living and making a life in community
- *Skill set:* Networking
- *Values theme:* Hope

Rights movement. In this way, time management is taken to a philosophical level and put in the context of community movements. Students use music and film clips to provide additional insights.

Project Community at the University of Michigan–Ann Arbor

Service-learning at the University of Michigan–Ann Arbor is headquartered at the Edward Ginsberg Center for Community Service and Learning, which engages students, faculty, and community members in learning together through community service, service-learning, and civic participation in a diverse democratic society. The center involves thousands of students each year. In addition, about a dozen University of Michigan students each year—Ginsberg Fellows—receive a stipend for undertaking a community-based initiative.

All departments, schools, and colleges that comprise the university offer service-learning courses. Offerings encompass more than 70 courses enrolling over 1,000 undergraduates. One student points out, "Service-learning takes place around Ann Arbor, in Detroit, and all over the U.S. Some examples are teaching children, building houses, working on organic farms, volunteering at homeless shelters and food kitchens, and working with people seeking political asylum."

Project Community, an undergraduate service-learning program, is one of the oldest service-learning programs in the United States.[1] It prepares undergraduate students as peer facilitators and coordinators of other students' experiences in service-learning classes. Each semester, the university prepares approximately 30 peer facilitators to work with 200 to 250 students in 30 different service-learning sites or seminars. Weekly seminars are taught by undergraduates who are previous course participants and have been through an extensive training program. Certain activities are hallmarks for peer facilitator preparation and support each semester. These include pre-semester retreats and in-semester meetings; icebreakers and tone-setters; assessments of students' skills in small group instructional leadership; work on diversity issues; and facilitator skill development.

Project Community has several objectives: (1) to develop some measures of sociological familiarity and expertise (the program is in the sociology department); (2) to ensure that students who facilitate others' learning activities have a high level of personal awareness of their own values, strengths, and weaknesses as students, as facilitators, as leaders, and as human beings interacting with others; (3) to develop and increase students' skills in guiding others through the service-learning process; and (4) to build a cooperative learning environment.

---

1. See Chesler, M., Kellman-Fritz, J., & Knife-Gould, A. (2003, Winter). Training peer facilitators for community service learning leadership. *Michigan Journal of Community Service Learning, 9*(3), 59–70.

Training Student Leaders at Saint Anselm College

The Meelia Center for Community Service at Saint Anselm College in Manchester, New Hampshire, has used student leaders to support community service and service-learning since 1991. The training described here represents the latest phase in efforts to develop and support student leaders, who in turn place and support their peers in the community. The focus is on training students to support service-learning. The training model considers the fact that service linked to coursework must meet strict standards for academic integrity. Once prepared to support service-learning, student leaders are well positioned to support other forms of community involvement, from civic engagement to community-based research.

CONTEXT FOR STUDENT LEADERSHIP

Campuses developing student leadership in service-learning must address certain requirements, including:

1. Appropriate support for service-learning from the academic dean and the academic departments where service-learning will occur.

2. General agreement regarding the definition of service-learning and the service-learning model(s) followed by the college.

3. Administrative structure to support students who are engaged in service leadership.

4. A willingness to allow students to play a leadership role.

Much of the growth in service-leaning at Saint Anselm is a direct result of an early agreement between the volunteer center and the academic dean about what service-learning is, how it fits with the college philosophy and mission, and how to administer it on campus. As a result, service-learning has grown from one class in the spring of 1987 to 25 courses and 15 faculty members in 11 academic departments. Approximately 10% of the student body engages in service-learning each semester, while 39% of the class of 2006 had at least one service-learning course. All this has been accomplished with a half-time administrator and a skilled corps of student leaders. This is a testament to the fact that if given the opportunity, students can and will play leadership roles.

ADMINISTRATIVE STRUCTURE

The Meelia Center, like many campus service and service-learning centers, turned to student leadership out of necessity. The college was genuinely interested in supporting service, and later service-learning, but resources were limited. The center was launched in 1989 with a half-time director. After several years, the call went out for student support. From the start, students gladly accepted leadership roles in support of community service and service-learning, and the center has worked over the years to revise administrative models to support their work. Following is a brief description of the evolution of these models:

- Office assistant model: A team of work-study students assists the director by working at the volunteer center; the students help with recruitment as well as support and organize service events.

- Affiliates coordinator model: Work-study students assume primary responsibility for placement and support of volunteers and service-learners, with each managing five to six sites that have limited service-learning or volunteer placements. Coordination with the agencies occurs from campus rather than on site.

- On-site and affiliates coordinator model: In this model, on-site coordinators are added to those sites that lack strong agency support structures or that require very close student supervision (e.g., correctional facilities).

- Comprehensive student leadership model: This model expands on-site student management to every community partnership and creates new levels office management for selected student leaders. The Student Assistant Director helps train and support the on-site and affiliates coordinators, while the Student Office Manager oversees office assistants and service events. Other management positions include information management, public relations, and web development.

- Comprehensive leadership model integrated with Federal Work-Study (FWS) and institutional advancement: This model enhances support to student leaders by collaborating with the campus work-study program and development office to give the service leaders higher pay, access to non–work-study payroll dollars, and service leadership scholarships. From the beginning this model required a special relationship with the office managing FWS. Saint Anselm has two distinct FWS components—campus work-study and community work-study; the latter has more flexibility in setting wages, hours, etc.

FOUR-PART TRAINING MODEL

In training, much of the focus is on preparing the on-site coordinators, who have the most direct role related to placement, support, and monitoring of service-learning students. For a college starting to develop a student leadership corps, the on-site model provides the tightest administrative structure for managing students engaged in weekly service.

At Saint Anselm, training for student on-site coordinators lasts 10 hours over four sessions. For the first two hours, students get to know each

The complete training and Leadership model is availale on the Meelia Center website, www.anselm.edu/administration/meeliacenter.

other and learn about basic skills in the administration of volunteers. In the second training session, lasting four hours, the students continue to build relationships, learn office policies and procedures, begin to work with office assistants, and reinforce the community nature of the work. In the third, two-hour session, students receive a fuller definition of the coordinators' roles, review support and resources available on and off campus, develop and refine skills to perform work, and meet with faculty, administrators, and community people for training and support. The final session, lasting two hours, fully defines roles of coordinators, site supervisors, service-learning faculty, service-learners, and the volunteer center; reviews support available to program participants and all forms and procedures for the semester's work; and allows the agency and on-site coordinator to begin to strengthen their partnership and volunteer center staff to meet and plan with service-learning faculty. The Sidebar that follows offers an example of a role-playing exercise that can help on-site coordinators feel comfortable in dealing with issues that may arise on site.

Sample On-Site Coordinator Role Play

On-site coordinator: You are a new on-site service-learning coordinator for the volunteer center's nursing home partnership. You placed 10 volunteers and service-learners in the first 4 weeks of the semester. You have called each of them to inquire about their placement, and you have spoken with the site supervisor. So far everyone seems happy, and you feel as if you are really getting a handle on the coordinating job.

You arrive at the nursing home today to spend a few hours in the Alzheimer's Unit, where you just love it. You notice that one of your service-learners is really not interacting much with the residents. You decide to talk with her about how things are going.

Service-learner: You are a freshman nursing student and this is your third time visiting the nursing home. You decided to challenge yourself when you took this placement by working in the Alzheimer's Unit. Even though you have never worked with the elderly, you thought as

a nursing student this would be a good population to get to know.

You had hoped that the work would get easier, but you continue to feel very awkward and self-conscious each visit. Your pattern has been to sit next to Alice, who would love to be wandering around the facility, but her seat is wired so that whenever she starts to stand an alarm goes off and she sits back down. You occasionally talk to her, but she does not seem to be able to engage in conversation. Still you feel that since she has this alarm thing on her chair clearly someone is concerned about her, so you will help to keep an eye on her.

Several other seniors have caught your eye, but you have yet to really talk with them. One man (Adam) strides up to you all the time, but you can't always make out what he is talking about, and that makes you nervous. Another woman (Marge) sits across the room mumbling and smiling at you, but when you approached her to say hi she thought you were her daughter, and you were not sure where to go with that. So you sit, feeling awkward and wondering if you are letting down yourself and the program. You are too embarrassed to talk with anyone about it, so you have decided to just stick it out. Maybe the elderly are not for you.

Alice: When ever you start to stand an alarm goes off. Make you own alarm sound, and use it briefly when you start to stand every couple of minutes. You pretty much ignore everything else except for the exchange with the alarm every couple of minutes.

Marge: You sit rocking in your chair, mumbling to yourself, and smiling at the two students. They remind you of your daughter, and some-times your thinking gets mixed up and you might think one of them is your daughter. But beyond that you are capable and interested in talking with people, especially young people.

Adam: You don't like to sit still. You pace around, and sometimes you pace up to the vol-unteers. You wonder about them, and would probably like to talk to them, but you really can't sit down. Too much sitting is not healthy, you know!

What facilitators may want to watch for:

- Did the coordinator allow the service-learner to really talk about how she feels?

- Did the coordinator help the service-learner come up with her own possible solutions before providing suggestions?

- Did the coordinator model ways of interact-ing for the service-learner?

- Did coordinator help the service-learner to identify available resources for additional support?

Training note: If you do not have experience processing role plays, get help from someone who has. Read the available literature for sug-gestions and tips. As a facilitator, model active listening by asking the group for their ideas before offering your own suggestions.

Daniel Forbes, Director of the Meelia Center for Community Service at Saint Anselm College, prepared the text for this vignette.

part

three

Students as Staff

STUDENTS PLAY MULTIPLE ROLES in the context of community-based learning. They navigate communities that are different from their own, address issues of power and injustice, and build relationships with a diverse group of people on campus and in communities—all while completing their other work as students. Although students often act as passive consumers of their education, in this section we highlight examples in which students fill the role of active *producers* of their education. The campuses and programs in this section allow students to "own" their education by enabling them to support the service-learning experiences of their peers.

In the first chapter, the authors describe the evolution of the role of students in the year-long practicum class for those majoring in public and community service at Providence College (the first public service major in the country). This program has deliberately shifted the focus of student responsibilities from course-based to community-based. With this shift, the emphasis has changed from classroom to community, allowing students to form deeper, more genuine relationships with those off campus and to spend more time where deep learning takes place—in the community.

In the next chapter, the authors describe efforts at Marquette University to include students as staff members in their service-learning program. Filled with rich quotes from students on the benefits of students working as employees in service-learning programs, this chapter also includes a concrete overview of the program's student staff structure.

The final chapter in this section focuses on student leadership efforts at Miami Dade College, the largest community college in the country. The authors describe successes and lessons from their student ambassador program. Student ambassadors, a paid position on campus using funds from the Federal Work-Study program, are an integral component of Miami Dade's large and successful service-learning program.

The section also includes a vignette describing the crucial role played by student staff at Boise State University.

The Community Assistant Model

Angela E. Kelly and Hugh F. Lena

A T PROVIDENCE COLLEGE, an ongoing experiment within an academic major in public and community service studies offers advanced students the opportunity to take on new roles in campus-community partnerships. The Feinstein Institute for Public and Community Service Studies was created a decade ago through the generosity of a local benefactor, Alan Shawn Feinstein, who envisioned an academic program that would prepare undergraduate students for careers while instilling in them a commitment to public service and a desire to improve the world. In June 1993, Feinstein awarded Providence College a $5 million grant to develop the program.

During the 1993–1994 academic year, a research team comprising nine faculty members and three students developed a liberal arts curriculum that used service-learning as a teaching method, conducted a national search for a permanent director, and designed a pilot program for the following year, to be preceded by a Summer Institute in 1994. A corps of 18 outstanding students was selected from about 60 applicants for the first year's activities. They joined six Providence College faculty members who enrolled as "students" along with the college's research and development team in a six-week seminar that included service, reflection, and an academic curriculum stressing the study of service and community. During the Summer Institute, the gateway course to the major—"An Introduction to Service in Democratic Communities"—and what became the year-long practicum course—"Public Service"—began. In addition, the six faculty members suggested ideas for service-learning courses they would offer in their own disciplines during the following year.

During the 1994–1995 academic year, the institute's permanent staff redesigned its major and minor programs and student corps, and determined strategies for supporting service throughout the curriculum.[1] Now, after 10 years of experience with the Feinstein Institute, there is an ideal opportunity to revisit the vision for a Public and Community Service Studies major in general, and the goals for student learning and leadership in community service in particular. (See the Sidebar on p. 123 for an overview of the major.) The evolution of the student role in the major's year-long practicum course is the focus of this chapter.

Practicum Development

After the initial pilot in the summer of 1994, the first practicum year began. The stated learning outcomes for the course indicated that students would provide leadership to student teams engaged in community service activities; recognize how their own values affect their interactions with others; develop an effective working relationship with faculty and community service sites; identify areas where students might need assistance during community service; facilitate reflection and discussion among student team members; provide leadership to service projects; and demonstrate effective communication skills.

In the early years of the program, students enrolled in the year-long practicum course were assigned to a faculty member and his or her service-learning course. Working in three or four sites in each course, these students coordinated the service work of students enrolled in that course in addition to attending class, doing the course readings, regularly leading reflection sessions, and assisting faculty with various substantive and team-building exercises. Because the students were closely associated with the course and faculty member, they started calling themselves teaching assistants, or TAs.

Even though these student leaders also spent about 10 hours at their affiliated community site, their allegiance seemed to be more to the course than to the community; they concentrated on being course liaisons to the community more than community liaisons to the course. Further hindering community partnerships was the fact that some TAs switched sites once the semester was over or were attached to two different community sites at the same time. After several years, it became clear that the practicum students did not connect to their community partners or gain the community-based experiences needed to develop the skills for which the practicum course was intended.

---

1. Hudson and Trudeau (1995) provide a full account of the events leading to formal approval of the major and minor in public and community service studies and the lessons learned creating the first academic major in this area.

The Providence College Major in Public and Community Service Studies

The interdisciplinary major in public and community service studies involves a systematic, rigorous exploration of the major conceptual themes of community, service, compassion, public ethics, social justice/change, and leadership. The principal goal of the major is to give students the tools with which to become fluent in these conceptual themes both academically and practically: students learn community-building skills and community action research skills, and also become conversant with models of leadership. To achieve these goals in a liberal arts tradition, the major emphasizes critical thinking, analytic and communication skills, and public problem-solving skills. In addition, the major includes strong field experience, complemented by ethical and reflective analysis components.

In the context of a developmental curriculum, the aim of the major is to provide a firm grounding in the concepts of citizenship, ethical behaviors, and the value of democratic institutions. It also aims to recognize contributions made by diverse people in a democratic society; to enable students to understand and become agents of change; to develop leadership skills; to provide decision-making opportunities in complex circumstances; to develop each student's ability to communicate effectively in written and spoken word and using the tools of mass communication; to provide concepts and skills in community-centered analysis and action research; and to understand the interdisciplinary nature of the study of public and community service.

The major is organized around four sets of courses: a core, an individualized track, leadership and field experiences, and a capstone experience. The six courses that make up the core include an introductory methods and organization course; "Introduction to Service in Democratic Communities"; "Foundations of Organizational Service," a survey of the history of community service in America; a diversity course; a course in ethics and service leadership; and Catholic social teaching.

Students then select three courses that integrate conceptual and methodological materials from other disciplines at the college, such as nonprofit management, environmental problems, or policy analysis. The third component of the major develops leadership skills and field-work experience through a year-long practicum course and a semester-long internship. The final set of courses is a year-long capstone seminar in which students synthesize and deepen their practical and academic experiences by developing an independent, community-based project.

During the year-long practicum course, students are paired with a community partner site and asked to learn all they can about the site and its needs. Their responsibilities include coordinating student volunteers from one of the other service-learning courses, working with faculty teaching service-learning courses, and developing new community-based initiatives by writing and executing a grant. They also provide leadership in evaluating existing community partners and proposing new sites. These duties are different from those fulfilled by the program's earlier students, who had worked with specific faculty members teaching service-learning courses but not with community partners.

From Teaching Assistants to Community Assistants

After considerable discussion at the Feinstein Institute's 2000 summer retreat about the tension between class-based and site-based community leadership, the institute decided to change the practicum structure. Instead of being attached to service-learning courses, students would be linked with a particular community site for the entire year. Thus, the teaching assistants became community assistants (CAs). In that role, practicum students are more fully immersed in the community that forms the context for their site work and can be integrated into the staff of the site to which they are assigned.

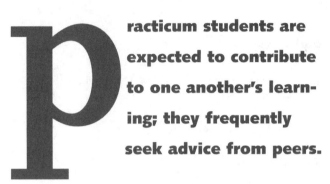

practicum students are expected to contribute to one another's learning; they frequently seek advice from peers.

As a CA, each student develops a year-long relationship with the mission, staff, and constituents at a particular site, such as a local school or nonprofit organization, with which the Feinstein Institute has a long-term relationship. The CA role entails a significant service commitment to the community partner, but it also entrusts each CA with the responsibility to lead and coordinate other students' learning. One CA commented:

> One of my favorite aspects of being a CA was the opportunity to play a role in facilitating other students' learning. This was a challenge, but also a lot of fun, and an experience that demonstrated to me that we as students have so much to learn from one another, as we do from faculty and community experiences. Students sharing their perspectives with one another is an important part of service-learning. It definitely opened my eyes to new insights and observations shared by my peers at our reflection sessions. Faculty and sites can also learn a lot from encouraging more student voice.

Each CA manages the service-learning of a group of student volunteers who are enrolled in another service-learning course, usually an introductory course, where they are required to serve three to four hours per week. Student evaluations of the CAs' contributions are uniformly positive. "The CA was very effective, organized and reliable," said one student. Another commented on the CA's multiple roles: "My CA brought me to the site every time and helped me out when I needed it and gave me suggestions for ways to approach helping kids in need."

CAs thus act as liaisons between a group of student volunteers and a community partner. Their responsibilities include designing meaningful projects for the student volunteers and scheduling and supervising their time at the site. CAs also serve as liaisons between student volunteers and the faculty member instructing their service-learning course, even though as CAs they are much less integrated into a particular course than they were as TAs. In addition, CAs lead student volunteers in reflecting critically on course-related issues raised in their service-learning experiences. A student in the introductory course commented:

> My CA was able to draw on her own past service-learning experiences to guide me through my first time combining academic studies of public service with community volunteer work. She shared her own questions and struggles and understood the challenges and concerns I had too and thus helped us to have more productive conversations. I felt like I was constantly looking at my service in a new way and from a new and evolving perspective.

Relationships and Responsibility

The CA is at the center of many key relationships: between faculty members and the student volunteers in their courses, between student volunteers and their community partner sites, and among the community partner, site staff, and the community members who are constituents of various sites (e.g., students in an elementary school or guests at a meal kitchen). In addition, CAs support their peers in the practicum course who are serving as CAs at other sites in the same neighborhoods. Because the role demands more deliberate involvement in the community itself, the CAs can learn from one another about the neighborhoods in which they are working, and about the connections between various sites in the same neighborhood. One CA wrote:

> Though we are all working with very different populations and types of organizations, the value of hearing about the challenges my fellow CAs are facing is great because, while I may not be working with a middle school or at an organic garden right now, perhaps one day I will. It will be useful to have heard the experiences and perspectives of others. Furthermore, it reminds me that the neighborhoods we work with are much more than the one site where we serve, but a complex network of people, organizations, and resources. Uncovering those connections is useful, even indirectly, for my own work.

Because the CA role is at the center of these diverse relationships, CAs generally begin each semester by drafting contracts with their primary site contact and with their assigned faculty member that clarify responsibilities. Some CAs also choose to draft reciprocal responsibility agreements with the student volunteers they supervise. These agreements outline communication plans, attendance policies, and the number of hours per week that the CA plans to spend at the site and in meetings and reflection sessions with faculty, other CAs, and student volunteers.

Developing Leadership through the Practicum Course

The practicum course helps CAs juggle these various responsibilities and ensures that the experience is one of learning and growth. It is a resource for the CAs as they develop and practice the skills necessary to lead, supervise, and facilitate the service-learning of other students and as they seek to advance the relationship between the Feinstein Institute and the community partner. Practicum students are expected to contribute to one another's learning; they frequently seek advice from peers, particularly about the challenge of supervising and managing student volunteers.

In terms of academic assignments, the practicum course provides a framework that engages CAs in developing a comprehensive knowledge of their community partners, the populations their sites serve, and the neighborhoods where their sites are located. To provide CAs with multiple perspectives, the Feinstein Institute has most recently adopted a team approach to instruction, with a faculty member, a community member, and the service-learning coordinator teaching the course in collaboration. (The service-learning coordinator is a permanent Feinstein Institute staff member who maintains and develops long-term relationships with all community partners throughout the year.)

Designing Grant Projects

The academic components of the practicum course include, in the first semester, a series of community action research assignments that foster the CAs' critical understanding of the mission, history, organizational structure, and challenges of their community partner. By completing these reconnaissance projects, CAs gain extensive knowledge about their partner that shapes the reflection sessions with student volunteers at that site.

The research projects, completed early in the year, lay the groundwork for an expanded leadership role in the second semester of the practicum course. At this time, each CA can apply for a small grant to fund a project that makes a lasting contribution to the site and furthers the relationship between the Feinstein Institute and the community partner. The CA is responsible for designing the project in conjunction with student volunteers and the community partner.

The grant project gives CAs hands-on experience in grant writing and evaluation. It also gives them a chance to create and lead a project of their own design—one meant to have a positive impact both on learning and on the community. The sites where CAs work vary widely, so the initial research projects are key to ensuring that all CAs can understand the unique complexities of the organizations to which they are committed for their year. The grant projects are informed by what the CAs learn during their first semester of exploring their assigned organizations and should reflect the unique challenges and assets of each agency.

In the past, grants to CAs have supported a wide variety of initiatives, ranging from health and beauty days at a women's shelter to murals painted on the property of a community development corporation in collaboration with youth from a local after-school arts program. Other grants have funded on-campus training and dialogue to reduce homophobia and support lesbian, gay, bisexual, and transgender (LGBT) youth, develop a community room and resource library at a food pantry, and purchase signs and supplies needed to make a local senior center accessible to wheelchairs.

A successful grant project draws on the many relationships CAs form. It entrusts the CA with leadership while also encouraging collaboration with students, faculty, and community partners and members. Throughout the practicum course, CAs are challenged to analyze all the stakeholders in the organization and the ways in which each will be affected by new projects, plans, and procedures. Sensitivity to the interests of various stakeholders is thus an important consideration in the formation of the CA's grant project.

Developing and Improving Partnerships

At the end of the academic year, CAs analyze the relationship between the Feinstein Institute and the community partner organization. They reflect orally and in writing on responsibility and impact at an institutional level and make concrete recommendations about how to advance the relationship.

Students' assessments are taken very seriously; CA input has led to important, concrete changes in community partnerships. For example, a CA who worked at a site that was clearly not interested in being a partner in students' learning recommended that the relationship be ended or transformed into one that no longer adopted the CA model. The following year, the site became an option for work-study students, with no CA assigned. In other instances, CAs have suggested changing the nature of the work done at a site or the size of the student volunteer groups assigned to each site. At one multi-service agency, work was restructured in response to a recent CA sug-

the relocation of student leadership to the community gives students numerous advantages in designing creative and effective programs.

gestion that students would be more effective and engaged if they worked in the meal kitchen rather than in the day shelter.

CAs develop relationships with new community partners as well. Toward the end of the spring semester, incoming CAs—students who will be taking the practicum course the following semester—meet with the practicum instructors and current CAs to consider what types of sites they might like to partner with. They are also invited to spend the summer months researching other organizations of interest and, in collaboration with the institute's service-learning coordinator, developing relationships with new community partners.

Some of the most successful partnerships in recent years have resulted when students identified organizations that address issues or work not yet represented by the current array of community partners. One student who spent a summer getting to know the neighborhood around campus identified a local food pantry and a public housing facility as organizations interested in working with CAs. Both have become successful partnerships. Another student identified new service-learning opportunities at a community center that supports LGBT youth. He formed a relationship with this organization and was the CA there for the first year; it too is now a thriving community partnership.

The relocation of student leadership to the community gives students numerous advantages in designing creative and effective programs. For example, this model allows CAs and volunteers to connect with other sites and the students serving there. One CA, who worked at an urban gardening organization, collaborated with a CA at an elementary school to create a garden club and playground garden at the school. A CA based at a senior citizen center connected with a CA at another elementary school to develop a service-learning project that brought fifth graders to the senior center to visit and entertain the elderly guests. The spirit of community-based leadership fostered by the CA model has also empowered students to take initiative in designing new projects, such as alternative break trips, new work-study and internship opportunities, student-run retreats, and international service-learning experiences.

These opportunities to identify and build new institutional relationships—while suggesting changes for existing relationships—allow students to lead and contribute to the overall work of the institute. The leadership, energy, and insights of new and former CAs drive the constantly changing dynamics of community partnerships and campus-community relationships, while helping the institute offer students a greater range in choosing where to serve.

Fostering New Leadership

Extending the two-semester academic year into a CA year that includes the previous semester and a summer has allowed CAs to contribute extensively to the program. Because incoming CAs meet one another as well as current and former CAs, community partners, and faculty members in the semester before their practicum course starts, they have a chance to reflect critically on what sites might be a good fit for them or to create new openings that will better reflect their own interests.

During the summer before they begin serving at community sites, incoming CAs also participate in a retreat at which they are oriented to the CA role, to the communities in which they will serve, and to the community partners with which they may work. This past year, instructors of the course, along with two students who had just completed their year as CAs, planned the retreat. The senior students decided a site fair would be an effective way for community partners and new CAs to get to know each before the CAs met to negotiate who would be based at which sites. The CAs' selection of their community site is often influenced by pragmatic factors such as transportation and scheduling; the fair better enabled them to consider where they would have the most to contribute. Allowing CAs to make more informed choices, in the long run, strengthens the relationships between community partners and the Feinstein Institute.

The students' involvement in planning the new CAs' retreat and orientation reflects the institute's larger commitment to fostering their leadership and initiative in service-learning. Similarly, CAs are responsible for orienting their student volunteers. Through these roles, CAs have the opportunity to identify community partners interested in actively fostering students' learning, and to draw on their knowledge of and experiences with community partners to educate and engage their peers. These exchanges happen more readily because student leadership is located in the community, rather than the classroom.

Meeting the Challenges of Community Work

While the CA model offers students opportunities for leadership, creativity, and a greater immersion into the community, it presents its own set of challenges as well. The tension between student learning and making a difference in the community is one ongoing challenge. To some extent, this tension is inevitable in campus-community partnerships, but CAs have come to understand this tension in a much deeper way than they could as TAs. Some of the other day-to-day challenges are described below.

Conflicting Schedules

The institute continues to struggle with the discontinuity between academic schedules and the cycles of need in community-based organizations. The academic calendar, with its vacation breaks and summers off, can create high turnover and gaps in service at the sites, thus exacerbating the tensions inherent in entry and exit. For example, summer and winter breaks for colleges and universities begin much earlier and generally last longer than do the breaks at local elementary and middle schools. Other organizations, such as food pantries, meal kitchens, and shelters, have their busiest seasons during the winter holidays or summer months when the college is not in session and no CAs are available to coordinate student volunteers.

In addition, with each new cycle of entry and exit, particularly at the beginning of each semester, new demands are placed on the staffs of the community partners, who must meet and orient an entirely new group to their organization. Still, the CA role is valuable because it encourages student leaders to share some of the burden with community partners; based on their deep knowledge of and close relationship with the organizations, CAs can help with transitions and with orienting new service-learners.

Student Turnover

These practical limitations related to the collegiate calendar are compounded by the personal challenges that student volunteers—and especially CAs—must face. Because CAs commit significant time and invest personally in building relationships and maintaining a presence at community partner sites, they often form close friendships with both the staff and constituents of community partners that are noticeably interrupted by students' schedules. Students often find it difficult to build authentic relationships of support with people in the community when their own schedules dictate that they are not as available and accountable as they—and their community partners—may think that they should be.

Students who form a close friendship with a particular individual or community group often have trouble ending their commitments when the semester or school year ends. Many say they will return to volunteer with the same organization or will maintain their community-based relationships, but new commitments, including new service-learning assignments, often make following through on these intentions impossible. At a recent freshman orientation to the Feinstein Institute, an incoming major, excited by the amount of community contact she would have through her service-learning courses, asked simply, "But how do you deal with leaving and moving on? Don't you feel guilty?"

Another introductory student reflected in her journal at the end of her first semester, "Just at the moment I feel I am connecting with the students I tutor, it is time for me to leave them." She wrote about one eight-year-old boy who had recently revealed to her many family challenges he had been facing, saying that he had "been wanting to tell somebody all year and especially [his tutor] for the three months they'd been working together, but it took him that long to feel comfortable sharing his feelings." With an entirely new student volunteer working with him the next semester, this young boy, like the constituents at many of the sites, may feel as if he has to start all over again in building new relationships. Trust takes time to build; with student volunteers entering and exiting service placements every few months, this is a challenge that colleges committed to community partnerships must consider.

Because CAs facilitate other students' service-learning, they can respond to doubts, questions, and concerns that volunteers raise when entering or exiting a new community assignment. They have had several semesters of service-learning before assuming this position of leadership, so they have faced similar challenges and can likely respond authentically. CAs can help volunteers confront their feelings, which can range from guilt or sadness to relief or eagerness to try out something new. CAs can also respond with a deeper sensitivity to the needs of the community partners because of their longer-term relationship with the sites and their staff. Together, community partners and CAs—with institute faculty and staff—can discuss how to minimize the negative impact of high turnover.

Short-Term Commitments

Of course, the CAs' commitment term ends all too quickly—at the end of each school year. But because the CA position is connected to a year-long course that runs annually, sites can expect a new CA to take over shortly after the current one leaves each spring. In this case, having service-learning staff is especially vital, because the coordinator meets with community partners repeatedly during the summer months so that the institutional relationship can be sustained despite breaks in the academic calendar. In addition, through their own involvement with community partners, many faculty members maintain partnerships even when school is not in session. Therefore, the CA model does overcome this problem to some extent.

Even when school is in session, CAs face a tension between how much they can be involved as full-time members of an organization while juggling the demands of other courses and campus activities. As one student noted:

> I am very satisfied with my CA experience but feel that I may have gained from it more than I gave. I could have made a much more useful commitment if only I didn't also have an on-campus job, clubs, activities, and four other courses to worry about. I wish I could have devoted more of my time to being a CA and was often frustrated with those other requirements of college life that prevented me from doing so.

Another student commented that the CA role encouraged her to venture off campus to form deep relationships with a new community, allowing her to have a greater impact than if she simply volunteered for a few hours each week. But, she said, "This is also one of the biggest challenges because you have to juggle this responsibility with so many others. I often felt most passionately about my responsibilities in the community, which made it even harder to achieve a balance."

Again, the institute's ongoing and extended commitment offers CAs some support in dealing with these challenges. The twice-weekly meetings in their practicum course seminars give CAs a chance to support each other and get support from institute faculty and staff as they negotiate conflicting demands. In class discussions, CAs often use problem-solving protocols to brainstorm strategies and solutions.

Limited Range of Sites

Although maintaining extended relationships with community partners enhances the institute's relationship with partnering sites, this model also limits to some extent the variety of opportunities available to students that a more diverse, fluid range of sites might provide. This is the tension between institutionalization and innovation. While students have recently been successful in creating new partnerships that address otherwise overlooked issues—such as a recent partnership with a political organizing project that engages volunteers in research, advocacy, and organizing for social policy issues—some challenges remain. Even diverse sites and longstanding relationships might not provide the depth of experience that students desire in every case. Support from the institution can help students in such cases gain the most from the experience. As one CA commented:

> Being a CA was one of the most frustrating experiences of my life. The staff at my organization didn't seem to take my leadership role as seriously as I felt they should. Thus, I often didn't have too much to do or enough of a challenge. Despite this, I learned so much anyway and did build great friendships with individuals at my site. And, because the voices and opinions of CAs are valued by the institute, the staff listened to my comments, concerns, and recommendations at the end of my year as CA. As a result, the nature of our relationship with the organization has since changed significantly.

Building Stronger Relationships

Not all institutions of higher education can integrate the CA model into their community-service activities, but the Feinstein Institute's experience suggests that experiments with new student leadership roles in service-learning hold promise both for closer relationships between students and members of the community and for stronger institutional relationships between academic institutions and community organizations. As the service-learning movement spreads, those involved should continue to seek new, more meaningful leadership roles for students in the process.

Reference

Hudson, W., & Trudeau, R. (1995). An essay on the institutionalization of service-learning: The genesis of the Feinstein Institute for Public Service. *Michigan Journal of Community Service Learning, 2,* 150–158.

The Student Coordinator Model

Bobbi Timberlake and Shelley Frank

T HE MISSION STATEMENT for the Service Learning Program at Marquette University was written by one of the program's creators, Grace Mazza Urbanski, who also helped develop the fledgling program. At the time, Urbanski was a junior majoring in English and theology. Her work is an example of the invaluable contributions students have made in the past 12 years as part of Marquette's Service Learning Program. This chapter describes the scope of student participation in the Service Learning Program at Marquette and the specific roles student staff members play.

The Service Learning Program, born of the Jesuit commitment to faithful service, works cooperatively with faculty, students, and community agencies to provide diverse ways for Marquette students to perform meaningful service to their communities while engaging in some form of academic reflection or study related to the service.

—Marquette Service-Learning Program Mission Statement

The Evolution of Service-Learning at Marquette

The Service Learning Program, housed within the Office of the Provost, was created in the spring semester of 1994 to facilitate service-learning in selected courses and departments throughout the university. From its inception, service-learning at Marquette has been an academic—not a co-curricular—program located under the umbrella of academic affairs. As a Jesuit university, Marquette considers the role of service to be among the four pillars that comprise the university's mission. In addition to the Service Learning Program, Marquette has Community Service and University Ministry offices, both of which coordinate volunteer efforts within the Division of Student Affairs.

The Service Learning Program has grown dramatically, from 164 students in 10 courses serving at 39 community agencies in that first semester to 800–1,000 students from 50 or more courses in more than 100 schools and agencies each semester a decade later. More than 180 faculty members have offered service-learning in nearly 200 different courses during the past 10 years. This expansion allows the program to reach many of Marquette's students: over one-third of the 2003 graduating class had participated in service-learning at some point in their four years.

Students were a vital part of service-learning at Marquette even before the program began. Two juniors, Samantha Adams and Grace Mazza Urbanski, participated on the management team. They assisted in program planning, interviewed and made recommendations on administrator candidates, and selected the first group of student coordinators. Once the program was under way, they became the staff managers for three semesters until they graduated. Since then, the Service Learning Program has continued to rely heavily on the work of paid student employees.

The current staff comprises two professionals (a program administrator and an assistant administrator) and 14 students (2 student staff managers and 12 student coordinators). The staff managers are promoted from the ranks of the student coordinators to oversee the coordinators and run the daily operations in the office.

Advantages of a Student Staff

Having student employees was always part of the plan for running the Service Learning Program. This model offers advantages both to the service learners and to the program. One former student staff member, Shelley Frank (one of this chapter's authors), described some advantages this way:

> No one is more qualified to work in such a program than students themselves. It is an efficient way of working with large numbers of agencies and service learners. It is hard to imagine one or two full-time employees juggling so many responsibilities and still maintaining a somewhat personal relationship with faculty, students, and agencies. Service learners appreciate that they are able to work with peers who have a better understanding of where they are coming from or problems they may be having.

The ability of student workers to relate to peers is a constant theme in student reflections. Student workers also best understand the concerns and time constraints their fellow students face. As another student, Kim Stein, pointed out: "Student workers have a better idea of what concerns or time constraints service learners have, and in many cases service learners feel more comfortable communicating with fellow students." Students also have a different perspective on the civic mission of the university. Kristine Pintor states, "As a student coordinator, I feel like I am contributing to the university in a stronger way than other students who just attend classes."

Alumni offer a long-term perspective on the benefits and talk about the values of service instilled through their experiences. Samantha Adams, who graduated in 1995, remarked:

> Student leaders see that a group of people working together really does make a difference. They realize, too, that the need for service doesn't end when a student gets a grade or graduates.... By involving student leaders in the Service Learning Program, you are educating and inspiring the next generation of service leaders, which is exactly the point.

Other alumni have pointed out that participating in service-learning allowed them to bring together academic work and real-world problem solving and have also discussed the importance of peer-to-peer relationships. Tricia Roehrig, a 1997 graduate, commented:

> Student staff can often see unique connections between classroom material and service opportunities. When I started my involvement with service-learning, I was a sophomore having difficulty making connections between my tutoring placement and my abnormal psychology coursework. I was experiencing firsthand how difficult it can be to incorporate classroom theories into the real world. I spoke to my student coordinator and bounced ideas off him. I just needed someone who could hear where I was coming from without judging me, but without letting me take an easy out. My student coordinator did that.

In addition to educational benefits, employing students offers a financial advantage to service-learning programs. Marquette's large program requires many people to manage all the details, but it does not have the financial resources to employ a large staff of professionals. Student workers, especially those receiving Federal Work-Study funds, provide excellent assistance at a reasonable cost. In addition, when funding for service-learning comes from the university, as is the case with Marquette, having some salary budgeted for students is a benefit because administrators favor funds that support students.

There are, of course, some challenges to having students staff service-learning programs. First, they don't stay around very long; thus, a constant hiring and training process must be built into program operations. During the program's first few years, most students stayed until they graduated and worked for an average of four semesters. Increasingly, though, students have left before graduation to study abroad or for an internship. Some have returned to work with service-learning; others have moved on.

Another challenge of having student workers is that they need more supervision and guidance because they have less work experience than professional staff. Because they are students first and employees second, they have many demands on their time:

papers and exams, basketball games, school breaks, and so on. However, these challenges are minor inconveniences compared with the many advantages.

Recruitment and Hiring

Each spring, the Service Learning Program recruits new student coordinators to fill the positions of those who are graduating or are leaving the program. (Mid-year hiring is also sometimes needed when staff leave for internships or study abroad.) Every effort is made to find student coordinators who have taken a service-learning class, because their understanding of the philosophy and the role makes their transition into the job much smoother. Job announcements are posted in service-learning newsletters, in the student newspaper, and on giant posters. Faculty encourage service learners to apply. Current student coordinators recruit strong candidates from the ranks of their service learners.

One goal of the program is to have student staff get to know and hear the voices of people whose cultural backgrounds are different from their own. Because the program is highly visible in Milwaukee, an all-white, female staff would not be well-received by the community partners who sometimes perceive Marquette as an institution lacking diversity. But without a proactive approach to hiring for diversity, this might be the most likely pool of candidates, since the majority of service-learning students fit that description. Therefore, the program actively seeks a diverse group, including men and students of color, by posting job announcements with the multicultural groups on campus and personally approaching good candidates. As a result, the staff has always had some level of diversity. The current staff includes four men, three African American students, and two Asian Americans.

The policy of hiring a diverse staff was established in the early years of the program, although the student staff on the hiring committee resisted at first. They thought that the "best" candidates should be chosen, defining *best* in terms of amount of service performed, talkativeness at interviews, and the ability to verbalize a commitment to service and social justice. Once administrators explained the importance of the policy, however, hiring for diversity became an accepted and expected practice of the Service-Learning Program.

After applications are reviewed, each qualified candidate has a group interview with the administrator, assistant administrator, and the two outgoing staff managers. The staff managers give a detailed description of the student coordinator position. All candidates are asked to discuss the following topics:

• Describe your own commitment to community service and social justice.

- After looking over the job description, what parts of the job do you think will be the most challenging for you?

- Describe your past leadership experiences.

- If you took a service-learning course, what did you get out of the experience? How did that experience affect you?

- Beginning a new job, such as this one, can be very stressful, especially since the busiest time in the semester is at the beginning. How do you handle stress, and how do you think you will handle the beginning of the semester here?

- When working as a member of a team, what role do you tend to play within group? Give an example.

- How would you approach a situation in which it is necessary to work with someone who has a completely different work style from yours, or with whom you have a personality conflict?

- How would your friends describe you?

- What else would you like us to know about you?

In addition to diversity, the program considers the candidates' year in school, major, other activities, GPA, punctuality and dress for the interview, ability to overcome nervousness and be articulate, and experience with or knowledge of service-learning. The student coordinator role is geared toward older, more experienced students, but increasingly we are finding freshmen who can handle the demands.

Because the job of student coordinator requires a 10-hour-per-week commitment, more than one coordinator has come into the office in tears about the demanding work. Combining a service-learning job with being a resident assistant, for example, can be done, but it is difficult and requires superior ability to organize and prioritize. We try to anticipate potential scheduling conflicts by asking students what else they'll be doing next semester and how many credits they'll be taking, among other things.

As much as possible, employment in the Service Learning Program is designed to mimic a real-world work experience, from the application process forward. All aspects of the employment process reflect this goal, from the written application, group interviews, and reference checks on top candidates to written job descriptions, dress codes for the office and for special events, joint supervisor-student performance reviews, and promotions and merit raises.

Two staff managers are promoted each year from the pool of student coordinators. Like the coordinators, they must complete a written application and group interview. The questions in both help candidates reflect on their vision for the program and the steps they would take to fulfill that vision.

Training

Training begins soon after new student coordinators have been hired, at the end of the semester before they begin their jobs. New coordinators spend an hour or two in the office with a staff manager who familiarizes them with the office layout, the database, computer system, files, and so on. At that time, the new coordinators receive training manuals that cover every aspect of the job, including a sample script for calling community agencies for the first time.

Formal training begins a few days before the first day of classes in the semester following recruitment and hiring. An all-morning orientation for new staff is held before the return of the veterans for the first all-staff meeting of the semester. Topics include office procedures, policies, and computer-related information; proper editing practices for placement descriptions; simulation exercises for calling community sites for the first time; tips on working with nonprofits and choosing placement sites; knowledge necessary to be an effective faculty liaison; and practice for doing in-class orientation presentations. Student feedback about the training regimen has been positive. One student, Kristine Pintor, remarked:

> The staff training was very helpful in making me feel comfortable at the office. I wasn't just thrown into the program. I was taught and prepared for the challenges the job entails. Coming into the job knowing it was going to be a challenge motivated me to do the best work I could once I started.

Because the roles and responsibilities change as the semester progresses, new staff consider their entire first term as training. Each new student coordinator is matched with a veteran staff mentor who is available to answer questions and further orient the novice. This relationship lasts all semester, but its intensity diminishes as the semester progresses and the new coordinators become more comfortable with their roles.

Office schedules are arranged so that mentors and mentees share several office hours together each week, making contact between the two more accessible and frequent. After training through this process, Rhegan Hyypio commented: "The most helpful aspect of this was the patience other staff members showed with questions. The shadowing of former coordinators worked well." Another student, Natalie Fuller, said: "It has been really helpful to me to have office hours with others on staff. If I have a question, it is easily answered by someone in the office. The staff trainings have...helped form a really nice staff community in which we are not just co-workers but friends."

Training of staff—both veteran and new—is ongoing and occurs in a variety of formats. The staff managers conduct biweekly staff meetings at which student coordinators receive information about upcoming activities and have an opportunity to raise problems and concerns with their peers. On alternate weeks when there are no staff meetings, each coordinator meets with a staff manager to discuss specific concerns. Twice during each semester, teams plan group training sessions for the staff. Topics for these trainings vary widely and include social issues such as racism as well as pragmatic topics such as how to produce an attractive newsletter.

Student Staff Roles and Responsibilities

Student Coordinator

The Service Learning Program employs 12 student coordinators. The coordinators serve as liaisons to three main constituent groups: partner agencies, service learners, and faculty. Each links 8 to 10 agencies, 40 to 60 service-learning students, and 3 to 4 professors with the Service Learning Program.

With participating agencies, student coordinators are responsible for forming a working relationship with the site coordinators, setting up orientations, and helping the site coordinators choose appropriate experiences for the students. Student coordinators make at least two site visits during the semester and check in with the site coordinators at other points to catch any problems and respond to concerns. They also provide site coordinators with forms at midterm so they can evaluate their service learners and exchange feedback with site coordinators at the end of each semester.

Student coordinators also provide information to service learners about their agencies and sign them up; attend site orientations with their service learners; participate in Beginner Service-Learning and Spanish Service-Learning Training; and assist service learners with logistics and problems (such as transportation, safety, or difficulties at the site). They check in with the service learners throughout the semester and help them connect their community experiences with their courses. These connections are shared at mid-semester reflection sessions, which student coordinators conduct. Finally, student coordinators handle all paperwork and records relating to their service learners and also promote other service-related opportunities to students.

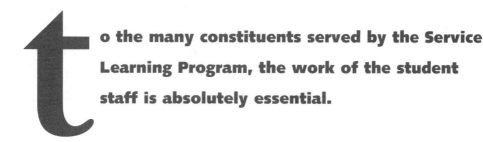

to the many constituents served by the Service Learning Program, the work of the student staff is absolutely essential.

Student coordinators also play an important role for faculty. They conduct service-learning orientations in their classes, collect contracts and timesheets, respond to concerns throughout the semester, offer extra support to faculty who are new to service-learning, and gather feedback from faculty at the end of each semester.

Staff Manager

The two student staff managers are part of the management team, along with the program administrator and assistant administrator. Their primary responsibilities are to help administer the program and manage the Service Learning office. Their duties are to:

- Work with program administrators and student coordinators to plan and execute student registration, orientation, training, and reflection sessions.
- Supervise and provide direction for student coordinators.
- Recruit, interview, and train new student coordinators.
- Plan the timeline of student coordinators' duties and tasks for the semester.
- Schedule staff and report their hours.
- Plan and lead staff meetings.
- Oversee student coordinators' management of service-learning responsibilities.
- Help student coordinators solve problems with sites or students.

The staff managers also have some office responsibilities, ranging from daily clerical duties to making phone calls to establish relationships with new sites.

Additional Staff Responsibilities

In addition to the responsibilities outlined above, all service-learning student staff are involved in a number of other activities, as needed. They may be called on to:

- Present at workshops or other events to agency representatives or high school students.
- Write newsletter articles, meeting minutes, memos, or letters to other staff, faculty, service learners, or agency representatives.
- Plan and lead staff training and team-building activities (such as social trips or group reflections).
- Staff service projects (such as serving meals at Ronald McDonald House, cooking for Campus Kitchens, or making a trip to Habitat for Humanity).
- Lead reflection sessions with service learners.

- Create bulletin boards in the office and displays about the Service Learning Program.
- Offer new ideas to improve the program.
- Perform skits for Beginner Service-Learning and Spanish Service-Learning Training.

Benefits of Employment for Students

To the many constituents served by the Service-Learning Program, the work of the student staff is absolutely essential. The benefits are not one-way, however; in addition to the satisfaction of working for the public good, students gain many transferable skills, including planning, organizing, problem solving, coordinating, public speaking, working with others, communicating orally and in writing, and coping with frustrations.

The value of this real-world work experience has been confirmed by student staff members. Kristine Pintor, a freshman, noted, "I have come to better understand and appreciate the work it takes to create a strong staff and to keep things running smoothly in the office. I have learned how to handle important matters in a more professional way." Another freshman, Natalie Fuller, was taken by the personal impact of her work: "I have gained an amazing outlook on how service plays a role in my life. By taking this position, I feel much more aware of the community needs and what I can do to make a difference."

Students have also listed confidence, communication skills, and connections as some of their biggest gains from serving as program leaders. According to Randell Irving, a junior, "I have gained experience in a leadership role. As a student coordinator, I feel I bring everything together. I get the chance to interact with service learners, agency contact persons, program staff, and faculty." Freshman Kim Stein was impressed with what she learned through such contact: "Personally I have gained confidence and communication skills from my interactions with students and people at the sites."

Many current student staff members describe service-learning as a foundation for continued service as they move into the workforce. "After two years in the Service Learning office, I feel that I am better prepared to serve—and perhaps work—in the nonprofit world," noted senior Craig Pierce. Shelley Frank, echoed this sentiment:

> Working for this program has increased my interest in and awareness of social justice issues in the Milwaukee community and the world. I have also gained a lot professionally, including better communication skills, organizational skills, confidence in my ability to work with those in higher positions, and experience with daily office work. I feel more prepared to enter the real-world workforce with my experience from this job.

"**most important, the Service Learning Program gave me an opportunity to develop a passion for promoting social justice.**"

Many alumni of the program have found that their experience prepared them for their lives after Marquette. Rhegan Hyypio, class of 2001, transformed the desire to engage in service that she developed in the program into working for a nongovernmental organization in the Dominican Republic. Other students applied the skills they gained to other fields. Tricia Roehrig, class of 1997, noted:

> Service-learning helped me see the value and real-world application of having an English degree. Everyone asked me, "Are you going to be a teacher?" as if that is the only way to use such a degree. How do you explain that there is value in getting an English degree if you're not going to "use" it? By having opportunities to apply communication skills in the real world—both as a student participant in service-learning and as a student staff member communicating with agencies, students, and professors—I learned that this was the most applicable degree for me. When do you not need to be able to communicate on the job?

Samantha Adams, class of 1995, found similar value in her experience:

> Service-learning taught me how to manage others, how to make cold-call contacts in the community, how to refocus and multitask. Most important, it taught me how to motivate others. This is my greatest asset as a leader in my community. I am able to keep the energy high and make the work important for the group. I developed this skill, in great measure, working with the Service Learning Program.

The quintessential example of the service-learning benefit to students is the current assistant administrator, Kim Jensen Bohat. Bohat began as a social work student at Marquette and participated in six service-learning classes. In the spring of her sophomore year, she joined the staff as a student coordinator and, in her senior year, was promoted to staff manager. After three years as a social worker in the community following graduation, Jensen rejoined the staff and now has two primary responsibilities: building relationships with community partners, and supervising all the student staff. Jensen commented:

> My own service-learning experience helped me to change my undergraduate major to social work. As a student worker with the program, I gained so many skills that helped me to be successful as a social worker and change agent after graduation: the ability to organize and develop programs, to help others to reflect on real issues, and to manage a caseload.

But most important, the Service Learning Program gave me an opportunity to develop a passion for promoting social justice. Now, as the assistant administrator, I help student workers develop these same skills and find the same passion for creating positive change that I have felt. We work hard not only to help the student staff members develop professionally, but also to help them discern their responsibility to their community in whatever profession they choose. This is central to the students' education, especially at a Jesuit institution or any institution concerned with developing the next generation of engaged citizens.

Challenges and Future Directions

The Service Learning Program at Marquette is constantly evolving. The program administrators are always looking for ways to improve job satisfaction and the quality of the students' performance. The goal is to broaden their horizons beyond service-learning and beyond Marquette.

One ongoing challenge is the unevenness of the workload each semester. The heaviest time commitment for all staff occurs at the beginning and end of the term. This distribution is especially difficult for new student employees, who must do their hardest work when they are learning the job. By mid-semester, when service learners are productively engaged at their sites or in their projects, the pace in the office slackens. In response to this downtime, the program has instituted staff service projects, ongoing training, and newsletters.

Future directions for student staff might include:

- Expansion of the reflections offered to service learners to include a series of themed reflections.

- More regional and national exposure, possibly through the Wisconsin or National Campus Compact or through organizations such as Idealist on Campus.

- Larger social justice issues, which might include choosing an issue (for example, racism) and creating training sessions, information, service projects, and reflections, possibly inviting that semester's service learners to participate.

Service-learning could not exist at Marquette without the work of the 100+ students who have assisted in running the program in its 12 years of operation. The students handle significant responsibilities with surprisingly little supervision. The program trusts the students and their work, and they respond to that trust with effort and professionalism beyond their years. Most have learned from the experience, made good friends, heard different viewpoints, grappled with thorny issues, and had fun along the way.

Acknowledgments

The authors wish to acknowledge the valuable input of present and former Service-Learning Program staff members Samantha Adams, James Austin, Chelsea Deiters, Natalie Fuller, Mallory Hager, Rhegan Hyypio, Randell Irving, Kim Jensen, Holly Kolanko, Craig Pierce, Kristine Pintor, Tricia Roehrig, Kim Stein, Grace Mazza Urbanski, Karen Vander Sanden, and Erik Wright.

The Student Ambassador Model

Katia Archer, Yleinia Galeano, Ossie Hanauer, Nicolle Hickey,
Michelle Lasanta, and Josh Young

MIAMI DADE COLLEGE (MDC) has earned a reputation for having one of the nation's largest, most respected service-learning programs. One key to the program's success is the students who have played a leadership role. Student voice and leadership are without a doubt essential for any institution of higher education that is serious about developing and institutionalizing service-learning—especially in this era of scarce resources. At MDC, we have come to realize that we could not run a service-learning program without student ambassadors. Students play a critical role not only in implementing and sustaining programs but also in serving as spokespeople for our efforts.

> The job of an educator is to teach students to see the vitality in themselves.
>
> —*Joseph Campbell*

This chapter describes MDC's service-learning student ambassador program—its history, rationale, and, most important, ways that other colleges and universities can build upon the concept of students as ambassadors to develop service-learning programs that empower students and foster their leadership skills.

Service-Learning at Miami Dade

MDC is a large, urban community college spanning all of Florida's Miami-Dade County. With eight campuses and several outreach centers, MDC is the largest institution of higher education in the United States, with more than 160,000 students taking classes at the college annually. The MDC Center for Community Involvement (CCI), created in 1994, uses the college's resources—faculty, staff, students, and physical infrastructure—to address the needs of the south Florida community.

The college recognized the potential, and indeed the obligation, to make education for the common good a hallmark of the institution. It is widely recognized that in recent years students and members of the general public have become more apathetic, less involved in the political process, and less informed about the demands of democratic citizenship. Higher education has the opportunity to be part of the solution for strengthening the democracy. At MDC, we believe that a fundamental role of the educational experience should be to prepare students for a life of informed, engaged citizenship. We want our graduates to have the skills, behaviors, attitudes, and knowledge that good citizens need—things such as a commitment to service, an understanding of community problems and mechanisms for bringing about change, listening skills, critical thinking, an understanding of the delicate balance between rights and responsibilities, and a commitment to the common good.

quality service-learning, by definition, expects and requires student voice, student leadership, and student empowerment.

CCI's mission is to promote the ethic of service and citizenship. This goal is accomplished through a college-wide infrastructure that includes three fully staffed comprehensive centers that coordinate service-learning, the Federal Work-Study America Reads program, and numerous other campus-community partnership projects.

Since 1994, more than 200 faculty members at MDC have combined academic study with course-relevant service projects. This has resulted in more than 30,000 students participating in service-learning projects, contributing more than 600,000 hours of documented service with approximately 500 community agencies. The program has grown exponentially, and now more than 4,000 students participate in service-learning annually, contributing in excess of 90,000 hours of service. With more than 500 classes a year offering service-learning, students provide many inspiring success stories. The development of the service-learning student ambassador program has enhanced these successes as student ambassadors convey the power of service-learning to their peers and, at the same time, provide faculty with invaluable support in providing these opportunities.

Why Student Ambassadors?

> No one is born a good citizen; no nation is born a democracy. Rather, both are processes that continue to evolve over a lifetime. Young people must be included from birth. A society that cuts itself off from its youth severs its lifeline.
>
> —*Kofi Annan*

Developing Citizenship

Quality service-learning, by definition, expects and requires student voice, student leadership, and student empowerment. In addition to enhancing academic learning and meeting community needs, a fundamental goal of service-learning is to foster civic responsibility. Service-learning aims to help students realize concrete contributions to their local community and beyond. It has the potential to prepare graduates who are informed, know how to get things done in the community, are concerned about the common good, and feel an obligation to be engaged in the community for the rest of their lives.

Often, service-learning practitioners and coordinators assume that leadership and civic learning simply happen when students are involved in service-learning. However, it has become clear that unless we are purposeful about leadership development, we will not fully realize these objectives. It was partly for this reason that Miami Dade began the student ambassador program.

Doing the "Work" of Service-Learning

In addition to addressing the broader need for developing citizenship skills and values, the student ambassador program provides essential assistance in helping the college do the day-to-day work of service-learning. CCI faces two major challenges in creating and sustaining service-learning at MDC. One is the size of the college: its eight campuses and several outreach centers are spread over the entire county. Although CCI offices on three campuses provide service to all campuses and outreach centers, it is difficult to build and coordinate a program in such a large, dispersed, complex institution.

The second challenge is the labor-intensive nature of service-learning. Administering a comprehensive program involves myriad tasks, and logistics can be quite complex. These tasks include creating an infrastructure to support faculty and students; building community partnerships; recruiting and training faculty; helping match faculty with service projects that meet their learning objectives; making class presentations; tracking and reporting on all service-learning activities; recognizing and celebrating program participants; and ensuring quality, impact, and sustainability.

The size of MDC, coupled with the complex logistics required, point up the tremendous amount of detail and behind-the-scenes work a high-quality service-learning program requires. The effort can seem overwhelming, especially for overworked campus service-learning coordinators, making them susceptible to burnout. CCI's student ambassador program began in response to a growing workload as more faculty became interested in service-learning as well as from the desire to provide more opportunities for student leadership and growth. The work of these ambassadors, and especially their assumption of leadership, is critical for CCI's programs to reach their potential and to remain sustainable.

Evolution of the Student Ambassador Model

Size and Structure

When the student ambassador program started, a handful of students on one campus spent three to five hours a week helping to coordinate the service-learning program. Now every semester, a corps of approximately 20 student ambassadors works college-wide to administer and lead the service-learning program. From the beginning, students have had to apply to be ambassadors, with previous experience in service-learning a requirement. Faculty helped recruit ambassadors from their service-learning classes.

In addition to student ambassadors, MDC has assigned Federal Work-Study (FWS) part-time student employees to work in the service-learning offices. Every college that receives funds for FWS is required to allocate at least 7% to Community Service Federal Work-Study (CSFWS). This provision offers a great opportunity for supporting student leadership. All the students who work in the service-learning program get paid through FWS. These students play an integral role in the program, maintaining partnerships with community agencies, helping counsel and place thousands of students in service-learning placements, and implementing campus-community partnership events.

When MDC's service-learning program began, FWS student assistants handled all the office work—entering data, filing, providing office coverage, preparing letters, helping students who came to the office, and so on—while the ambassadors took on more complex leadership projects such as delivering class presentations, calling community partners and students, and communicating with faculty. As the program expanded to eight campuses and the corps of CSFWS student coordinators grew to more than 15, they became effective, dynamic, and committed service-learning student ambassadors who each put in more than 20 hours as paid employees every week.

Throughout the years, the student ambassador program has grown, offering students more opportunities to travel to conferences, make public presentations, and gain leadership skills. Ambassadors now have public-speaking opportunities at regional and national conferences, as well as at training sessions for faculty and community partners. Ambassadors lead and coordinate service-learning not only at their home campus but also at the other campuses where there is no on-site service-learning office. For example, the Wolfson campus located in the downtown Miami area also supports and coordinates activities for the Medical and InterAmerican campuses. Student ambassadors must therefore be flexible community builders who are responsible for working with faculty, community partners, and students in multiple locations across the county.

**tudent ambassador reports include evaluations from both the students and the agency supervisor. These reports often become part of faculty portfolios and annual performance reviews.**

Duties of Student Ambassadors

Student ambassadors spend 15 to 25 hours a week coordinating service-learning and campus-community partnerships. When someone calls or visits any of the campus CCI offices, a student ambassador greets and assists them. Ambassadors therefore serve as the face of MDC's service-learning program. They also take the lead in listening to and encouraging students, assisting professors, and administering the program.

In addition to staffing the offices and offering frontline support, each ambassador is assigned approximately six service-learning faculty members whom they assist during the semester. The ambassador meets with the faculty members, reviews their plans for using service-learning, and provides feedback. After an initial presentation to the class, the ambassador does follow-up visits, creates a file for each class, tracks applications and placement confirmations from that class, enters all the information into the program's database, and sends the faculty member bi-weekly status reports. Reports give the faculty members a written record of how many students from their class participated in service-learning, how many hours they volunteered, and which community partners they worked with. The reports also include the results of the students' questionnaires at the end of the term and transcribed evaluations from both the students and the agency supervisor. These reports often become part of faculty portfolios and annual performance reviews.

Student ambassadors are the program's chief representatives for the service learners. When students want more information on service-learning, they contact the ambassador who made the presentation to their class. Ambassadors handle questions from students about community opportunities and help counsel them to find the most appropriate home for their class. Ambassadors also maintain essential communication with students working in the community, including helping to identify and solve problems students may encounter with their placement. For example, when an agency gives a student a negative evaluation or vice versa, the ambassador follows up with the student to address the cause of the dissatisfaction. Ambassadors also make follow-up calls to clarify information about students' service placement and ensure that they complete their service-learning projects.

Administrative duties are also important. The ambassador-managed database is invaluable for organizing and retrieving information efficiently. For example, when a student has not received a certificate of completion for the service-learning project or has any questions about paperwork, the database enables the ambassador to find the service-learning course, the community partner, and the number of hours completed.

Student ambassadors assist with myriad other tasks. Faculty rely on them to be their liaisons with CCI and to consult with them during their service-learning courses. Ambassadors also help organize faculty workshops and gather data and prepare reports summarizing service-learning activities for each faculty and the campus. In addition, they maintain a comprehensive listing of all faculty involved in service-learning each semester, including their course meeting time, room number, hours required, and special instructions.

Among other benefits, the involvement of student ambassadors helps recruit new faculty. One ambassador informed her political science professor, who was not aware of service-learning, that CCI was organizing a month of activities around the concept of civic engagement. This topic led to a broader discussion about service-learning on campus; the professor came to CCI later that same day to learn how he could get involved.

Another key role for the ambassadors is serving as advocates and spokespersons for the service-learning program. In working with community organizations, ambassadors help organize community partner workshops twice a year to train agencies interested in becoming an approved service-learning placement site. Their presence inspires agency supervisors, who report that the student ambassador presentation is one of the most effective parts of the workshop they attend. Ambassadors represent the student perspective with agencies, letting them know what they should keep in mind when working with service-learners. Ambassadors also keep in contact with community partners to check the status of the service-learners.

More detailed information on the role of student ambassadors—including forms, applications, and job descriptions—may be found at Miami Dade College's Center for Community Involvement website, www.mdc.edu/cci.

Finally, ambassadors play a key role in organizing a service-learning celebration every semester. This event celebrates and recognizes students, faculty, and community partners. It is an invaluable opportunity for reflection on the accomplishments of the semester.

Benefits of Being a Student Ambassador

For their hard work and efforts, and in addition to their regular CSFWS pay, each ambassador receives a polo shirt with the student ambassador logo that they wear to class presentations and program functions, a $250 stipend each semester, recognition, and letters of recommendation for their portfolios. Their pictures are also prominently displayed in the service-learning office.

Equally important and rewarding is the personal, professional, and academic growth the students achieve through their participation in the program. Student ambassadors have been nominated for numerous national, state, and local awards, received scholarships to four-year institutions, gotten jobs, and become more confident students, citizens, and leaders as a direct result of their leadership in the program.

Some MDC student ambassadors commented on the power of this leadership experience:

> I have gained many valuable technical and communication skills as well as a clearer understanding of responsibility. Most importantly, I have gained friendships with a unique group of dedicated and hardworking individuals who have helped shape my view of a leader.
>
> —*Yleinia Galeano*

> [Being a] student ambassador means to explore your horizon and have other ambassadors join with you in your pursuits to encourage and guide service in the community, as well as in everyday life.
>
> —*Jonquila Williams*

I've always thought that school prepared you to claim a place in society and in your community. How can you claim that position if you cannot interact with your community? That is what being a student ambassador has exemplified for me—the ability to communicate and the importance of human relations.

—Michelle Lasanta

Being a student ambassador allowed me to grow as an individual. It was a fulfilling experience because I was able to help both faculty members and students become more involved in the community through service-learning.

—Katia Archer

Recommendations Drawn from the Student Ambassador Program

Creating a student leadership model can be straightforward and manageable. Based on the lessons from MDC's program, some suggestions are:

1. Form a service-learning advisory committee with faculty, community partners, key administrators, and students.

2. Create a job description for the CSFWS service-learning student position (sample available on MDC's website at www.mdc.edu/cci), and plan how to utilize and staff the campus service-learning office.

3. Meet with financial aid representatives to determine where the institution is directing the 7% mandated for Community Service Federal Work-Study.

4. Advocate for one or more CSFWS positions to help coordinate service-learning. Emphasize the benefits to students, the institution, the community and, most important, to the growth and sustainability of service-learning. Secure support and involvement from the deans or the president.

5. Plan a comprehensive orientation and leadership development program for student leaders.

6. Seek ways to empower students to take on as much leadership in the service-learning program as possible.

7. Make the most of student leaders as spokespeople for the program and as examples of the possibilities service-learning offers.

Conclusion

We challenge you to ensure that the next year's entering students will graduate as individuals of character more sensitive to the needs of community, more competent to contribute to society, and more civil in habits of thought, speech, and action.

—Wingspread Group on Higher Education, 1993

Are colleges doing enough to guide students to become "individuals of character more sensitive to the needs of community, more competent to contribute to society, and more civil in habits of thought, speech, and action"? What more can they do to make student leadership a focal point? How can they create the next generation of leaders who will fully embrace service-learning as an even more accepted and widespread pedagogy, and who will ensure that the entire education system embraces the concepts and goals of service-learning? How can students graduate with strong civic skills and a commitment to civic engagement? An important first step is to explore the possibility of creating a service-learning student ambassador program.

Reference

Wingspread Group on Higher Education. (1993). *An American imperative: Higher expectations for higher education, an open letter to those concerned about the American future.* Racine, WI: The Johnson Foundation, Inc.

Students as Staff

Professionalism of Student Staff at Boise State

Boise State University's service-learning program has a reputation for innovation, both on campus and nationally, in large part because of the professionalism of its student staff. The only full-time employee, the service-learning director, coaches a staff of six students to run the service-learning program. Students coordinate class-agency partnerships, marketing, orientations, and service-learning class support. They also train, coordinate, and mentor new student staff.

New staff members are recruited as freshmen or sophomores, so they can be groomed as trainers within two years. With this system, cycles of students develop skills in program development, management, collaboration, training, and service-learning pedagogy. From 2003 to 2004, six Boise State student staff, each working 15 to 20 hours per week, successfully coordinated more than 60 service-learning classes, 1,000 service-learning students, and 50 community agencies.

How were they able to accomplish so much? Student staff perform professional-level work because the service-learning director invests in them through high-quality infrastructure, professional development opportunities, personal mentoring, and collaborative problem-solving.

INFRASTRUCTURE

The service-learning database streamlines administrative tasks, allowing student staff to focus on program implementation rather than menial work. Coordination of agencies, projects, classes, students, and faculty is all facilitated online. This comprehensive database also decreases loss of institutional knowledge when students eventually leave.

Personal space and equipment are also vital. Each student has his or her own individual workstation, phone, and personally decorated area in one of two staff offices.

PROFESSIONAL DEVELOPMENT

Student staff members are given a segment of the program to manage on their own. According to Kelly O'Rourke, returning student and coordinator of the Community Work Study Program:

> Each staff member is responsible for the management, development, and function of their part of the program. Because of this, I am provided with an opportunity for independence, self-responsibility, and creativity that most campus jobs do not offer. These qualities create an invaluable learning experience that push me to grow as a person and a professional and will leave me with skills I will use for the rest of my life.

The service-learning director guides them in their new roles as managers and also pays for training in service-learning, technology, community-building, or other topics suggested by the student staff. Management training begins when students ask: "What did I need to know to be successful with this project?" and "How would I improve the management of this project?" Their reflections are used as a basis for writing or improving a manual on their program area. Because of this personal ownership and investment, students often return year after year.

PERSONAL MENTORING

The service-learning director also helps the students learn about delegation, training techniques, supervision, and mentoring. The director meets weekly with each staff member to discuss goals, accomplishments, challenges, and personal growth. With this coaching, each student practices project management and trains, coordinates, and mentors two tiers of new student staff. The first tier of mentored students is hired to replace the core staff after graduation. The second tier of student staff is composed of former service-learning students who applied to be service-learning teaching assistants. This two-tiered system provides a pool of potential recruits and an initial screening and training mechanism.

COLLABORATIVE PROBLEM-SOLVING

Because most student staff members were once teaching assistants as well as service learners, they bring many perspectives to their administrative roles. In weekly group meetings, the service-learning director and the student staff solve problems and brainstorm together. The student staff makes the service-learning program at Boise State University becomes stronger, bigger, centered more on students, and, most importantly, more effective.

part four

Student-Faculty Partnerships

P
ARTNERSHIPS BETWEEN STUDENTS AND FACULTY are a core component of engaging students as colleagues on campus. More than simply including students as assistants to faculty, this section describes efforts to make students a fundamental part of curriculum design as well as course development and implementation—the very heart of colleges and universities. Although students find that the curriculum is often the hardest part of the institution to engage, the four chapters and shorter vignettes in this section provide powerful examples of institutional commitment to these partnerships.

The first chapter in this section, from the University of North Carolina at Chapel Hill (UNC), describes the APPLES program, in which students supported the creation of one of the nation's first student-led service-learning programs. The unique structure of APPLES includes two key committees: a university-wide Courses Committee that oversees the administration of all university courses with a service-learning component and distributes funding for course development and enhancement, and a Reflections Committee that coordinates student-led reflection sessions for the service-learning efforts. It is clear from this chapter that institutional support for students in service-learning is essential for flourishing partnerships. The chapter concludes with the story of the development of a student-led course, "Reflection and the Service-Learning Experience," which provides training for student reflection facilitators.

Like UNC, Allegheny College has been host to a student-developed initiative, the Service-Learning Challenge. Launched in 1999, the program empowers students as co-educators. Student Service Leaders (SSLs) are involved in every aspect of the program, from training to offering a course on service-learning theory. The SSLs then use their knowledge and expertise in the community to pair with faculty in service-learning classrooms. Pointing out the importance of having involved, dedicated students on campus—as reflected in the first section of this book, "Identifying Student Leaders"—this chapter also provides advice for replicating the Allegheny model on other campuses.

The third chapter describes the unique university studies program at Portland State University. This program demonstrates that student-faculty partnerships can be an essential element of an overall institutional commitment to civic engagement. The authors outline four key programs: the Freshman-Senior Capstone Connection, where senior student leaders connect their coursework with the work of freshmen in first-year classes; the Student Leaders for Service program, which focuses on student-led efforts to help other students engage in this work; Senior Capstone Design, where students actually design new courses for implementation by faculty; and the Mentor Program, where student leaders support freshman- and sophomore-level service-learning courses.

Finally, students and staff from the Center for Community Partnerships at the University of Pennsylvania describe how students have served as both colleagues and catalysts in three university-community partnerships: a cluster of linguistics courses in which a faculty member and students have designed a cutting-edge reading improvement program for local schools; a community health and disease prevention program organized by students and faculty; and a student-facilitated course to promote democratic participation in the classroom and the community.

Two vignettes close out this section, one a university-based program from the University of Richmond's Jepson School of Leadership Studies and the other a community-based program in St. Paul, Minnesota, from the Jane Addams School for Democracy. The Jepson School demonstrates how student-faculty links in service-learning provide critical leadership experiences and educational value for students. The Jane Addams School, in partnership with the University of Minnesota and other local colleges and universities, is an example of truly integrated learning, where college students, faculty, and community partners work together to create a learning community.

Merging Students, Faculty, Community, and University

Dac Cannon, Emily Cupito, Janaka Lagoo,
Kasey Q. Maggard, Leslie Parkins, and Beth Payne

A SSISTING PEOPLE IN PLANNING LEARNING EXPERIENCES IN SERVICE (APPLES), a student-led program at the University of North Carolina at Chapel Hill (UNC), engages students, faculty, and community agencies in service-learning partnerships. According to its mission statement, its goal is "to foster socially aware and civically involved students through participation in an enriched curriculum and hands-on experiences that address the needs of North Carolina communities." The program also has a comprehensive system of organizational beliefs and values, including (Boynton et al., 2004):

1. Sustained commitment to public service integrated in academic curricula

2. Maintenance of a student-led program

3. Responsiveness to community needs

4. Decision making by consensus

5. Equal partnership with university and community

6. Teamwork and mutual respect

> For more information about the APPLES program, see www.unc.edu/apples.

History of APPLES

The strength of APPLES comes from merging students with their faculty, communities, and the university as a whole. Early in 1990, an ambitious student named Tony Deifell perceived a disconnect between service and learning within the university community and envisioned a program to connect the two. In the spring of that year, he organized the Student Action Group (SAG). This group of students, dedicated to increasing the presence of service-learning on campus, worked to connect their ideas with the university. A task force of faculty members, administrators, and community members also formed to help SAG gain support.

However, the program fostered its own questions and concerns. Task force members were concerned that providing academic credit for service would affect students' motivations for volunteering. Moreover, they wondered if the faculty would integrate service into their courses. Such questions helped SAG focus its objectives and vision. Although the process was not simple, the students persevered.

The next semester, things began to fall into place. A national organization, Campus Outreach Opportunity League (COOL), gave APPLES its first grant. APPLES also found a home at the Center for Teaching and Learning (CTL) on campus. The CTL was a perfect fit, because the program wanted to be recognized as both an academic organization and a student organization. Deifell also felt that the CTL would support the organization's student-run structure.

Despite this progress, the students involved quickly found that full-time staffing would be necessary for the program to succeed. The APPLES program was then presented to the student body for the first time in a referendum that asked students to add 90 cents to their fees to support a service-learning coordinator. Students voted to pass the referendum, demonstrating their support for this new idea of service-learning. The idea of APPLES was one step closer to becoming a reality. In spring 1991, six service-learning courses were finally introduced with great success.

Through the hard work of many dedicated students, the idea of service-learning was introduced in a way that focused on the relationship between the community and the classroom. As Deifell stated:

> I believe the student ownership . . . reveals the strength of our program. Our motivation is contagious. . . . Students working to influence the quality of their own educational experience can be a powerful catalyst for improvement of that experience." (Quarles, 2001, p. 40)

APPLES Structure

APPLES now has two full-time professional staff and three part-time staff members. It fits into the university structure as both a registered student organization and a unit within academic affairs (see Figure 1). Student fees, state funds, and private donations support the programming and administrative budgets.

Outgoing seniors recruit and select the executive cabinet and the committee chairs, also known as APPLES organizers, each year. These students plan, implement, and evaluate the programs with the guidance of the staff.

Two of the major committees, the Courses and Reflections Committees (described below), each have two co-chairs responsible for their respective programs. Typically, six

FIGURE 1: **APPLES Organizational Chart**

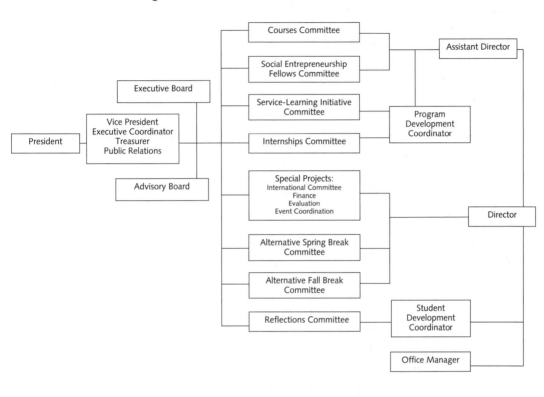

students sit on the committee, working on specific projects and planning new directions.

APPLES Courses Committee

The Courses Committee oversees the administration of all university courses that have a service-learning component through APPLES. In addition, it is responsible for awarding Course Enhancement and Ueltschi Course Development grants.

APPLES COURSES. The largest number of students involved in APPLES are either taking or organizing courses. These courses either are traditional university courses enhanced with a service component or are specifically designed with service-learning in mind. APPLES courses are offered in a wide variety of disciplines and levels of advancement. Student service experiences include creating a public relations campaign, promoting tissue donor registration, providing child-care services to young mothers in need, and working with relocated refugee families to find area resources and assistance.

Service-learning courses integrate a service project into the traditional curriculum for the course. APPLES connects the students and professors of these courses with local community groups and organizations. Some placements operate on a week-to-week basis, while others involve a project that spans the entire semester. In both cases, students complete approximately 30 hours of service over the course of the semester.

One of the Courses Committee's responsibilities is to ensure that students are aware of available APPLES courses by listing them on the APPLES web page. All the courses have a footnote attached to online listings indicating their service-learning component. Currently, approximately 20 APPLES courses are offered each semester, with an enrollment of 20 to 40 students per section.

The demand for APPLES courses increased with the introduction of the Public Service Scholar (PSS) program. All participants in the program, which focuses on and recognizes students consistently and actively engaged in service during their UNC career, are required to take at least two APPLES courses, in addition to a number of independent service requirements.

COURSE GRANTS. The Courses Committee distributes grants through two different grant programs: Course Enhancement grants and Ueltschi Course Development grants. Course Enhancement grants are available annually for faculty who seek to improve their current APPLES class. The Courses Committee requests and reviews these applications to evaluate the projects and determine funding, up to $500, to cover books, field trips, student travel to sites or conferences, or other educational expenses.

The Ueltschi Grants provide opportunities for new faculty to develop APPLES courses. To recruit faculty, students plan and facilitate information sessions and send personalized invitations to faculty members recommended by fellow students. The Courses Committee chair is one of the student representatives on the Ueltschi Grant selection committee.

APPLES Reflections Committee

Within the APPLES community, reflections are often described as the hyphen between service and learning. The phrase encapsulates the meaning of reflection as a bridge that connects what students learn in the classroom to the community service and activism they conduct outside the classroom. The Reflections Committee engages students in an effective dialogue that connects learning with experience. Specifically, the committee routinely works on the coordination of reflection sessions for all APPLES classes, training of facilitators, and the incorporation of reflection into other service programs.

Reflection sessions generally accompany APPLES courses to create a concentrated time to focus on making the connection between service and learning. APPLES provides volunteer reflection facilitators for the professors. Three structured student-led reflection sessions are conducted for each class during the semester. The first reflection session, titled "Thinking about Service," explores the meaning of responsible, engaged service. Students have generally begun volunteering in the agencies at this point, and the session enables them to discuss with their classmates the rewards and frustrations they have already experienced in their placements. A recommended activity is to use a formal rubric to examine the question, "How do you define service?" The goal of the exercise is to encourage students to see their personal connection to service and leave the first session motivated to serve and excited about their APPLES placement.

reflection is a bridge that connects what students learn in the classroom to the community service and activism they conduct outside the classroom.

The Reflections Committee also recruits facilitators who have taken an APPLES course, are participants in the reflections course, or are involved in other aspects of the program. The committee facilitates training workshops at the beginning of each semester. The workshops address the logistics of facilitation and teach skills for leading a productive discussion. Reflection coordinators receive guidelines on setting up a physical environment in which students can comfortably share ideas, building group camaraderie, encouraging a variety of discussion styles, and allowing students to lead the discussion (see the Sidebar on p.166). Students create facilitator notebooks that provide forms, logistics, contact information, and specific ideas for each session. In addition, the notebook contains activities for leading discussions and general principles on how to be an active listener, provide constructive feedback, and attend to the needs of all students.

REFLECTION LEADERSHIP. Reflection sessions exemplify student leadership in the APPLES program. The sessions are usually held without faculty; thus, the undergraduate facilitators have the challenge of engaging their peers in constructive, reflective discussion on their own. During the three sessions, the students in the courses analyze what it means to serve responsibly, develop a better understanding of their agency, and end with a desire for continued service. The students often realize the greater implications of their service through their discussions during these sessions.

APPLES Guidelines for Facilitating Reflection

I. SETTING UP THE DISCUSSION AREA.

- Room setup is important for the discussion dynamic. A circular arrangement is best, so that every student can see every other student.

- Plan your meeting for a place that is easy to find and where students will feel physically comfortable during the sessions.

- Encourage students to feel free to put their feet up, sit on the floor, or any other arrangement that makes them feel "at home" during the discussion.

II. GETTING TO KNOW THE GROUP.

- Knowing names is a key for success during reflections. Work hard to learn reflectors' names quickly.

- Interns may be less likely to share if they are afraid of forgetting names. Help the students learn each other's names by addressing each reflector by name. Making name signs is useful.

- Also learn the personalities of the reflectors. Know who will be open to questioning, who is shy, who might get defensive, etc.

III. ENCOURAGE SPECIFIC, PERSONAL, AND CONCRETE DISCUSSION.

- Ask reflectors to back up statements with specific, personal, and concrete examples.

- People tend to relate to real-life stories better than broad, abstract statements.

- Small groups are good.

- Make sure everyone gets a chance to speak.

IV. HE WHO FACILITATES LEAST, FACILITATES BEST...

- Expect some awkward silences. Do not feel responsible for filling them with babble. Be patient and people will almost always step forward.

- Don't feel it necessary to respond immediately to each comment. Such responses tend to create a teacher-student, question-answer dynamic that limits real, meaningful discussion.

- Avoid putting a value judgment on reflectors' comments. In an unfamiliar situation, people will be less likely to contribute if their comments are immediately judged or evaluated. Remember, we are encouraging people to do real critical thinking in these sessions, so they must feel comfortable to experiment with their opinions. Reflectors should be excited, engaged, and spontaneous with their comments.

- Whenever possible, allow one of the reflectors to lead part of the discussion. If someone raises an interesting issue and appears to have knowledge about the subject, let him or her run with it. Don't feel the need to direct the conversation at all times.

During the semester, facilitators get constant feedback from the Reflections Commitee Chair, who sends weekly emails reminding facilitators of their reflection dates. Committee members create a blackboard site containing all pertinent forms and extra resources on conducting reflections. They sponsor a lunch to discuss and evaluate the past semester. At the end of the semester, each facilitator meets with an APPLES staff member and the faculty member teaching the course in a debriefing session, so all three can evaluate the past and plan for the future of the class.

THE REFLECTIONS ROAD SHOW. Reflection sessions extend beyond courses, within APPLES and externally. The idea of spreading the message of reflection as an integral component of service has been a recent goal of the committee. The Reflections Road Show was initiated as a way to spread the idea of reflections with service to other campus organizations.

The Reflections Road Show emphasizes the importance of reflection in enriching a service experience and facilitating productive discussions. It divides reflection into two complementary areas: reflection on service and facilitating group discussions. A website that combines resources and group facilitation of reflection is the backbone of the road show and is a source of reference for all campus organizations. The presentations conducted for campus groups communicate information from the website through activities tailored to fit the specific needs of each organization.

A Student-Led Course: Reflections and the Service-Learning Experience

Although students lead many parts of the APPLES program, their involvement is most evident in the creation of the fall 2003 course, "Reflections and the Service-Learning Experience." Offered jointly by UNC and neighboring Duke University, the course aimed to make students aware of the importance of reflection to the learning process in service-learning. The class was advertised heavily to North Carolina teaching fellows—students receiving scholarships in exchange for promising to teach in the state's high-need schools after graduation—because the committee believed they would most benefit from learning techniques and getting hands-on practice at group facilitation.

One graduate student adviser and two passionate undergraduate student leaders planned and led the course, in collaboration with 16 students from the two universities who attended. Students played additional roles as well, as the UNC students facilitated reflection sessions for APPLES courses at UNC, and students from both schools participated in direct service in both communities.

Every week, the graduate student adviser, Brian Pittman, reminded participants that the class was about student empowerment; therefore, the success of the course fell on the students' shoulders. Although Pittman did many of the administrative tasks for the

Students weren't content just to learn; they wanted to change things for the better.

class, he ultimately left the direction and content of the class to the students. In a typical class, Pittman would facilitate a brainstorming session about a particular topic and would then ask simply, "What else?" until ideas covered two whiteboard panels. When deciding whether the class should participate in a service project, for example, he allowed the students to debate the pros and cons, rather than forcing his original plans through. On the last day of class, as the students reflected on the success of the course, he finally added his opinion: "The reason this class was a success was not anything that I did. It succeeded because you, the students, made it do so."

Course Development

The initiative and eagerness of the participants made the class work. How can this be replicated for future classes? Many aspects of the course's design encouraged such student leadership and participation.

The spring before the class began, Pittman called all potential participants, selecting those who could add most to the the the class, based on student initiative. The class was self-selective as well, because it consisted only of those students willing to travel biweekly to another campus.

The summer before the launch of the course, the group collaboratively developed a packet of readings as a textbook. After the first few weeks, though, the readings were discarded as the students developed their own theory on how the class should be run. Students began to research topics on their own and share them with the rest of the class. They even decided which speakers would come to class and how class time would be spent.

Course Goals

One of the course's main goals was to prepare students to facilitate group discussion and reflection. Thus, about halfway through the semester, a handful of students began leading a half-hour reflection exercise at the end of every class. In the spring, UNC students applied these new skills by becoming reflection leaders for the overall APPLES program, infusing the program with well-trained, dedicated leaders.

Instead of the typical college lecture, the reflections course revolved around discussion among the students. Discussion was based on experience, rather than memorization. Often the class would begin with a vague topic such as, "What is service-learning?"

From there, the discussion would take off, tying in the assigned readings, ideas from the numerous speakers the class heard throughout the semester, and students' personal experiences. The discussion would move from the large group to smaller focus groups and back to the large group again until every definition had been challenged and altered.

The strength of the students was apparent in all parts of the course. Not willing to take anything for granted, they boldly challenged anything and everything they felt wasn't quite right. At one point in the semester, the director of a service-learning program at a local high school came to speak to the class about the successes and challenges of having a mandatory service-learning component in high school. The session raised important questions: Why did they call it service-learning, for example, when the program had no academic component? What happens to the students who aren't able to meet the basic requirements, for financial or other personal reasons? What actually counts as service, and why? Mostly important, why didn't they lead reflections about the students' service experience? This session is one example of a common theme of the reflections course: students weren't content just to learn; they wanted to change things for the better.

Any doubt that the class is student-driven has been erased as students have moved from the theoretical discussions in the classroom to practical, individual projects. One student is contacting the agencies with whom APPLES students work in order to assess their needs. Another is creating a best-practice model for ridding workplaces of discrimination. One is developing a brochure for Chapel Hill High School on how reflection can enhance service-learning. All the projects stem in one way or another from the reflections course; they give the students the opportunity not only to develop their own ideas and initiatives but also to contribute to the community.

The Future of APPLES

In the 2003–2004 school year, 36 faculty from 16 different departments taught service-learning courses through the APPLES program. During that year, 759 students served 133 organizations through their courses. In the future, APPLES will develop new ways to connect additional disciplines with service-learning, improve reflection activities, and improve the community partnerships.

References

Boynton, L., Eapen, R., Harris, K., Huq, J., Kirk, L., McLaughlin, G., Pittman, B., et al. (2004). *APPLES service-learning program strategic plan.* Chapel Hill: University of North Carolina, APPLES Service-Learning Program.

Quarles, A.E. (2001). *Bringing service-learning and student empowerment to fruition: The history of the APPLES service-learning program at the University of North Carolina at Chapel Hill.* Unpublished undergraduate thesis, University of North Carolina, Chapel Hill.

Capitalizing on Student and Faculty Strengths

Andy Bennett, Michelle Ferry, Karen Hoerst,
Rebecca Milbert, and David Roncolato

T HE ALLEGHENY COLLEGE Service-Learning Challenge is a relatively new student initiative to improve the quality of service-learning. More than 60 students are in service-leader positions at Allegheny College, including AmeriCorps Bonner Leaders, Bonner Scholars, Peer Project Leaders, student supervisors of a computer literacy program, and student supervisors of America Reads. Many partnerships between the college and the community have developed through these strong service leaders.

Allegheny's Service-Learning Challenge was shaped by a vision of civic engagement shared by college students across the country at Campus Compact's Wingspread Summit on Student Civic Engagement in 2001. The report from this conference (Long, 2002, p. 7) notes:

> Service-learning has been called a "strategy for civic engagement." Through service-learning, we have the opportunity to share and relate our experiences with others and to explore the broader context of our service activity. Service-learning, with its rich integration of readings, reflection, and class discussion, offers feedback and recognition and makes us realize that collectively we are a powerful force for social change.

The Service-Learning Challenge pairs faculty and students to capitalize on their respective strengths. Faculty members, well versed in their particular academic fields, have a firm grasp of the discipline and the learning goals of their courses. But they come from graduate schools across the country and around the globe, and the professional and academic demands placed on them make it difficult for them to become engaged in the community. Student Service Leaders (SSLs), on the other hand, have gained extensive experience and knowledge of the community through involvement in ongoing community service programs. Their respective expertise can facilitate fruitful discussions about how service-learning fits into course objectives and what community needs can be met while accomplishing those objectives.

The Service-Learning Challenge is not the only student and faculty joint endeavor at Allegheny. Other programs, including the First Seminar Advisors and the teacher assistant programs, also partner faculty and students. However, the Service-Learning Challenge is a unique collaboration in that it empowers students to be co-educators *in the classroom* through service-learning.

Program History

In the fall of 1999, two students, with entirely different motivations, had the vision that evolved into the Service-Learning Challenge. After the annual Make A Difference Day, one student became enthusiastic about the idea of mobilizing every Allegheny College student to serve the Meadville community during the spring semester of the new millennium. As the philanthropy chair of the student government, he was in an ideal position to motivate many students. Another student had spent part of the previous summer as a service-learning intern with the Corporation for National and Community Service. She felt that Allegheny College had a strong community service program but lacked an equally strong service-learning program.

Both students became convinced that 1,800 students pouring into Meadville for a one-time service event was not the best use of the school's resources. The pair assembled a group of committed service leaders and began to hammer out a plan that would introduce more students to service through service-learning.

The group decided to target the first-year seminars held during the second semester. These seminars would expose first-year students to a culture of service. It would also assist faculty members in shaping courses that had service-learning potential to incorporate a service component. Six faculty members agreed to the experiment, and the Service-Learning Challenge was off the ground.

During the first two years, the SSLs worked only with professors of the first-year seminar courses. In the third year, the program expanded to include other courses. In spring 2002, the SSLs were given the option of enrolling in a concurrent independent study seminar to examine service-learning theory while working with their faculty partner to apply that theory. The fall of 2005 marked a further step toward institutionalizing the Service-Learning Challenge. The faculty approved a two-credit, two-semester service-learning course sequence, "Service Learning: Theory and Practice" I and II (INTDS 201 and INTDS 202). The courses, taught each semester, are open to all students who have previously taken a service-learning course. This sequence fulfills a requirement for the Values, Ethics, and Social Action minor.

The impact of Service-Learning Challenge has continued to grow since the program's inception. During its first five years, the program supported more than 40 courses taught by more than 20 different faculty members.

Structure of the Service-Learning Challenge

During the prior semester, the faculty members whose classes will have a service-learning component and who will collaborate with the Service-Learning Challenge are selected. They are chosen for their willingness to work with students and for their knowledge of service-learning. Those who have attended training on service-learning have priority. SSLs are also recruited at this time. The selection criteria include completion of INTDS 201, knowledge of the community, willingness to work with faculty members, and academic abilities. The coordinating team, composed of two students and the program adviser, administers an interview process for qualified students.

*t*he Service-Learning Challenge is a unique collaboration in that it empowers students to be co-educators in the classroom through service-learning.

After the students are selected, they participate in four hours of training that focuses on the key concepts of service-learning using Andrew Furco's model (1996, pp. 2–6). The coordinating team discusses the five components of the organization: working with professors, introducing service-learning to a class, preparing and facilitating the service projects, monitoring the projects, and reflecting and assessing. After the SSL training, students and faculty partners meet at a luncheon to review the basic concepts of service-learning and the design of the Service-Learning Challenge. The faculty and students have a chance to build relationships, share service experiences, and get a brief overview of each course. After faculty and students list their partnership preferences, the coordinating team pairs faculty with SSLs based on these preferences and areas of interest and expertise.

Course Structure

In INTDS 201, which is co-taught by a veteran SSL, students study the theory behind service-learning, methods of implementing it, and what makes it work well. As a final project for this first course, students recreate a syllabus for an actual Allegheny College course to include a service-learning component. The course professor may choose whether to accept the suggested changes.

In the second class, INTDS 2002, student leaders are paired with professors who teach service-learning courses. The student meets with the professor and plans the service-learning component. They work together to understand and develop the learning objectives of the class and how they can meet the needs of the community. This stage is key: the service-learning component must meet course objectives while addressing a real community problem. Collaboration is essential throughout the semester, since the professor and the SSL are jointly responsible for monitoring the project and integrating the experience into the classroom. The student and faculty member develop a plan for dividing responsibilities for the service-learning portion of the course.

The SSLs introduce the service-learning component to the class early in the semester. Hearing one of their peers get excited about service-learning helps engage other students. The SSLs are responsible not only for explaining service-learning and the class's specific projects, but also for introducing the class to the community. They talk about stereotypes that Allegheny students might have of Meadville residents, and vice versa, in an effort to dispel both stereotypes. The SSLs also administer a pre–service-learning evaluation for all the students, which is revisited after the service experience (see the section on "Reflection and Evaluation," below).

Together, the professor and the SSL set up sites with community partners, take students on site visits, and serve as contacts for the agency. Often the SSL already has connections to the agencies where the service-learning will occur. Throughout the semester, the SSL monitors the service by communicating with students, the professor, and the community partners. The professor and SSL together address any problems that might surface throughout the semester.

Reflection and Evaluation

One important piece of the Service-Learning Challenge—as with any service-learning—is reflection. SSLs facilitate at least one in-class reflection, generally near the end of the service-learning. Professors also may facilitate formal or informal reflection during the rest of the semester. Reflection includes a discussion of the overall experience—connecting the service experience to classroom learning—and encourages students to think about how to improve their involvement.

At the end of the semester, the faculty members evaluate the program in order to improve their experience. Along with the evaluation, there are two reflection activities: one in which the SSLs reflect on their own efforts in class, and one in which students and professors in all of the Service-Learning Challenge courses meet over lunch.

Finally, SSLs administer a post-service evaluation. The pre-and post-service evaluations are then matched, and statistical analyses are done to assess the effectiveness of the service-learning component. Information from the evaluations (by students, professors, and SSLs) is assessed and integrated into the following year's program.

Service-learning will always be a work in progress because of the changing needs of the community, the objectives of the curriculum, and the interests and needs of the service learners. Evaluations help faculty and students gauge this progress.

Having professors and service-learners evaluate the service component in a particular course serves several other purposes. Service-learning should be a positive experience for all: the service learners and leaders, the professors, and the community agencies. Evaluations assess whether the service component enhanced the professor's course curriculum or detracted from it. Equally important is ensuring that the service-learning is meeting a real community need and that the service component is running smoothly. In addition, evaluation allows students to express their opinions honestly, while making suggestions without pressure.

Pre- and post-service evaluations reveal whether student notions of the community, community service, and service-learning change as a result of the service experience. The pre-service evaluation also helps students formalize their expectations about service. By thinking about what they want from the experience, students are better able to ensure that they accomplish their learning objectives. The post-service evaluation gives valuable feedback on problems and how they were handled. It also illuminates the aspects of the service-learning that were most effective in providing a valuable experience for the students and the community. It enables students to step back and review their experiences. Examples of statements from pre- and post-service evaluations (which students and faculty rate on a scale from "Strongly Disagree" to "Strongly Agree") appear in the Sidebar on the next page.

Some Criteria for Replication

From the seven-year experiment with the Service-Learning Challenge, it is possible to distill some criteria for successfully replicating the project. Because a student-led service-learning effort is shaped by students working in particular communities in collaboration with faculty members, the project will be quite different on different campuses. The following criteria—for student, community, faculty, and institution—are meant to assist others who might want to undertake a similar project.

Students

The first criterion is the presence of a significant number of students engaged in the community on an ongoing basis. What student leaders bring to the partnership with

Examples of Pre- and Post-Service Evaluation Statements

(rated from "Strongly Agree" to "Strongly Disagree")

PRE-SERVICE EVALUATION	POST-SERVICE EVALUATION
"The service-learning component in this course will help me to see how the subject matter I learn can be used in everyday life."	"The service-learning component in this course helped me to see how the subject matter I learned can be used in everyday life."
"I think service-learning will help me to better understand the lectures and readings in this course."	"The service-learning project I did helped me to better understand the lectures and readings in this course."
"I probably won't volunteer or participate in the community after this class."	"I probably won't volunteer or participate in the community after this class."
"I feel I would learn more from this course if more time were spent in the classroom instead of doing service-learning in the community."	"I feel I would have learned more from this course if more time were spent in the class- room instead of doing service-learning in the community."

faculty is knowledge of the local organizations, agencies, community dynamics, and community needs. The students who function effectively in the challenge are drawn from a wide pool of service leaders. Allegheny College could not have successfully launched the Service-Learning Challenge in 1990, when it was just beginning to develop a base of Student Service Leaders. A decade later, a pool of sophisticated, committed leaders enabled the Service-Learning Challenge to get off the ground.

A second requirement is having academically strong students who are interested in the program. Because faculty members rely on the students to help accomplish the academic goals of their courses, the students themselves must have done well academically and have good communication skills, troubleshooting abilities, and a record of dependability. An ill-prepared student can turn a previously interested faculty member away from future involvement with the program.

Finally, the students must be highly motivated. They spend extra time meeting with faculty, which they could otherwise offer to service sites. They must feel it is worth the sacrifice. At Allegheny, the service-learning program began as a student-initiated project; on other campuses, the idea might first capture the interest of faculty members or administrators. Either route can work, but administrators must first gauge the degree of student motivation.

Community

With regard to the community in which the service is performed, the first criterion is the community's positive attitude toward the students. If the agencies have experienced poor follow-through by students in existing programs, they will be reluctant to consider initiating a new program. A positive reputation earned by students helps when a new service-learning course seeks to develop community partnerships.

A second criterion relates to the service model: Do the service agencies and organizations see themselves as partners with the school, or do they see themselves merely as recipients of service? Partnership is particularly important for two reasons: First, the community organization ought to view itself as a co-educator. SSLs can facilitate this by sharing the goals of the course and, whenever possible, a copy of the syllabus with agency staff. Second, partnership implies equal, open communication between the partners. If an agency is reluctant to share constructive criticism for fear of losing student volunteers, the entire program suffers.

The third criterion has to do with addressing the needs of the community. Are there critical needs, defined by the community, that students in service-learning courses can help the community address? Can students be partners in addressing these needs?

Faculty

Three additional criteria for success focus on faculty culture. The first is whether faculty respect the SSLs' ability to help implement service-learning. In the process of shaping a course, a professor must have trust in the student. This is the most radical aspect of the Service-Learning Challenge because it blurs the line between the traditional roles of the student and the professor. Can a faculty member accept a creative alternative to traditional academic structures, especially when the alternative is offered by a student?

A second criterion has to do with whether the structure of service-learning on campus offers a niche for student leadership in cultivating service-learning. If an institution has established expectations for service-learning and structures to support it, faculty might be able to get what they need to initiate programs from peers or other resources on campus. Faculty who are not experienced in service-learning but would consider teaching a service-learning course are ideal targets for student leadership. At Allegheny,

Can a faculty member accept a creative alternative to traditional academic structures, especially when the alternative is offered by a student?

the main obstacles for faculty in pursuing service-learning are lack of knowledge of the community, time constraints, and other commitments—not lack of interest or an aversion to service-learning. Students provide the assistance that faculty members need to offer a service-learning course for the first time.

The third criterion is a basic faculty-wide service-learning literacy. All faculty members should be made aware of service-learning as a tool, even if it may never be appropriate for one of their courses. This basic literacy offers an important endorsement that supports the students and faculty involved in the program. Having service leaders make a presentation about the program at a faculty meeting helps build basic literacy.

Institutional Culture

The final set of criteria for success involves the overall institution. First, how does service-learning fit into the school's overall mission? Is the program essential or tangential, or is the institution opposed to it? It may be difficult to find faculty willing to risk incorporating service-learning into their courses if the institution is opposed or sees the program as unimportant. At Allegheny, service-learning is one of six cogs in the wheel of civic engagement that embodies a commitment to civic responsibility. The other cogs are the Center for Political Participation; the Values, Ethics, and Social Action minor; the Center for Economic and Environmental Development; the Writing Center's "Engagement Through Writing" program; and "Community-Based Research: The Marketplace of Ideas." Each cog supports the others in strengthening the civic education of students.

Second, is there an office or department to support the service-learning program? Administrative help is essential, along with transportation and other logistical support. Will the institution support vans, buses, or public transportation? Can the administration underwrite some costs involved in the projects?

Third, does the institution recognize and reward students' initiative and faculty members' willingness to try innovative teaching techniques? Awards that recognize outstanding partners—including community partners, students, and faculty members—are important for demonstrating institutional support.

An Evolving Challenge

While many good things are happening with the Service-Learning Challenge, the program has room for improvement. The recent shift from offering independent study credit for the service-learning course to offering a two-credit, two-semester course sequence will stregthen the program. This sequence makes it possible for the trained SSL to begin to work with the faculty member on course design the semester before the course is offered. The challenge is to maintain students as co-leaders in the program as the effort becomes increasingly institutionalized at Allegheny.

A second positive development is the use of special flags for service-learning courses in the online registration process. Students now have the option to select sevice-learning courses. Further, faculty are more willing to make the service-learning component a requirement rather than an option because students know at registration that they are taking a service-learning course.

In the future, the campus-community partnerships need to be strengthened, with an enhanced role for community partners as co-educators. Currently, the SSLs explain to the community partners how service-learning students are different from those simply volunteering at the site. The program hopes to develop joint training for community partners, faculty, and SSLs to encourage cooperative planning among the three constituencies. Another possibility is to host a symposium at which the service-learning work of the semester would be shared with community partners and other members of the college community. The program is also working to create a community partner evaluation to gather more systematic feedback.

Conclusion

In *The New Student Politics: The Wingspread Statement on Student Civic Engagement*, Sarah Long (2002) writes:

> Through service-learning, important relationships between professors and students are developed, evidenced in some instances as mentoring. Service-learning also builds bridges and pathways to career possibilities. By merging academics and service, service-learning makes systemic social and political issues an obvious extension and duty of higher education. (p. 7)

This has been the experience of the Service-Learning Challenge at Allegheny, as many students experience personal efficacy—that is, the ability to have a positive impact. This sense of student efficacy extends not just to service in the community but also to the educational efforts of the college. The program has contributed greatly to students' development as agents of positive social change.

References

Furco, A. (1996). Service-learning: A balanced approach to experiential education. In B. Taylor (Ed.), *Expanding Boundaries: Service and Learning* (pp. 2–6). Washington, DC: Corporation for National and Community Service.

Long, S. (2002). *The new student politics: The wingspread statement on student civic engagement*. Providence, RI: Campus Compact.

Partnering with Faculty and Community

Dilafruz Williams, Kevin Kecskes, Christopher Carey,
Adam Smith, Candyce Reynolds, and Ronnie Craddock

MORE THAN A DECADE AGO, Portland State University (PSU) developed a historic agenda of comprehensive institutional transformation. Reflecting its commitment to a newly defined urban mission, PSU aligned its curriculum, undergraduate and graduate academic programs, scholarship and research, and community outreach and partnerships to explicitly place learning and experience at the core of its educational effort. PSU's downtown location enhances its possibilities to be *in* and *of* the city and the metropolitan region. Its motto, "Let Knowledge Serve the City," symbolically captures its commitment to the communities in which it participates. Several presidential initiatives, such as calls for internationalization, diversity, sustainability, and assessment as well as the "Great City, Great University" project, have enabled faculty, students, and community partners to reflect on PSU's purpose.

PSU's student population of more than 23,000 consists mostly of commuters. While graduate programs that have a professional emphasis have long been community-based in terms of their internship opportunities and practica, the undergraduate program—University Studies—has emerged only recently as a model for the integration of student learning with service in the community (Colby et al., 2003; Ehrlich, 2000; Williams & Bernstine, 2002). Integrated into the University Studies program are four primary areas: inquiry and critical thinking; effective communication; the variety of human experience; and ethical issues and social responsibility (see www.ous.pdx.edu). The University Studies program has the following components:

- Freshman inquiry (FRINQ) is a 15-credit, year-long, thematic sequence taught by teams of faculty from different disciplines. A peer mentor works with faculty members and links them with students in courses such as "Human/Nature,"

"Faith and Reason," "Cyborg Millennium," "Columbia Basin," and "Knowledge, Art, and Power." Approximately 80% of these classes have some form of community-based learning (i.e., service-learning) in order to engage students with the community from the beginning.

- Sophomore inquiry (SINQ) allows students to choose three courses from different interdisciplinary clusters. All have sessions in which peer mentors link students with faculty.

- Upper-division junior cluster courses extend and develop a theme that students began in the previous year.

- The senior-level capstone course, the culminating service-learning experience for students who collaborate on community-based projects, brings different disciplines to the problem they have chosen (with faculty guidance) to address.

This chapter describes the four models of student leadership that have emerged as students and faculty have worked together to address community needs. These models reflect the ongoing commitment to students and faculty as copartners and co-creators (see Figure 1). When they leave PSU, students will have gained the skills they need to participate effectively in complex democratic, economic, and social systems.

Freshman-Senior Capstone Connection

In Spring 2003, Chris Carey, who taught "Faith and Reason," casually discussed with Kevin Kecskes, director of PSU's Community-University Partnerships for Learning, their shared interest in hiking in the old-growth forests of the Pacific Northwest. Carey mentioned that his senior capstone students also enjoyed hiking while learning about themselves and the politics of environmental activism in class, and invited Kecskes to join him and his students on their next hike. Carey's senior students would guide the hike, and several first-year students would join as part of a new experiment to connect the community-based learning aspects of the senior capstone course with the content of first-year courses. The themes of student leadership, informal mentor relationships, and connective and sequenced learning emerged as Kecskes met the students and learned more about their experience.

Faculty Reflection

Chris Carey reflected on his simple idea to connect freshmen and seniors via community-based learning:

> As I watched my eight senior students in the "Environmental Advocacy Capstone" present their final projects to community partners, faculty, and administrators, they seemed to glow. They shared many experiences: getting to know the forest around Portland; adopting a timber sale slotted for harvest; surveying the trees, plants, and

FIGURE 1: **Models of Student Leadership for Community Engagement at PSU**

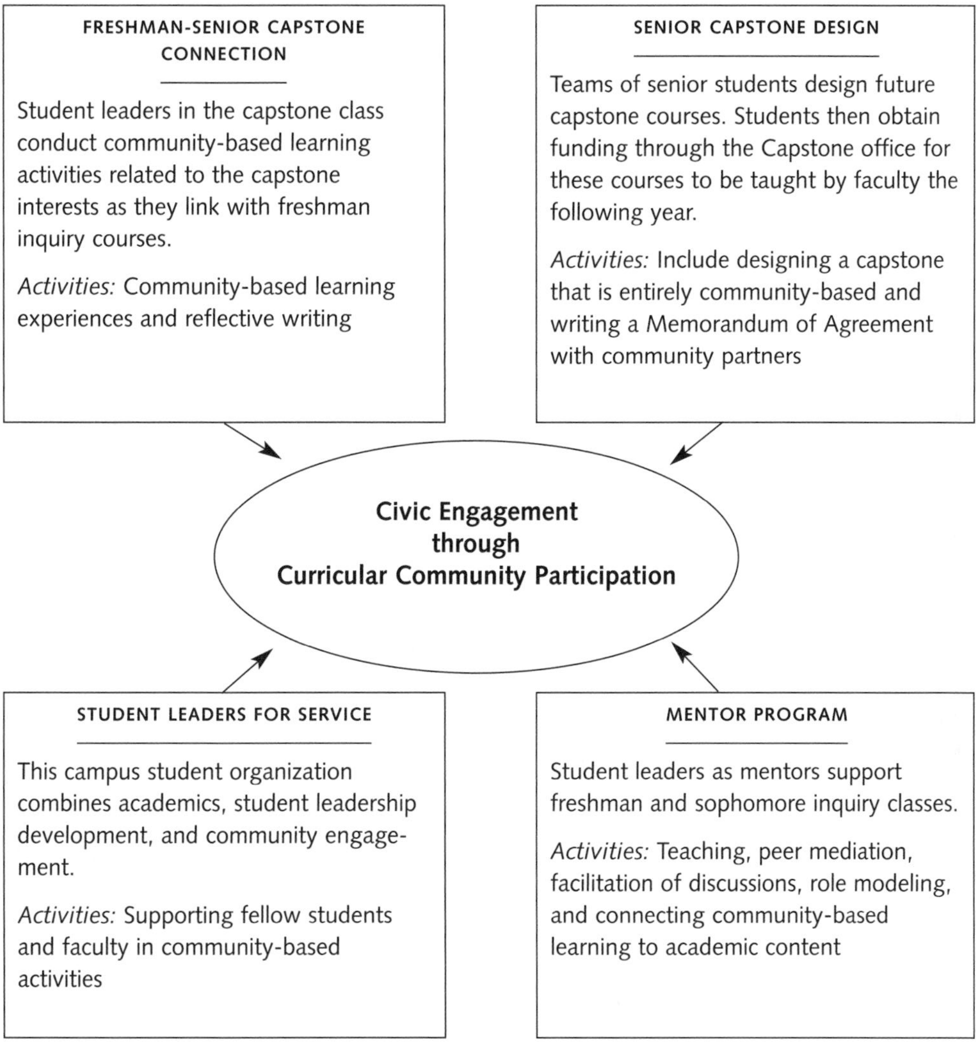

FRESHMAN-SENIOR CAPSTONE CONNECTION

Student leaders in the capstone class conduct community-based learning activities related to the capstone interests as they link with freshman inquiry courses.

Activities: Community-based learning experiences and reflective writing

SENIOR CAPSTONE DESIGN

Teams of senior students design future capstone courses. Students then obtain funding through the Capstone office for these courses to be taught by faculty the following year.

Activities: Include designing a capstone that is entirely community-based and writing a Memorandum of Agreement with community partners

Civic Engagement through Curricular Community Participation

STUDENT LEADERS FOR SERVICE

This campus student organization combines academics, student leadership development, and community engagement.

Activities: Supporting fellow students and faculty in community-based activities

MENTOR PROGRAM

Student leaders as mentors support freshman and sophomore inquiry classes.

Activities: Teaching, peer mediation, facilitation of discussions, role modeling, and connecting community-based learning to academic content

---

lichens; searching for animals and signs of forest health; incorporating their scientific and emotional findings into letters to the forest service to become part of an environmental impact statement. Their presentations were polished, rigorous, and persuasive, and conveyed that their experience was more than a superficial assignment for class.

After their presentations, we discussed their experiences in the class and plans to continue working with the community partner. We also discussed how Portland State had prepared them for life after college. They kept returning to the metaphor of a doorway.

They had loved the capstone experience, which integrated classroom and experiential learning, but they wished they had gotten it (or at least part of it) when they were entering the university as freshmen instead of when they were exiting. Thus, the students and I developed a plan to sequence the service-learning experience. The senior capstone students would organize and lead the FRINQ [Freshman inquiry] students on a hike to the timber sales that they had adopted. I agreed to integrate readings and materials into my FRINQ curriculum, provided the seniors would teach those sections. We would give the FRINQ students a taste of what to expect in later years at PSU. We hoped the experience would spur some first-year students to become involved in the community before their capstone experience.

The following quarter, we put the plan into action. The hike was voluntary for the FRINQ students. Ten FRINQ students, the community partner, three student leaders, and I headed off to the Mt. Hood National Forest, where I took an informal role at the back of the hike. When we arrived at the timber sale, the student leaders reviewed the rules with the FRINQ students: "Do not go off on your own. Make sure you are always in sight of someone else. If you fall behind, yell out." We would be off the trail almost the entire time, so the instructions were essential. The student leaders explained forest health and ecology and discussed the economics and politics of Northwest timber sales. They spoke about engaging the forest service and speaking at public hearings, and of becoming attached to a place through an academic course.

> **"I now feel a need to be a part of a group of activists that looks for solutions to this problem."**

I watched the FRINQ students respond to the capstone student leaders and vice versa. The symbiotic process was magnified by the fact that it was happening in an old-growth forest, while the students were crawling over fallen logs, moss-covered rocks, and dried-up streambeds. As we hiked up and down the hills of Cascadia, we contemplated what would be lost if this timber sale proceeded. Many FRINQ students spoke of living in the Northwest but rarely venturing into the woods and never off the trail. They spoke of the treasures we came across: the trout in the stream, the mushrooms sprouting from the decaying trees, and the owls that greeted us. They also spoke of the miles of stumps, the dried-up earth, and the mudslides from lack of forest cover.

As the hike ended, the student leaders gathered us in a clearing, pulled out paper and pens from their rucksacks, and asked the students to write letters about their experiences, how they felt, what they saw, and what they, as citizens of the Pacific Northwest, wanted done with the land. Did they want this timber to be harvested? They sent the letters to the forest service, other regional representatives, and politicians.

The next week, back in the classroom, I asked the freshman students to reflect again on their experiences. The FRINQ students reacted strongly because they were led by students, not faculty members, making the experience seem more relevant. The capstone student leaders, by sharing the knowledge they had gained, felt a sense of completion.

Student Reflections

Freshmen and seniors alike found the experience valuable. A freshman student commented:

> The forests of Oregon are an important part of the atmosphere of beauty here. It was heartbreaking to see the clusters of tall healthy trees separated by brown patches of nothingness. I began to worry that someday soon this beautiful foliage might be replaced by small new trees planted by foresters. These petite and awkward things, just beginning their lives, cannot compare to their seemingly ancient predecessors.

> Perhaps forest companies really believe that by planting these small trees, they are replenishing the areas that they have destroyed. They are replacing the trees, but all the small animals and plants that depend on these large trees for their survival have been forced to relocate or have died off. How can a squirrel make his home in a tree that is five inches in circumference? Perhaps the logging companies feel that this is the best way to make money manipulating earth's resources and still save face.

> I am increasingly worried that the beauty of these local forests will not exist when my children are old enough to appreciate them. I now feel a need to be a part of a group of activists that looks for solutions to this problem without violence, to find a way that we can meet our needs for these kinds of resources without destroying what is most precious to us. Our children deserve all the beauty we see and more.

Ronnie Craddock, one of the capstone student leaders, described the experience of leading the younger students on the hike:

> I grew up with Mt. Hood and the surrounding National Forest as my backyard. We hiked, camped, fished, and swam all over the area. I was unaware of the significance logging had for the area I loved.

> At first, the capstone course material was overwhelming; there was a lot of history and scientific knowledge that I had to learn. Even more, the politics and policymaking procedures that I had to learn in order to understand the timber sale process were challenging.

> My first hike as a leader was an opportunity to share what I had learned. The freshman students seemed to enjoy the physically challenging hike, and I enjoyed teaching them in the field. The expressions and concerns I had seen and heard from the students were enough to change some of my ideas.

> Currently, I am continuing to work with the community partner, other capstone students, and the public on leading hikes. Also, I am spending more time teaching and working with other senior capstone students so that they can lead hikes themselves.

This is an opportunity that all college students need to have, not just with timber sales, but working with others in the community and other students.

Ongoing Development

One faculty member's creative teaching in his two classes was only the beginning. The university studies program recently received a three-year grant from PSU's Center for Academic Excellence to support a diverse, dedicated cohort of first-year and capstone faculty interested in using community-based learning to connect senior capstone students with first-year FRINQ classrooms.

Four FRINQ and several capstone courses have adopted the FRINQ-capstone connection model. The FRINQ courses are "Meaning and Madness on the Margins," "The Constructed Self," "Pathways to Sustainability," and "The Columbia Basin." The capstone courses are "Juvenile Justice," "Community Food Security," "Reflecting on Community," "Somali Refugees," "Global Portland," "Connecting with Diverse Populations," "Social Change through Music," and "The Politics of Immigration." To facilitate discussions, integration of content, and community building among the instructors, speakers are invited specifically to address FRINQ and capstone faculty. Further, a series of monthly lunches is held to facilitate these course and curricular connections.

As these FRINQ-capstone courses are being taught and students enter the community together, many questions are emerging. How will faculty intentionally connect the content of previously disconnected courses? What is the appropriate role for students of varying ages as co-teachers or co-learners? How might the relationship with the community partners associated with the various courses change? And, finally, how should this initiative be assessed?

Student Leaders for Service

PSU students have many opportunities to serve in the community and train to be student leaders. Adam Smith describes his experience as a member of Student Leaders for Service (SLS):

Student Leaders for Service is a student organization that combines academics, student leadership development, and community engagement. For the past three years, I have been involved in the program. Initially a group of four students, the organization has grown to 20 socially aware students who have a strong desire and commitment to offer their talents and time to serve the greater metropolitan community. They also encourage fellow students to get involved in service.

Students serving in multifaceted leadership roles contribute to the achievement of the program's goals. SLS members spend a minimum of five hours every week providing direct service in their designated community-partner site in the Portland metropolitan area. The sites include public schools, social service agencies, and other nonprofits. Each site is interested in working with university students but, because of limited staffing, is not able to provide the support needed to work effectively with multiple student volunteers or other service-learning students. Thus, SLS not only provides a consistent level of service throughout the entire academic year, but also recruits and supports other volunteers and service-learning students.

We are required to enroll in a class about community leadership, a venue in which to discuss and address the challenges and develop leadership skills. I helped design this course and have co-facilitated it with our graduate student SLS coordinator. We balance the course time between allowing students to develop problem-solving strategies with one another and providing community leadership skills that include volunteer coordination, fundraising, working with the media, exercising collaborative leadership, and resolving conflicts. The combination of applied experience and community-leadership skill development helps the program connect our daily work with the overall concept of being civically engaged, responsible citizens.

SLS provided me with the structure to begin engaging in the community in a targeted, useful way. It guided me to a service project that was meaningful both to me and to the community. This was my first step in taking responsibility for my education and realizing my potential for academic achievement and community leadership. Being a part of a group of motivated peers created the perfect environment for me to experience new situations, learn from others, and understand the importance of engaging in my community.

Senior Capstone Design

The senior capstone course, entitled "Community Development" and offered through the Department of Urban Studies and Planning, is the third in a series of courses that begins with the history and theory of community development and then explores its methods. The course unites the concepts in the first two courses with community development activities in the Portland metropolitan area.

Students work in groups of four to six and conduct research in the community, examine community issues, locate community partners, develop the syllabus for the instructor to use the following year, and also design the advertisement for the course. Six different courses designed by students and taught the following year are summarized below.

BUILDING HOUSING–BUILDING BRIDGES: COLLABORATION BETWEEN HABITAT FOR HUMANITY AND PSU. Capstone students address, analyze, and discuss the need for affordable housing in the Portland metropolitan region. They assess how Habitat for Humanity is meeting the housing needs in northeast Portland, gain a historical overview of the organization, and create a written and pictorial story of the effects of a Habitat home in a given neighborhood.

ENVIRONMENTAL JUSTICE AND COMMUNITY BUILDING. This course links environmental justice and community building, specifically to a low-income community of color in Portland. In the first phase, students and community members learn the basics of community building, the complexities of environmental justice, and the skills of an effective facilitator. In the second phase, students assess area residents and existing organizations and associations for current involvement, interests, and concerns while also working to educate the public about an environmentally contaminated, abandoned property in their neighborhood. Phase three consists of evaluating the experience and compiling the information gathered through focus groups, surveys, and interviews into a handbook, to be publicly presented.

THE TRANSPORTATION CREATION. This partnership with the Lloyd District Transportation Agency, a nonprofit group, seeks to promote awareness of alternative modes of transportation. The course furthers the goals of the agency by working on a program with businesses and employees in the Lloyd Center Mall, the largest building and largest employer in the area.

CONNECTING TO COMMUNITY THROUGH WRITING. Classroom work includes reading texts of both theoretical and practical inquiries into personal empowerment through writing. Students participate in training for individuals from diverse backgrounds. Partnering with Write Around Portland (WRAP), students produce an anthology of their work. The student project culminates in an anthology of their community partners' written works.

COMMUNITY GATHERING PLACES. Students from many backgrounds share the vision of various organizations involved in developing and strengthening neighborhoods, such as the City Repair Project. In this two-term course, students examine the use of space as a public gathering place. The students incorporate theory with community experience to create a handbook that neighborhoods can adapt to their own unique needs in creating and governing community gathering places.

RENTERS' RIGHTS: FIGHTING INJUSTICE THROUGH LEGISLATION. This course helps students understand the issues of eviction and renters' rights, both in Oregon and in other states. They ultimately use the information from readings, research, focus groups, interviews, and work on the Community Alliance of Tenants (CAT) hotline to propose changes to legislation in Oregon regarding evictions and renters' rights. The proposals are presented to CAT for consideration.

Mentor Program

For the past few years, students acting as mentors have enhanced the success of the freshman and sophomore courses in civic engagement. Upper-division undergraduate

"theoretical discussions pale next to a thank-you and a hug.**"**

students serve as mentors in the yearlong interdisciplinary FRINQ courses, and graduate students serve as mentors in term-long interdisciplinary SINQ courses.

Peer mentors and graduate mentors attend a three-hour section of their course taught by their faculty partner and then lead sessions once or twice a week for one hour with smaller groups of students. The mentor sessions enable students to connect with each other in small groups and receive help from mentors and fellow students on the coursework and adjustment to college. Mentors partner with faculty to deliver the curriculum. But they are also friends, facilitators of discussion and activities, technology trainers, role models, and guidance counselors.

Currently, the program employs 57 upper-division undergraduate peer mentors and 33 graduate mentors. The highly competitive positions draw some of PSU's most talented, well-rounded students. Mentors are chosen for their academic skills (3.0 minimum GPA), interpersonal and problem-solving skills, and commitment to program goals. A majority of the peer mentors and many of the graduate mentors have been enrolled in the University Studies general education classes. They describe their motivation to be mentors as a way to give back to a program that was helpful in their own academic and personal development. Peer mentors receive a state-funded academic scholarship that pays for their tuition and a small monthly stipend as compensation. Graduate mentors are hired as teaching assistants and receive tuition remission and a monthly stipend.

Because a faculty member and a mentor partner to work on a course, the role of the mentor depends on what each person brings to the enterprise. This makes the mentor program unique and increases its success, since there is no one correct way for a mentor to work. Faculty and mentors create strategies together that allow their personalities and strengths to contribute to their students' success. Mentors often design and deliver the civic engagement curriculum.

Mentors usually take active leadership roles in their FRINQ and SINQ courses to help students learn about and manage the community-based projects. While faculty usually assign the students to a project, the mentor helps students learn from direct experience in a smaller group setting. For example, in a SINQ class titled "Understanding Communities," students research a particular community group in the Portland metropolitan area by observing and working in the community. Layne Newton, a graduate mentor for one section of this course, helped students break down the steps in the process; they chose the community, defined the research questions, developed questions for key players, and crafted a final presentation. "The ability to think through a project and plan for its outcome is a skill in and of itself," says Newton. "Without that support and guidance, I don't believe the learning gained from the experience would have been as great. To become engaged, we need to understand the complexities of a project and a community and learn and practice skills to help us engage. The process has to be intentional. I need to constantly be reminded of this, too."

Mentors also help students connect the course content with the community-based learning project. Alison Elliot, a graduate mentor in a SINQ course called "Leadership for Change," recalls that the deepest learning about community leadership came from going out into the community and observing and interacting with leaders and others in various community organizations and then discussing the experiences in subsequent mentor sessions. "Being able to see and experience the things we were reading about helped students to really understand the abstract concepts. In the discussions that followed, we learned from each other," she notes. Carrie Sanders, a peer mentor in a FRINQ course called "Meaning and Madness on the Margins," believes that the class's research project—which looked at the impact on marginalized populations of the failure of a statewide funding measure—was an opportunity for both the mentor and her students to examine the impact of policy decisions and to understand the importance of voting.

Mentors also actively engage students in designing and creating their own community-based learning projects. Ariana Kramer, a graduate mentor for a SINQ "Leadership for Change" course, helped a student develop a creative, meaningful strategy for completing the required community-based leadership involvement project. The student, who worked in a coffee shop, asked her manager to give several *baristas*, including herself, time to read to children in a local elementary school.

Jason Damron, a peer mentor for a FRINQ course called "Sex, Mind, and the Mask," worked with his students to develop a community-based learning project from their interest in exploring the role of religion. The mentor and students developed a community-based research project examining how faith-based social services address the needs of marginalized groups such as transsexuals and teen mothers.

Civic engagement can also easily happen outside the formal class structures. In March 2004, Multnomah County began issuing marriage licenses to gay and lesbian couples. Peer mentor Damron, his faculty partner, and some students in his mentor sections went to the courthouse. Damron (2004) wrote in a column in the student newspaper: "This was a learning experience unrivaled by any classroom discussion that I have ever participated in at PSU.... The abstract was realized. The theoretical discussions pale next to a thank-you and a hug."

Conclusion

The students' experiences represented in this chapter are merely samples, because during each quarter for the past decade, hundreds of PSU students have participated in the community as course content is linked with experiences. Often, the distinctions between community and classroom are blurred, as real-life experiences become the context for academic undertakings.

For successful experiences, however, students have to be prepared to work in teams and also to honor different disciplinary perspectives and prior experiences. Sometimes, mentors assist students in planning activities and also in resolving the conflicts that arise when students work in groups. Further, students must learn to address the issues of diversity they face in the community. Civic engagement requires that individuals come to a common understanding of public issues; to do this, they need to be able to communicate and be inclusive. Practicing leadership through curricular service in the community has the potential for developing a lifelong commitment to service and leadership, democratic political awareness, and a deepening of student commitment to democracy.

References

Colby, A., Ehrlich, T., Beaumont, E. & Stephens, J. (2003). *Educating citizens: Preparing America's undergraduates for lives of moral and civic responsibility.* San Francisco: Jossey-Bass.

Damron, J. (2004, March 9). Gay marriage: Community based learning . . . and no more apologies. *The Vanguard.*

Ehrlich, T. (Ed.). (2000). *Civic responsibility in higher education.* Phoenix, AZ: Oryx Press.

Williams, D.R., & Bernstine, D.O. (2002). Building capacity for civic engagement at Portland State University: A comprehensive approach. In L.A.K. Simon, M. Kenny, K. Brabeck, & R.M. Lerner (Eds.), *Learning to serve: Promoting civil society through service learning.* Norwell, MA: Kluwer Academic Publishers.

Developing Students as Catalysts *and* Colleagues

Jennifer Bunn, Mei Elansary, and Cory Bowman

THE UNIVERSITY OF PENNSYLVANIA's Center for Community Partnerships (CCP) has long worked with Penn's students and faculty, West Philadelphia K-12 students and teachers, and other community partners to put the concept of "students as colleagues *and* catalysts" into practice. We have found that creating ways for students and faculty to work together as colleagues both advances the core research, service, teaching, civic engagement, and democratic development missions of education (K-16+) and creates effective community-university partnerships that improve local quality of life.

Working collaboratively and democratically to bring about concrete community improvement (on and off campus) is both a major organizing principle and an end of our work. Among other things, it builds successful partnerships, improves teaching and learning, and develops positive habits of civic engagement. The resulting quality of life improvements in turn improve the conditions for education so we can increasingly realize the multiple missions of our institution and of education as a whole.

Overview of the Center for Community Partnerships

Founded in 1992, CCP is Penn's primary vehicle for bringing to bear the broad range of human knowledge needed to solve the complex problems facing American cities so that West Philadelphia (Penn's local geographic community), greater Philadelphia, the university, and all of society benefit. CCP is based on three core propositions:

1. Penn's future and the future of West Philadelphia/Philadelphia are intertwined.

2. Penn can make a significant contribution to improving the quality of life in West Philadelphia/Philadelphia.

3. Penn can enhance its overall mission of advancing and transmitting knowledge by helping to improve the quality of life in West Philadelphia/Philadelphia.

In his vision of a Penn education, Benjamin Franklin (1749) envisioned a college that would develop students with "an inclination join'd with an ability to serve mankind." CCP is helping to put in practice this "great aim and end of all learning" as it works across campus with faculty, staff, and students to engage them creatively with West Philadelphia and to take those lessons learned nationally and globally.

Academically based community service (ABCS) is at the core of CCP's work. ABCS is service rooted in, and intrinsically linked to, teaching and/or research. It encompasses problem-oriented research and teaching, as well as service-learning that emphasizes student and faculty reflection on the service experience. ABCS courses involve hands-on, real-world problem solving and help students become active, participating citizens of a democratic society. More than 160 ABCS courses from diverse schools and disciplines across the university have engaged in work in West Philadelphia through CCP. During the 2004–2005 academic year, 2,118 ABCS students were involved in 46 undergraduate courses across 19 departments and 16 graduate courses involving 8 of the professional schools.

For more information about the University of Pennsylvania's Center for Community Partnerships, see www.upenn.edu/ccp.

Our problem-solving approach includes making the organization of undergraduate academic programs and campus culture an appropriate focus ("problem") for collaborative academic study. Undergraduates have taken the lead in conceptualizing, initiating, and implementing some of the most substantial developments in Penn-community partnership projects as well as in developing their own role as partners in the classroom. The primary mechanisms for helping students become agents of change are ABCS courses where students explicitly focus on bringing about the organizational changes on campus necessary to support the implementation of partnership projects. Often support takes the form of additional ABCS courses.

CCP has worked with students, faculty, and community partners to develop a series of supports for ABCS projects, including developing the role of students. These projects include the allocation of core university funds and Federal Work-Study funding, as well as grant and alumni fundraising for the following:

- Undergraduate internships to develop and implement programs;

- Grants for faculty and faculty-student applicants to develop new ABCS courses, support existing ABCS courses, and create undergraduate teaching assistantships; and

- Infrastructure to create networks of student and faculty leaders across departments and schools engaged in similar work.

CCP also has full-time staff members who are based at local schools, nonprofits, and communities of faith. These staff members help establish partnerships and support course and program implementation.

Following are three specific examples of how students use these mechanisms and support structures to build their roles as colleagues and catalysts in the classroom and the community.

Linking Research, Service, and Linguistics to Improve Reading

Since the mid-1990s, Penn undergraduates have focused their work on identifying problems, creating new courses to address problems, and developing comprehensive programs from the courses to help solve problems. One example is Penn's program to increase reading achievement in the early grades among students from disadvantaged communities.

Course Development

Bill Labov, a distinguished sociologist and professor of linguistics who directs Penn's Linguistics Laboratory, instituted the reading achievement program at the suggestion of students. Labov, who had long had a theoretical and empirical interest in African-American linguistic patterns, was also intensely troubled by the low reading achievement of African-American youth in poor urban school districts. His decision to focus on "solving the reading problem" of West Philadelphia teachers and schoolchildren was spurred by Hesham Alim and Timothy Durkin, two undergraduates who were members of a 1997 seminar. As part of that seminar, they proposed that Labov offer an academically based community service course that would go beyond the Ebonics controversy and make positive use of African-American cultural and linguistic patterns to improve reading performance. Impressed by the students' ideas and passionate engagement with the problem, Labov hired one of them as an undergraduate teaching assistant (with support provided by CCP) and offered the course in the spring of 1998.

One of the main goals of Linguistics 161, "The Socio-Linguistics of Reading," was (and still is) to make a detailed, action-oriented study of reading difficulties among African-American children in nearby public schools. Undergraduates in the course met with children experiencing reading problems to diagnose the source of their difficulties. Using sophisticated measurement techniques, the Penn students obtained samples of reading errors committed by children. Once they analyzed their findings, Labov and his students developed a program to overcome the difficulties observed in the school-children.

Encouraged by the work of the spring 1998 semester, Labov and the students decided to expand the project considerably during the 1998-99 academic year to include four undergraduate and graduate linguistics courses. One course focuses on developing linguistically and culturally appropriate narrative texts and illustrations to teach reading to inner-city African-American children. Another course trains Penn students to work as tutors in the schools and as trainers of other tutors. Labov's courses are connected to after-school tutoring programs (also designed by ABCS students) and to Penn's America Reads Federal Work-Study program.

Program Results

Early results from these courses have been impressive. Reading scores at participating schools have improved substantially; one school's scores saw the greatest one-year improvement of any school in Pennsylvania. A school-day program has since been added in which approximately 100 Penn students, supported by America Reads funds, are placed with classroom teachers at local elementary schools at least one day per week. Curricula and program trainings and structures are being generated for national dissemination and adaptation.

The Labov reading improvement project—initiated, and still coordinated, by undergraduate students—is extraordinarily comprehensive. It has effectively integrated a major action research project with a strong theoretical basis, a series of Penn undergraduate and graduate seminars, and volunteer and work-study programs into an innovative and effective model. Combining the skill, expertise, and cutting-edge theoretical work of a senior faculty member and intensive collaboration with graduate and undergraduate students, the program exemplifies in practice the valuable results that can be achieved when students, faculty, and community partners collaborate to solve real-world problems. Given the importance of ending the "minority differential" in reading, the findings from this project have major national significance.

The Sayre High School Health Promotion Program

A second model of students partnering with faculty is illustrated by the successful work of Penn undergraduates in creating a health promotion and disease prevention center at Sayre High School in West Philadelphia. This program has galvanized schools from across Penn (including the schools of Arts and Sciences, Medicine, Nursing, Dentistry, Social Work, Engineering, and others) into a new, permanent collaboration resulting in major change at the university.

Far from being harmoniously integrated, American universities tend to be remarkably specialized, fragmented, and competitive, both internally and externally. Yet it will take the resources and expertise of virtually every university unit to develop solutions for globally significant problems, which tend to be highly complex, multifaceted, and continuously evolving. Thus, greater institutional alignment is absolutely necessary. Students working as colleagues are a key vehicle for bringing about such alignment, as well as for supporting the development of effective, ongoing, collaborative problem-solving partnerships that genuinely improve the quality of life and learning on campus and in the community.

the students' work and research led to a successful proposal for a health promotion and disease prevention center at Sayre High School.

From Research to Practice

The poor health status of the West Philadelphia community illustrates the pathogenic role that social inequalities play in urban America. Until recently, the situation of West Philadelphia also reflected the striking disconnect between the tremendous health resources of urban research universities and the substantial unmet needs of their local communities. In 2002, however, a group of undergraduates enrolled in an ABCS seminar decided to focus their research on the complex urban health problems of the local community.

The students were troubled by the state of community health in West Philadelphia and recognized the need to develop a model for substantially engaging Penn and other universities in addressing health disparities. The leadership work of Mei Elansary (winner of Campus Compact's Howard R. Swearer Student Humanitarian award in 2003) on the Sayre program is illustrative. Building on the momentum of the Sayre project, Elansary mobilized a group of peers to work on designing a course that would provide undergraduates with opportunities to learn significant research skills and apply them to the complex, interdisciplinary issues involved in implementing the Sayre program. They designed a syllabus, persuaded a Health and Societies faculty member to join the team, and recruited students from different undergraduate schools.

By all measures, this pilot course was a tremendous success. Students from diverse disciplines took active roles in all aspects of course planning and implementation, from inviting guest speakers to leading individual sessions. The seminar, "Improving the Quality of Health and Status of Life in West Philadelphia," produced significant research papers that informed the development and expansion of health promotion activities in the community. The course continues to be offered in an expanded form, with students and faculty from various undergraduate and professional schools developing innovative approaches to improving the health status and quality of life of those living in West Philadelphia.

The students' work and research led to the proposal for a health promotion and disease prevention center at Sayre High School, a large public school serving one of the poorest communities in the city, with 50% of the population living at 200% or below the Federal Poverty Index. Today, the initiative serves hundreds of Sayre students and their families through comprehensive school-day, after-school, and evening programming. Moreover, the center recently expanded to offer primary care services under a $1.5 million grant awarded to Sayre by the U.S. Department of Health and Human Services.

Students as Bridges

The rapid growth of the Sayre Health Promotion and Disease Prevention Center is the result of the successful integration of health promotion and advocacy into the curriculum of both Sayre High School and the University of Pennsylvania. Far from being merely passive recipients of information, Sayre students are agents of health care change who deliver information and services to improve their own and their community's health literacy. Sayre's health promotion and disease prevention activities have been incorporated into the educational experiences of Penn students in Arts and Sciences, Medicine, Nursing, Social Work, and Dentistry. Curriculum reform has served as a powerful vehicle not only for engaging Sayre and Penn students in collaboratively improving the quality of life in West Philadelphia and improving learning, but also for attracting significant additional resources.

The number, variety, and integration of Penn's new ABCS courses provide the support that make it possible to operate and develop the Sayre Health Promotion and Disease Prevention Center. Hundreds of Penn students (professional, graduate, and undergraduate) and dozens of faculty members, from a wide range of Penn schools and departments, work at Sayre. Since they are performing community service while engaging in academic research, teaching, and learning, they are simultaneously practicing their specialized skills and developing their moral and civic consciousness and democratic character. And since they are engaged in a highly integrated common project, they are also learning how to communicate, interact, and collaborate with each other in unprecedented ways that have measurably broadened their academic horizons.

University-community partnerships are often initiated by individual faculty members and remain largely isolated from each other as a result of academic and hierarchal barriers. Such challenges hampered earlier attempts by Penn faculty to develop a university-community school health program. How is it that undergraduates were able to overcome such barriers and institutionalize the Sayre program as a site for interdisciplinary learning opportunities? One may argue that undergraduates are in an ideal position to bring their knowledge and experience to serve as a bridge between the university and local community and among various academic communities. Students are often more attuned than faculty to the needs and interests of the local community, and many have developed strong relationships with community members through service activities. As a result, linkages between university resources and local needs are often more transparent to undergraduates. In addition, many faculty members are particularly receptive to student-led initiatives that connect substantial academic work to real social problems.

Faculty-Student Collaborative Seminar

Students like Elansary and others who have developed ABCS courses and programs laid the foundation for a third, overlapping approach to "students as colleagues and catalysts," one that far more dramatically and deliberately emphasizes the democratic development of students. In this approach, students are involved in a course creation and implementation process that is democratic from start to finish, particularly in the course's actual instruction.

Democratic Education and Pedagogical Development

In the fall of 2004, student author Jennifer Bunn undertook an independent study research project under the guidance of Ira Harkavy, Director of the CCP, with the goal of finding a way to increase the democratic development of Penn undergraduates. The solution that she identified was an adaptation of an existing program at UC Berkeley, Democratic Education at Cal (DeCAL), in which undergraduate students initiate and facilitate their own courses under the limited supervision of a professor. The program takes the concept of an independent study course, where an individual student studies a topic not offered as part of the university's curriculum under the guidance of a professor, and expands it to include a group of undergraduates studying a topic of common interest.

After discussions with Harkavy, Bunn realized that Penn's pilot student-initiated, student-facilitated course should be an ABCS course for a variety of reasons. On a practical level, ABCS was the natural home for such a course because Harkavy and others in the CCP who oversee ABCS courses already supported the concept and could champion the idea to other critical decision makers whose approval was necessary. On a more theoretical level, service-learning is a pedagogy that emphasizes democratic development (Colby et al., 2003), and thus is a natural fit with a course that employs a democratic learning process from course creation through implementation. The goals of both service-learning and democratic development are met to a greater extent when the two are employed together in the same course than when employed individually.

In spring 2005, Bunn was again studying under the guidance of Harkavy, this time as a student in Harkavy's "Urban University-Community Relations" course. While working on a group project to increase civic engagement among students at Sayre High School in West Philadelphia, Bunn met a fellow student, Elizabeth Curtis-Bey, who became interested in the concept of a democratized learning process. Bunn and Curtis-Bey collaborated to design and co-facilitate an ABCS course on improving education in West Philadelphia. The course would implement Bunn's research from the previous semester, drawing on concepts from democratic education and peer-assisted learning (PAL); i.e., the "acquisition of knowledge and skill through active helping and supporting among status equals or matched companions" (Topping & Ehly, 1998). It also served as the next step in Bunn and Curtis-Bey's research on civic engagement among Sayre students. Students from diverse academic backgrounds, representing each of Penn's four undergraduate schools, were recruited for this course.

Course Description

With the support of Harkavy and Benson, the course, "A Faculty-Student Collaborative Seminar to Improve West Philadelphia Education," was approved as a Benjamin Franklin Seminar, one of a group of small courses that explore subjects through in-depth discussions. It was also approved and cross-listed by the Urban Studies and Africana Studies departments. The official course description highlights students' leadership role:

> This course is an interdisciplinary seminar that seeks to engage undergraduates in problem-solving learning in public education. By exploring the history of African-American education in Philadelphia from Benjamin Franklin to the present, as well as political, economic, legal, psychological, and other aspects of public education, the seminar will generate solutions to improve Philadelphia public schools. A significant part of the course will be the engagement of students, parents, and teachers at Sayre High School as partners in the problem-solving learning process. This seminar will employ a democratic learning process in which students will play a major role in facilitating and guiding the course.

Because it was not politically feasible to have a course with only undergraduate facilitators, Harkavy, Benson, and two other professors, John Puckett and Matthew Hartley, were listed as the professors of the course, while Bunn and Curtis-Bey were listed as "facilitating associates." As the course description suggests, however, Bunn and Curtis-Bey, as well as the other students enrolled in the course, took major responsibility for the learning process with the support and guidance of the four professors.

the goals of both service-learning and democratic development are met to a greater extent when the two are employed together in the same course.

The course comprises a weekly two-hour seminar at Penn and a weekly meeting at Sayre High School with a class of ninth grade African-American history students. The Penn seminars are multi-purpose: they provide an opportunity to explore dimensions of public education through discussions of readings; they serve as a time for undergraduates enrolled in the course to engage one another in discussing ideas for improving education in West Philadelphia; and they offer students a time to give and receive support on their projects at Sayre. During the first few weeks of the course, discussions focus on the history of local black education, including Benjamin Franklin's vision for black education in Philadelphia.

The student facilitators are ultimately responsible for facilitating these sessions, but each undergraduate has an opportunity to lead discussions and to teach fellow students by bringing in outside material that others may not have read. In addition, the syllabus is flexible, with all students having a voice in what is discussed each week. The professors occasionally sit in on the class, especially during the first few sessions, but otherwise play a limited classroom role.

Penn students spend the first few weeks at Sayre acquainting themselves with the students, teachers, and staff, and, more important, beginning to understand the history of the school and the challenges that Sayre and other public schools in West Philadelphia face. After this introductory period, these meetings involve a team of two or three undergraduates working with a group of four or five Sayre students (depending on the size of the class) on a civics-like project to improve their high school educational experience. Projects may include changing a school policy or lobbying the school's administration for the addition of a particular elective course.

While the goal of the course is to improve education in West Philadelphia on a grander scale than these initial projects entail, the organizers chose to undertake these types of projects because they produce positive outcomes for the high school students, which is a prerequisite to any activity that Penn undergraduates engage in at Sayre. At the same time, this work prepares the undergraduates and Sayre students for drafting broader proposals to improve education because it gives them a deeper understanding of the issues involved in local public education, particularly from the perspective of the Sayre students themselves, and of the political landscape in which they will ultimately have to work to effect change.

As a final product, each undergraduate team in the course is required to write an article-length paper outlining a proposal for improving education in West Philadelphia. The proposals outline an "ideal" local education system as well as what they as individuals and what Penn as an institution can do to move toward that ideal state. These papers must draw on the undergraduates' experiences working with the Sayre students on their projects as well as on the readings and discussions during sessions at Penn.

One inevitable question that Bunn and Curtis-Bey receive about the course is, How are undergraduates in the course assessed? To address this issue, facilitators use a type of peer-assisted learning system, in which peers evaluate the learning of others in the group. In this case, the students assess each other's participation in discussions and their final papers. The Sayre students also have an opportunity to assess the Penn undergraduates with whom they work. Finally, Harkavy and the other professors review these peer assessments and assign grades accordingly.

Course Outcomes

OUTCOMES FOR UNDERGRADUATE STUDENTS. In addition to promoting learning about issues in West Philadelphia public schools, the course envisions two major outcomes for participating undergraduates. First, democratizing the learning process across the board should encourage the democratic development of the students in the course. A second, related outcome is fulfillment of the mission of all ABCS courses, which is to realize Benjamin Franklin's vision for higher education of joining the inclination and the ability to serve mankind. Although this course won't enable students to solve the issues facing public schools in West Philadelphia in one semester, we believe the course may inspire them to continue to serve mankind, especially in the area of public education.

OUTCOMES FOR STUDENT FACILITATORS. The course model offers an unparalleled opportunity for the student facilitators to exercise and further develop leadership skills, especially their ability to motivate their peers. It also affords them an opportunity to take full ownership for their education and guide that of their peers—an opportunity that may prove to be the most intellectually rewarding experience of their careers as undergraduates (Whitman, 1988). The student facilitators also have an opportunity to learn by teaching (or facilitating), which allows for a powerful learning experience, since people learn material differently when they know they are responsible for helping others to learn it than when they are learning solely for their own benefit (Gartner, 1995).

OUTCOMES FOR HIGH SCHOOL STUDENTS. The primary benefit for the Sayre students is their exploration of civics through the projects that the Penn undergraduates lead. While many civic education programs focus on federal government, students actually learn civic skills better when they engage in projects close to home, such as changing a policy within their school. The Sayre students, like the high school students who have been involved in other ABCS courses, also gain from their exposure to college students, especially if those students challenge them to think and write critically as they engage in their civic projects.[1]

Looking Forward

It has been particularly important that the course's student facilitators, Bunn and Curtis-Bey, were involved in ABCS courses prior to developing their own course. At the risk of stating the obvious, we note that it is crucial for student facilitators to have been involved in service-learning, understand the community in which they are serving, and, perhaps above all, be familiar with the work of other students who have made significant contributions to the community through service-learning.

On a related note, having two students leading a course is helpful so that they can look to one another for support, both logistical and academic. Such joint leadership also enables a more interdisciplinary approach to the topic, especially when the students come from different academic backgrounds. While professors are often wedded to their disciplines, undergraduates are much more willing to bridge disciplinary boundaries.

As matters now stand, Bunn and Curtis-Bey have had that opportunity only because they know professors who support this type of work. In the future, we expect many more students to have an opportunity to create, implement, and facilitate courses addressing a range of real-world problems. We envision creating a program within the Center for Community Partnerships that will institutionalize democratization of the learning process within ABCS. Such a program will help students create courses and provide them with resources for facilitating those courses effectively, including support from other student facilitators. As more students become involved, the program will foster an interdisciplinary community of scholars that may even serve as a model for interdisciplinary exchange among professors.

It is important to recognize that student-facilitated ABCS courses will never supplant professor-taught courses, but will instead serve as additions to the curriculum. Lest

---

1. For a discussion of the benefits to high school students from a similar ABCS course, see Von Joeden-Forgey, E., and Puckett, J. (2000), "History as Public Work," in I. Harkavy and B. Donovan (Eds.), *Connecting Past and Present: Concepts and Models for Service-Learning in History*. Washington, DC: American Association for Higher Education.

cost be a deterrent, we might add (with some hesitation in this era of cost-cutting in higher education), that student-facilitated courses are a cost-effective way to add high-quality courses to the curriculum (Topping & Ehly, 1998, "Summary Conclusions"). Of course, student-facilitated courses should never be added simply for that reason; their other benefits are far more compelling from a pedagogical standpoint.

Although we wholeheartedly believe we should be able to test the merits of our proposed democratized learning process with a substantial number of experiments and variations, it may be difficult to expand from a single pilot course to an institutionalized program. Peer-assisted learning, and especially an entirely democratized learning process, calls into question the very nature of authority and the process of knowledge creation (Whitman, 1998). It is predicated on the belief that students are able to engage one another to create meaning and understanding (Cooper, 1999)—a belief that may well find resistance in higher education. Even for the most idealistic, accepting a democratized learning process will require a shift in thinking about what it means to teach and, more important, what it means to learn. In the end, we hope that skeptics and idealists alike will critically explore the pedagogical advantages of students as active colleagues in their own education and the education of their peers, especially in service-learning.

We look forward to working with and learning from other colleagues, locally and nationally, who are engaged in these and other approaches. While "students as colleagues and catalysts" has come far in a short time, we feel we are just scratching the surface of this work.

References

Colby, A. Ehrlich, T., Beaumont, E., & Stephens, J. (2003). *Educating citizens: Preparing America's undergraduates for lives of moral and civic responsibility*. San Francisco: Jossey-Bass.

Cooper, M.A. (1999). Classroom choices from a cognitive perspective on peer learning. In A.M. O'Donnell & A. King (Eds.), *Cognitive perspectives on peer learning*. Mahwah, NJ: Lawrence Erlbaum Associates.

Franklin, B. (1749). *Proposals relating to the education of youth in Pennsylvania*. Philadelphia: University of Pennsylvania Archives (http://www.archives.upenn.edu/primdocs/1749proposals.html).

Gartner, A. (1995). *A new approach to peer tutoring: Reciprocal tutoring as a learning strategy.* New York: Peer Research Laboratory, Center for Advanced Study in Education, the Graduate School and University Center, The City University of New York.

Topping, K., & Ehly, S. (Eds.). (1998). *Peer-assisted learning.* Mahwah, NJ: Lawrence Erlbaum Associates.

Whitman, N. (1988). *Peer teaching: To teach is to learn twice.* ASHE-ERIC Higher Education Report No. 4. Washington, DC: Association for the Study of Higher Education.

Student-Faculty Partnerships

The University of Richmond's Jepson School of Leadership Studies

The Jepson School of Leadership Studies at the University of Richmond is the first undergraduate school of leadership studies in the United States with the mission of educating people for and about leadership. The school provides a rigorous upper-division course of study in the history, theory, ethics, and techniques of leader-follower relationships and maintains an active outreach effort. The school gives students a liberal arts education through a multidisciplinary course of study around the single theme of leadership. The curriculum has five questions at its core:

- What is leadership? What are its processes?

- What are the purposes and ethical obligations of leadership?

- What competencies does one need for the socially responsible and ethical leadership process?

- How do others and I exercise leadership?

- How can I analyze, incorporate, and generate knowledge about leadership?

JEPSON CURRICULUM DEVELOPMENT

Jepson students routinely partner with faculty on curriculum design, and joint development of projects is common. Student-faculty partnerships may emerge through a request from the community, the school's active student government council, a class, an internship, or independent study. Faculty offer topics that encompass a broad range of interests, including constitutional history, international conflict, organizational change, religious values, moral responsibility, social movements, public service, good government, politics, and public policy.

At the heart of its efforts, the Jepson School has an interdisciplinary, integrated curriculum focusing on active learning. The curriculum prepares students to:

- Serve groups as leaders.

- Help groups envision, articulate, and reach goals of increased inclusiveness, equity, ecological sustainability, and democratic practice.

- Pursue these goals through ethical, socially responsible practices.

- Evaluate and analyze ideas, including their own, with exacting rigor.

- Pursue a scholarship of discovery in graduate and professional education.

Service-learning is considered key to the formation of ethical, imaginative leaders. The school's signature service-learning class, "Service to Society," precedes formal admission into the Jepson School and signifies its approach to leadership. The course uses readings, class activities, experiences in the Richmond community, and assignments to offer students explicit perspectives on leadership as service in various organizational settings.

Student service, a 30-hour requirement, is the central "text." The course emphasizes the clarification of values during the semester and is structured as a seminar in which participants share responsibility for learning. Although there is a syllabus, the content and direction evolve according to class composition and ability to move from theory and experience to the capacity for empathy and an understanding that values are central to leadership.

STUDENTS' RESPONSES

Students find the course to be a valuable learning experience on many levels. Cristin Kane, a sophomore, notes:

> My volunteer work at the Virginia Rehabilitation Center for the Blind and Visually Impaired showed me that the most important element of service-learning is the two-way exchange between the individual serving and the individual being served. I learned a great deal about people living with disabilities, and my expectations were surpassed as I began to learn that I was not the only one with something to give.

Elleni Ghebremicael, a freshman, found similar value:

> Though my service site, I worked with homeless children at the YMCA. This opportunity began as an assignment, but developed into a remarkable lifelong learning experience. Working with the children allowed me to help them do better academically, but I learned from them as well. Readings and class discussions, along with the community service opportunity, taught me about servant leadership. Service to Society has been my most valuable, rewarding class at the University of Richmond.

Community Relationship Building at the Jane Addams School for Democracy

The Jane Addams School for Democracy (JAS) in Minnesota began as a grassroots initiative by a diverse group of people—some from the local neighborhood, others from area institutions of higher education. The purpose was to co-create a community school where new immigrants, neighborhood residents, college students, and faculty could learn the arts and skills of democratic citizenship. Located in St. Paul's West Side neighborhood, JAS is an intergenerational environment in which people learn languages and share cultures; prepare for the citizenship test; develop skills for civic participation; and engage in public work together.

JAS began as a collaborative effort among Neighborhood House, the neighborhood settlement house; leaders of the local Hmong and Hispanic communities; the College of St. Catherine; the University of Minnesota's College of Liberal Arts; and the Center for Democracy and Citizenship at the Humphrey Institute of Public Affairs. Each brought important perspectives and resources to the effort. The organizational sponsors have always remained in the background, brokering resources but not dictating policy or priorities.

After nine years, JAS participants have developed and refined a practice of bringing together immigrant families with college students and faculty to engage in dialogue, public work, and education grounded in the principle that "everyone is a teacher and everyone is a learner." JAS now has six learning circles: two Hmong adults' circles, an East African circle, a Spanish-speaking circle, an organizing circle, and a children's circle. Each comes together to work on public issues and participants' individual learning goals.

Student-faculty partnerships have played a key role from the beginning. John Wallace, a University of Minnesota professor of philosophy and JAS founder, has partnered with many students. Aleida Benitez, then a student at the University of Minnesota, was the first person to recognize the importance of creating a space with children, thus beginning the children's circle. See Moua, as a college student, acted as the first interpreter of language and culture, helping connect her Hmong elders with the non-Hmong participants at JAS.

The number of college students at JAS has continued to grow, with about 50 college students participating each semester. JAS is reaping the benefits of college students serving within the JAS community where they can contribute, learn, and build relationships with people different from themselves. Students participate through university classes, work-study jobs, and internships that last at least one semester. Many stay much longer.

JAS deliberately helps students put theory into practice in a real neighborhood with people of diverse cultures. In this way, students have an ongoing opportunity to stretch their undergraduate and graduate learning to something larger—to tangible people and places.

Students as Academic Entrepreneurs

T HIS FINAL SECTION CONTAINS FOUR CHAPTERS describing the work of students who are creating community-based programs, teaching classes, building civic infrastructures, and conducting engaged research. In each chapter, we hear about students who are not only personally engaged but who are also building within the fabric of the university sustainable structures that will last beyond their time in school. These articles present transformative research and practice by entrepreneurial student leaders.

The section begins with the service-learning efforts at Duke University initiated by students in the mid-1990s. One result of these efforts is "Scholarship with a Civic Mission," an innovative program that prepares students to conduct research of value to community partners. The chapter includes inspiring examples of the ways in which six students at Duke are producing high-quality research addressing issues such as literacy, the psychological needs of refugee children, food insecurity, Mexican migration, and HIV/AIDS.

The next chapter vividly describes what happens when students have not just token authority but real ownership over a service-learning course. The authors describe the possibilities and challenges presented by a professorless class at the University of Massachusetts Amherst, offered through a program called UMass Alliance for Community Transformation (UACT). In describing the passion and growth that take place when students take ownership of their education, the chapter challenges readers to rethink in fundamental ways what is possible in the classroom.

In the next chapter, students, staff, and faculty from the University of Utah tell the story of their journey to create a student-initiated program that connects an impressive group of service-learning programs associated with the university's Lowell Bennion Community Service Center. The Service-Politics and Civic Engagement (SPACE) program is an initiative that allows students to address controversial issues and to create an integrated program that promotes systematic change by linking service and politics. The work of students at the University of Utah also serves as a reminder that entrepreneurial student engagement initiatives connected with the curriculum are not regionally or ideologically limited.

Finally, a 2004 graduate of Miami University of Ohio (and a winner of Campus Compact's Howard R. Swearer Student Humanitarian Award) writes about his experiences organizing for social justice both at the university and in a neighborhood in Cincinnati. He describes his role in researching and then creating a series of programs to support student learning and action, including a weekend service-learning experience, a year-long service-learning program, and a Student Action Center on campus. The author concludes with a core lesson, also central in the University of Utah chapter, that speaks to anyone working to promote students as agents of social change: the importance of collaboration among those working on different approaches to social issues.

This section also includes vignettes describing the community-based service-learning theses written by students at Bates College; the student-faculty summer research conducted at Macalester College; students integrating social justice into the curriculum at Georgetown University through initiatives such as the John Carroll Scholars Program and the Center for Social Justice Research, Teaching and Service; and Princeton University's Community-Based Learning Initiative. Each vignette highlights promising ways in which colleges and universities support entrepreneurial student research and activism.

A Continuum of Engagement

Betsy Alden and Julie Norman

STUDENT LEADERSHIP AT DUKE UNIVERSITY affected both the initial creation of the service-learning program in 1997 and the recent launch of a more comprehensive research service-learning program called "Scholarship with a Civic Mission." From the original vision of a few student leaders who wanted to change Duke's approach to education, Duke has welcomed student initiatives to improve and deepen civic engagement. Because students wanted to pursue their commitments to a community partner or a social issue beyond a particular course, the program was reconfigured to provide for a continuum of service-learning and research service-learning options.

Research service-learning (RSL) promotes the goals of producing knowledge and contributing to the local community by bringing together community and university representatives to identify emerging issues and unmet needs that will benefit from sustained study. RSL students engage in research embedded in the context of a civic partnership, exploring the links between their coursework and their ethical and civic responsibilities. Simultaneously, RSL prepares students for positions of leadership and responsibility, as participants become leaders for service initiatives on campus and in the community.

> Full details of Duke's RSL program are available at http://rslduke.mc.duke.edu.

Origins of Service-Learning at Duke

Service-learning emerged in 1996 from the initial efforts of a group of students who appealed to Dean of Faculty William Chafe to sponsor their attempts to "change the way Duke does education" (this became an early mantra). With his encouragement, they formed LEAPS as a chartered student organization, recruited professors, found community placements through Duke's Community Service Center, and served as a volunteer squad of reflection facilitators. Within a year, they realized they would need staff support to manage the administrative aspects of this new educational venture, so they wrote a grant proposal to the brand-new Kenan Institute for Ethics (KIE) at Duke, successfully making the case that service-learning necessarily included critical ethical reflection and that it could be instrumental in KIE's mission of "infusing the curriculum with ethical discourse."

KIE's new director, Elizabeth Kiss, agreed to provide a staff person (Betsy Alden, a supporter of service-learning programs at other colleges for 20 years and one of the authors) to work with LEAPS and build on its efforts to establish a broader investment in the teaching of service-learning among Duke faculty. Dean Chafe created an advisory committee on service-learning—which has always had student representation—and the student-staff partnership was established.

LEAPS Development

The education and work history of LEAPS co-founder Glenn Gutterman reveals the evolution of his leadership as an engaged scholar-activist. After graduating from Duke in 1998, he taught in Ecuador before receiving his M.A. from Princeton's Woodrow Wilson School of Public and International Affairs. He is now working with the American Jewish World Service, a nonprofit organization. In the following paragraphs, he describes his work at Duke in creating and developing LEAPS.

> In my first semester at Duke, I took an ethics course with Professor Thomas McCollough that really shook me up. Like a lot of college students, I began looking at my own privilege and my responsibility to community. Early on in that first semester, I began tutoring once a week at a high school in Durham. It was community service as I had always known it, but it didn't feel as fulfilling. There was nothing holding it together; each week drew a different crew of volunteers to tutor a new group of students, which didn't allow for meaningful relationships to be built. It seemed like a lot of first-year students at Duke had been active in service in high school, but were wary of becoming overcommitted amid the wide array of activities in college.
>
> There were structural barriers as well. I lived on East Campus, which is encircled by a three-foot stone wall. Although easy enough to hop over, it serves as a literal and figurative barrier keeping out Durhamites and hemming in Duke students. You can do your grocery shopping, your dry cleaning, or get a haircut all without ever leaving campus. Part of the premise behind developing LEAPS was that students learn best when stretched beyond their comfort zone.
>
> In the spring of my first year, I enrolled in William Chafe's course on modern American history; he proved to be a staunch ally for integrating service-learning into the Duke curriculum. In a freshman seminar, "Insight and Responsibility: Perspectives on Community Service," I met Dan Kessler; we talked at length about the readings as well as the challenge of discussing community service in a seminar setting without the

students having any shared service experience. In the fall, Dan and I together launched LEAPS.

In the summer between my first and second years, I was living in Durham, taking classes, and training to be the student director of the Community Service Center (CSC). I benefited from time spent strategizing with CSC staff about how to mobilize Duke students to be more active and involved in Durham. I read a lot about the pedagogy of service-learning and got my hands on a three-ring binder from APPLES, the service-learning organization at the University of North Carolina at Chapel Hill. Over the summer, I wrote the proposal for LEAPS and began passing it around and meeting with administrators and faculty to talk about who could breathe life into this initiative. Janet Smith Dickerson, vice president for student affairs, welcomed innovative thinking and helped point out faculty who would be interested in a LEAPS component.

Dan and I went to an APPLES retreat and got acquainted with a version (albeit with a different model and ethos) of what we aimed to become. We focused on facilitating the LEAPS component in Dr. McCollough's course, building a staff, getting approval from the dean of student affairs as a bona fide student organization with the capacity to raise funds, and recruiting faculty. We also learned a great deal about leading reflection sessions from Claudia Horowitz, who has since written a book, *The Spiritual Activist* (2002).

Results of Early Efforts

The early efforts of LEAPS student leaders were essential to the development of Duke's service-learning program. They petitioned President Nan Keohane to join Campus Compact, a national association that works with colleges and universities to educate students for civic and social responsibility; they instituted, developed a curriculum for, and taught a half-credit course called "Service-Learning: Expanding Your Education Beyond the Classroom"; and they continued to recruit new professors to join the ranks of service-learning faculty, increasing the number of courses to 15 a semester by 2000. The Kenan Institute for Ethics provided funding for a part-time coordinator to manage the selection of community partnerships and follow up with placement sites.

Scholarship with a Civic Mission prepares undergraduates to produce a substantial research product to benefit community partners.

Simultaneously, the Hart Leadership Program in the Terry Sanford Institute of Public Policy created a model for engaged scholarship called Service Opportunities in Leadership (SOL). SOL had created a model for engaged scholarship that involved an intensive 12-month leadership program for Duke undergraduates that combines academic study, community service, mentoring, and leadership training. It includes a half-credit course in the spring, a community-based internship in the summer, and a research seminar in the fall. Interns work with community development initiatives, organizing efforts, refugee and immigration issues, clinical health programs, and a range of service projects. Critical reflection, documentary writing, and small group discussions support the learning process throughout the year. Students have served in community organizations in Central America, Namibia, and South Africa, as well as in Charlotte, Chicago, Pittsburgh, Albuquerque, and New York.

Scholarship with a Civic Mission

As service-learning continued to grow and expand—with as many as 25 courses and 500 students each year, and more than 25 community partners—momentum began to build in a different direction, fueled by the students who had enjoyed their introductory courses in service-learning, but who wanted to go deeper into some of the social and policy issues raised in their work with community partners. The arrival of new curriculum requirements at Duke precipitated a need for more research-designated courses, and students wanted options for nonclinical, community-based settings to fulfill this requirement. The new dean of arts and sciences, Robert Thompson, suggested that the program apply for a Fund for the Improvement of Post-Secondary Education (FIPSE) grant to create a research service-learning model at Duke. The program received a FIPSE grant in September 2002.

Scholarship with a Civic Mission, Duke's unique research service-learning model, is now becoming institutionalized through a process of increasingly profound research service-learning opportunities throughout a student's academic career at Duke. At the heart of Scholarship with a Civic Mission is a three-stage model designed to prepare undergraduates to conduct thorough research and produce a substantial product to benefit community partners. The three stages are designed to help students gain skills as well as a deeper understanding of research methods, community issues, and civic engagement:

- The Gateway Course, which includes a service-learning component, introduces students to basic research skills and ethical issues. The course requires students to complete a research proposal based on their service experience.

- The Community-Based Research Opportunity can be an internship or an academic course that includes field research the students conduct in collaboration with a community partner under the direction of a faculty mentor. The course requires students to keep a research journal that addresses intellectual, ethical, and civic issues.

- The Capstone Course allows students to pursue an independent research project that builds on their collaboration with the community partner and culminates in a final thesis paper or other major research product. This course also requires students to keep a research journal that addresses intellectual, ethical, and civic issues.

As students move through the three stages of the research service-learning model, they develop deeper understandings of the intellectual issues, ethical concerns, and questions of civic responsibility related to their research topics. The project provides funds for students who wish to pursue projects within this model, faculty who wish to support projects or courses within the model, and community partners who are interested in participating.

Students enter this new arena through a gateway service-learning course, identify a research question that interests them and their community partner, pursue that question with a faculty mentor over several semesters, and then complete a capstone course and produce a research product that is returned to the community partner. The following case studies illustrate how the process works in the lives of individual engaged scholars.

Case Study 1: Julie Norman, Class of 2002

Julie Norman (one of the authors) was one of Duke's first Civic Scholars, having designed and implemented a research service-learning program of study before the Scholarship with a Civic Mission initiative was officially launched. Norman developed a project combining her interests in media studies and local and international children's issues as part of a self-designed interdisciplinary B.A. degree in Media, Education, and Social Activism.

Norman entered Duke with an interest in communications and youth issues, including child policy and education. In the spring of her freshman year, she enrolled in her first service-learning course, "Educational Psychology," offered through the Program in Education. The class introduced her to the pedagogy of service-learning in the context of education theory, while providing practical experience through a one-on-one tutoring placement in a local elementary school. She continued her service-learning through courses in public policy, psychology, and education. Norman expanded her service activities to include coordinating a reading group for young women at a local middle school and teaching photography and writing skills to sixth graders.

Having gained a solid understanding of child policy and education in theory and practice, Norman became interested in researching the services that public schools and alternative education programs provide to at-risk refugee youth. She pursued a summer internship after her junior year with Global Action Project, Inc. (GAP). GAP works with at-risk youth in the United States and overseas through summer and after-school programs to create documentary media projects such as photographs, videos, and websites on topics identified by the students. During Norman's internship, she assisted with video projects by at-risk New York City youth on teen pregnancy, smoking, and cultural exploitation; assisted with a video project on refugee issues by youth from Kosovo; and helped develop an educator's guide for a video created by Israeli and Palestinian youth.

Norman applied the knowledge gained at GAP in a senior thesis project with Professor David Malone, in which she coordinated a video project with local refugees as a capstone experience and wrote a formal paper integrating a literature review on youth media and alternative education, particularly in relation to refugees, with qualitative research collected during the video project. With grants from the Kenan Institute for Ethics at Duke and the International Rescue Committee, Norman worked with a group of high school students at Sanderson High School in Raleigh, North Carolina, to create a film about their experiences as refugees in an American high school. She facilitated the project, teaching the students interview skills and documentary techniques, and assisting them in brainstorming ideas, writing questions, and collecting footage.

After taping, Norman worked with the students to edit the video to a 30-minute format and create a website and educator's guide to supplement the video. She also helped the students coordinate two public screenings, one at Sanderson and one at Duke, and presented and distributed the video and guide to secondary school educators in Raleigh, Durham, and Chapel Hill.

Norman notes that in addition to giving her the opportunity to develop skills in critical thinking, writing, and research methodology and implementation, her service-learning experiences were an integral factor in shaping her academic and professional goals. After graduation, she spent a year in Cairo as a Lewis Hine Fellow through Duke's Center for Documentary Studies. She was partnered with Children of the Nile, an Egyptian NGO focusing on early childhood development, where she produced photographs, a website, a video, and a brochure for the organization, in addition to writing lesson plans, training teachers, and assisting in an Egyptian kindergarten. She also completed an independent video project in which she interviewed Egyptian college students about their perceptions of the United States.

Norman is pursuing a Ph.D. in international conflict resolution at American University and traveling in the Middle East. She plans to pursue a career in international conflict resolution with a focus on nonviolent activism and children's issues.

Case Study 2: Tori Hogan, Class of 2004

Tori Hogan also focused her RSL experiences on the topic of refugee children, incorporating RSL into her self-designed interdisciplinary degree on Global Health and Human Development.

Hogan became interested in refugee issues in a service-learning gateway course called "Refugee and Immigrant Children: The Politics of Displacement," part of an intensive freshman program on "Humanitarian Challenges at Home and Abroad." She worked with Lutheran Family Services (LFS), a refugee resettlement agency, serving as a home-work tutor for two Burmese girls, Wine and Cha-Cha. While the placement started as a tutoring position, the girls began to see Hogan as a mentor and close friend. Hogan continued her relationship with Wine and Cha-Cha through all four years at Duke.

In addition to continuing to serve with LFS on a local level, Hogan became increasingly interested in addressing international refugee issues. She spent a semester abroad in Uganda where, in addition to taking classes, she served as a researcher for the C.H.I.L.D. project in Mbarara to assess the status of development among Uganda's children. The next semester, she spent her spring break researching the status of child development among Palestinian children in Lebanon's Shatila refugee camp as part of a course. The following summer, she worked with Save the Children on an assessment report for child protection needs in Kenya and Somalia. All these experiences built on her knowledge from her gateway course, providing Hogan with the theoretical and practical background to pursue a community-based research (CBR) project as part of the second stage of Duke's three-stage model.

The summer after her junior year, Hogan worked with psychology professor Bob Thompson to design a CBR project in Durham addressing the psychosocial needs of refugee children. Hogan stated in her proposal that "one of the greatest deficits that I have noticed is that of mental health assistance for refugees who have experienced stress and trauma. While programs such as the Bridges Project [run by LFS] are good starting points for psychosocial recovery, they have yet to find ways of effectively reaching children who are most in need of such services." To address this issue, Hogan proposed to work intensively with LFS during the summer to conduct interviews and col-

hogan stated that her initial gateway service-learning experience was the key factor in influencing her to pursue the field of refugee studies.

lect data on refugee children in the Raleigh-Durham area, and to help LFS improve methods for identifying the types of trauma children had faced and their subsequent psychosocial needs.

Hogan realized that her original goals were not compatible with the needs of LFS or with her own capabilities. She thus shifted her focus to identifying the sources of stress for refugee youth and then determining the necessary support services that could be accessed within current systems. The new approach focused on literature review and extensive interviews with caseworkers, school counselors, and mental health professionals and was refined through weekly meetings with her faculty mentor and through a journal in which Hogan documented her "observations, questions, frustrations, and insights."

The result of Hogan's research was the development of a school-based mental health model, consisting of training sessions and packets for school counselors, administrators, and teachers. She helped Durham Public Schools develop a waiver to identify refugee students, so that teachers might be better prepared to recognize symptoms of psychosocial problems in traumatized students and be more sensitive to their needs. She also worked to educate counselors and principals on the meaning of the term *refugee* to help them better understand the background of this student population. Hogan coordinated training sessions with counselors in Durham to teach them how to identify needs of refugee students. Her recommendations were based on her field research and literature review, guidance from her faculty mentor, and consultation with LFS and the International Rescue Committee.

Throughout her senior year, she completed and disseminated training materials, led training sessions, and presented her research at various conferences. She also extended her research to the international level by writing a thesis on "Responses of International Agencies to Psychosocial Programming." Her focus on international organizations in her thesis complemented her assessment of local services in her CBR project to provide her with a sound understanding of child refugee issues both at home and abroad.

Hogan stated that her initial gateway service-learning experience was the key factor in influencing her to pursue the field of refugee studies. Along the way, she gained insights about her own strengths and limitations as a researcher and change agent and a nuanced understanding of the strengths and weaknesses of aid organizations.

After graduating from Duke in 2004, Hogan won a Fulbright Scholarship to study forced migration and refugee studies at the American University in Cairo. She is currently working with refugees in San Diego and has been admitted to Harvard University to pursue a master's degree in international education.

Case Study 3: Joseph Lee, Class of 2004

Joseph Lee built on his high school experience of working with a food bank in western North Carolina to design his RSL project. A Spanish major, Lee used his language skills and interest in Latino migrant and immigrant issues to assess emergency food provider perceptions of Spanish-speaking clients and to develop Spanish-language food bank resources.

Like Hogan's, Lee's service-learning experience began in the "Humanitarian Challenges at Home and Abroad" freshman focus group. Lee's service-learning placement was with Student Action with Farmworkers (SAF), a nonprofit organization that works to bring together students and migrant farmworkers in eastern North Carolina to learn about each other's lives, exchange resources, improve conditions for farmworkers and their families, and work collaboratively for social change. Lee worked as an assistant ESL (English as a second language) instructor in SAF's "English-into-the-fields" program, which provides meals to farmworkers along with language instruction.

His first activist project was to co-found the Duke-Durham Hunger Alliance, in which Duke students contribute their unused food points (worth thousands of dollars) at the end of the academic year to Durham hunger programs. Lee became interested in food insecurity issues during a field trip to the Capitol Area Food Bank in Washington, DC, and he became further interested in health issues facing the Spanish-speaking community during a course on health policy.

Having worked as a fundraising intern for two summers with MANNA, a food bank in western North Carolina, Lee designed a CBR project with Professor Kate Whetten's guidance to assess emergency-food-provider perspectives of Spanish-speaking clients. He conducted informal interviews with food pantry staff in four counties. He particularly identified a lack of adequate translated materials and a need for client access to recipes and food education. He reflected throughout his research by taking notes and communicating with his faculty adviser.

During his senior year, in a capstone independent study with Whetten, Lee created resources based on his summer research findings for emergency food providers, members of the Spanish-speaking community, and other regional food banks and researchers. The core product was a resource translation website that allows agencies to choose frequently asked questions (in English) and receive the questions and answers in Spanish, formatted for immediate printing and dissemination to Spanish-speaking clients. In a mailing to MANNA's affiliated agencies, Lee offered information on current food bank projects, county-based Latino demographic information, a summary of research findings, and suggestions for serving Spanish-speaking clients; he also promoted the website as an additional resource.

Lee felt that his initial gateway course made it possible for him to see the connection between politics and social service. His field research, combined with his review of health disparity literature, enabled him to connect his research project with broader academic and social issues and gave him to skills to investigate issues of unequal access in food distribution programs.

Lee is now a 2005–2006 Bill Emerson National Hunger Fellow at the Congressional Hunger Center in Washington, DC, with a fellowship field placement at Farm to Table in Santa Fe. He has been accepted to the University of North Carolina at Chapel Hill to pursue a master's degree in public health with a focus on maternal and infant health. His study on North Carolina food banks may be found at www.ibiblio.org/wncstudy.

Case Study 4: Vicki Kaplan, Class of 2004

Vicki Kaplan also focused her RSL project on Latino communities, researching the causes and effects of Mexican migration to the southeastern United States. A cultural anthropology major, Kaplan concentrated her studies on Latin America and Latino migrant and immigrant issues. She also addressed these issues outside of her classes, founding MANO (Mujeres Aprendiendo por Nuevas Oportunidades), an ESL tutoring program for Spanish-speaking women, and becoming a student leader in numerous social justice causes, particularly those related to the Latino community.

Kaplan's RSL experience began with a cultural anthropology gateway seminar on farmworkers in North Carolina. Her service-learning placement was with the Action, Inspiration, Motivation (AIM) Club for migrant students in Sanford, North Carolina. The AIM Club is a dropout prevention and academic achievement program for middle- and high school migrant students that provides members with educational, social, and cultural activities. Kaplan worked with students at East Lee Middle School to create documentary projects on their experiences of migration. In addition to her gateway course, Kaplan took a number of classes on Latin American society and politics, as well as advanced Spanish language courses. She also became involved in several other Duke service-learning initiatives, including Students of the World, in which she taught classes and led student delegations to Peru and Mexico; and Service Opportunities in Leadership, in which she developed an extensive portfolio on agricultural labor law history and its effects on the unionization of farmworkers. Kaplan also spent time abroad studying the relationship between CARE, an international humanitarian organization, and the residents of the rural village of Pampamaca, Peru.

With the help of faculty mentor Diane Nelson, a professor of cultural anthropology, Kaplan spent the summer after her junior year researching the causes and effects of increased migration from Guanajuato, Mexico, to the southeastern United States, particularly North Carolina. As she noted, "Mexican immigrants are changing the political, social, cultural, and economic landscape of North Carolina.... In order to understand these local changes and to devise strategies for addressing North Carolina's new cultural landscape, it is necessary to understand the changes occurring on the other side of the 2,000-mile border." Kaplan spent the summer in an agricultural region in Guanajuato, Mexico, with La Fundación Comunitaria del Bajío (FCB). She interviewed local residents, lived with an agricultural family, and traveled to other regions of Guanajuato to talk to factory workers, managers, farmers, community leaders, teachers, students, and politicians.

After returning to Duke, Kaplan interviewed immigrants from Guanajuato who currently reside in North Carolina, culminating her research with a senior thesis connecting the rapid changes that Guanajuato and North Carolina are experiencing. Her thesis examined the changing needs of both the sending and receiving communities, and identified the causes and effects of migration from Guanajuato to North Carolina. Kaplan shared her thesis with FCB and other organizations and individuals with whom she worked, presented her research at conferences, and also produced an audiovisual exhibition of oral histories.

Kaplan's RSL experience gave her a personal understanding of the experiences of people in Guanajuato, particularly women, elders, and children. Coupled with her work in Durham, her CBR experience helped her gain a unique understanding of the causes of immigration and its effects on both communities, and gave her an opportunity to pursue quality anthropological research through ethnographic methodology. In addition, Kaplan's work shed light on how larger political and policy developments, such as NAFTA, affect people and communities at home and abroad.

Kaplan is working as a national organizer for Food and Water Watch in Washington, DC. She plans to extend her interest in migrant issues in the future by attending law school and seeking a career as an immigration lawyer.

Case Study 5: Courtney Crosson and Michele Lanham, Class of 2004

Courtney Crosson and Michele Lanham worked within the "Public Health Inequalities" pathway to address informational gaps in knowledge about HIV/AIDS among college students in Kenya. Crosson, an art and architectural history major, and Lanham, a comparative area studies major and biology minor, were students in Professor Sherryl Broverman's gateway biology class, titled "AIDS and Emerging Diseases." Crosson participated in the service-learning aspect of the course by tutoring an HIV-positive patient at the Infectious Disease Clinic at Duke Hospital. She also coordinated a forum, fundraiser, and dinner event for World AIDS Day entitled "When the Global Epidemic Hits Home: AIDS in Our Community."

The following summer, Crosson and Lanham traveled to Egerton University in Kenya with Broverman for three weeks. Egerton is unique in Kenya because of its commitment both to gender issues and to HIV/AIDS education. They worked with faculty members and students at Egerton to assess HIV/AIDS education needs by engaging in discussions, participating in university classes, assessing facilities, and visiting community organizations concentrating on HIV/AIDS work. The goal of the CBR project was, as Crosson explains, "to empower students, specifically women, to alter their own risk or their community's risk of HIV infection through access to cutting-edge, current information." The project aimed to create a partnership between Duke students and students at Egerton. Crosson and Lanham met with many individuals, organizations, and agencies and took notes on different opinions, experiences, and understandings of HIV/AIDS that were expressed in the conversations.

One of the primary goals of the summer CBR experience was, in Crosson's words, to "link the cultural consciousness of the Kenyans with the wealth of information available to Duke students in order to collaboratively create a culturally sensitive informational resource about HIV/AIDS." Crosson, Lanham, Broverman, and Dr. Rose Odhiambo, a professor at Egerton, decided that the resource should take the form of a CD-ROM, which was cost-effective, environmentally sound, transportable, and easy to store and reproduce.

Crosson and Lanham led a section of Broverman's "AIDS and Emerging Diseases" course in the fall and worked with Duke students to facilitate the production of a culturally sensitive textbook in CD-ROM format that was delivered to Kenya. They also worked with Broverman to arrange for Odhiambo to visit Duke's campus in the spring to share her experiences and insights. In addition, Lanham worked with Broverman to produce a capstone research paper comparing the perception of and care for HIV/AIDS in the United States and Kenya, based on her research in Kenya and a subsequent internship with Legacy Founder's Cottage, a Dallas-based nonprofit organization that focuses on HIV/AIDS.

For both students, RSL provided a unique opportunity to develop community-based research skills and to ask new questions about HIV/AIDS. As Crosson writes, "My heart was broken by the wide-reaching effects of AIDS. It touched everyone's life there. As the Kenyans say, 'If you're not infected, then you're affected.'" The students also learned about structural problems such as poverty, lack of housing, lack of clean water, lack of education, and gender inequality.

The RSL experience influenced both Lanham's and Crosson's career goals and future plans. Lanham is pursuing a master's in public health at UNC–Chapel Hill and planning a trip to Tanzania to do related research. Crosson also plans to continue international development work through a year-long Hart Fellowship in Kenya working on urbanization and HIV/AIDS projects. Afterwards, she plans to pursue a career in architecture and urban planning, focusing on sustainable development and poverty reduction.

Final Reflections

These and many other students have provided guidance and inspiration for finding ways to support their passions and creativity. What key components establish an environment in which students like these can flourish? Committed faculty, both as teachers and mentors, are essential; small grants for undergraduate research are useful; and collaboration with community partners is integral. Of course, the college or university also needs service-learning research program staff to help students clarify and focus their topics of inquiry and lead them through a research methodology appropriate to their projects.

This chapter illustrates the fundamental role of students in this work. From the initial founding of LEAPS to today's ambitious capstone projects, students have led the way for service-learning and community-based research at Duke with their vision, focus, and determination. When research is joined with service-learning, students have the opportunity to engage in a deeper level of inquiry-based field research that not only builds leadership and life skills but also helps shape students' identities as leaders and change agents in both the local and global community.

Reference

Horowitz, C. (2002). *The spiritual activist: Practices to transform your life, your work, and your world.* New York: Penguin.

Acknowledgment

Research Service-Learning Coordinator Vicki Stocking contributed to this article.

The Professorless Classroom

Danyel Addes and Arthur Keene

O NLY MINUTES INTO THE FIRST CLASS MEETING *of the spring term, the classroom for Anthropology 397H: "Grassroots Community Development" is alive with activity. Twenty-five students have divided themselves into groups of five. Each group sits on the floor attempting to build a four-foot tower out of note cards, tape, and paperclips. The classroom is loud, and students struggle to make themselves heard as they compare ideas, share resources, and race against the time limit. Three of the groups decide to pool their resources and expertise to build a single tower. Another deliberates whether building a tower from the ceiling toward the floor violates the given instructions. This room is easily distinguishable from other classrooms on the corridor by the general din, the high level of activity, the simultaneous participation of every person in the room, and most notably, by the absence of a professor.*

What would make undergraduate students attend a three-hour class every Sunday night for a full academic year and complain that a three-hour time slot was too short? What would make students cheer when they discover that they have an extra class meeting before they are free for the summer? Why would graduating seniors commit to participating in the class again, after they have graduated, without the incentive of credits or a stipend? What would make graduate students consider an undergraduate class the most intense, meaningful class of their semester?

The Alternative Spring Break (ASB) program at the UMass Alliance for Community Transformation (UACT) at the University of Massachusetts Amherst is the answer to all these questions. The program combines rigorous academics, critical pedagogy, praxis, meaningful community building, work for social justice, and large doses of fun, passion, and hilarity into a process of student empowerment.

How the Program Works

UACT is the coordinating organization for curricular spring break programs at the University of Massachusetts. It is a collective, run by a steering committee of 7–10 student leaders—all alumni of UACT alternative breaks—working in partnership with a faculty adviser (anthropology professor Art Keene, one of the authors, who developed the program in conjunction with students). The primary project is the alternative break, which combines a four-credit honors course in grassroots community development with a week-long spring break trip to the rural South, where students work side-by-side with a grassroots organization.

"Grassroots Community Development" (GRCD) is a four-credit honors course with a substantial workload. The class meets on Thursday afternoons for three hours during the spring term. Students read four books and a selection of articles (see the course website at www.courses.umass.edu/anth397h for a complete reading list). Students write 21 short (one-page) papers and two longer papers (7–10 pages each). They also keep a journal during their week in the field and attend a weekend retreat during the fourth week of the semester. They engage weekly in a series of intellectually challenging, in-class exercises and discussions and participate in informal, student-generated, out-of-class group activities. And, of course, they spend their spring break with a community organization, often working long days and living in rudimentary accommodations.

The course differs from all other advanced courses at UMass in that it has no prerequisites, although students must apply in the fall to gain entry in the spring because the number of students interested exceeds the number of seats available. The course brings together undergraduate students of all years, from dozens of different majors, as well as an occasional graduate student. Because the GRCD classroom operates as a learning circle, it can accommodate these differences in background and expertise.

Each participant is expected to come to every class prepared to be a teacher and a learner. The students share expertise, connect course readings to life experiences, and are mutually accountable to each other. A senior economics student with experience in development might help a freshman understand the intricacies of micro-credit, while a freshman from a rural community whose mother works at Wal-Mart can provide powerful insight into the impact of retailing giants on small communities. One student explains:

> It was really important to hear the personal stories of other students in the class, because for me it is hard to completely understand something if I can't see or interact with it. We could have read 10 million case studies about redlining [the illegal practice of a lending institution denying or restricting loans to certain areas of a community] in Boston and I would never have fully grasped the concept if there hadn't been a student in the class to talk about his own experience with redlining.

The class is modeled on the kind of asset-mapping and asset-based development central to a grassroots approach (Kretzman & McKnight, 1993). With this approach, students are challenged to rethink the "banking" model of education that views teachers as experts depositing information into students (Freire, 1993). Every aspect of the course is about praxis—the connection of thought to action and theory to practice.

In his book *When Students Have Power,* Ira Shor (1996) recounts the disaster that befell his class at the College of Staten Island when he offered to share power with his students before they understood what they might gain (or lose) from such empowerment. Shor thought that given an opportunity to vote on how the class should be run, students would take a responsible approach and act in their collective interest. Without the cultural or political experience to make sense of his offer, students instead chose to cut back on course requirements and used their power to subvert their own learning. Students at UMass who enroll in GRCD may experience a very similar kind of dissonance at the outset. The facilitator-leaders endeavor to model, in their own behavior and in the structure of the class, what empowerment means.

It's approaching 10:00 on a Sunday night and the leaders for GRCD are sprawled on the floor of Professor Art Keene's family room, trying to wrap up their weekly seminar. During the course of the evening they have debated two challenging readings on interracial alliance, participated in a role-play to prepare for a difficult lesson on white privilege, discussed the previous week's classes, and established key learning objectives for the week to come.

It's been an intense and fulfilling evening, and although the time has passed quickly, people are tired and it's time to go home. But Nick resists. "We haven't mapped out our lesson plan yet. We can't afford to do this at the last minute. This is going to be a challenging week for us and for the students. We need to do this now!" No one disagrees, so they get to work, trying out different ideas for accomplishing the learning objectives they had set out earlier in the evening. They continue to work until 11:30, when Keene begins to nudge them toward the door. They will reconvene for another four hours on Wednesday evening in preparation for Thursday's class.

The Professorless Classroom

Perhaps the most unusual aspect of the ASB class is the absence of a professor. The classes are made up of sections of 12 to 25 students. Teams of two or three student leaders who have previously taken the course work with the faculty adviser to plan the program, design the curriculum, recruit students, and facilitate classes. The student leaders and the faculty adviser meet weekly on Sunday evenings from September through May. They also attend three weekend retreats in addition to the GRCD student retreat.

They are required to read and understand course material, identify learning objectives, create a lesson plan, design activities to fulfill the stated objectives, and co-facilitate each class. They also read and comment on student reflections and write their own weekly reflection on the teaching process.

Each team of leaders works from a binder that has been assembled by previous leaders. Thus, each group leaves a legacy of what they have learned so the next group will not have to start over. Each successive group of leaders vows to raise the bar for their class and achieve a higher standard of learning and community. This keeps the class exciting for all the students as they connect with previous ASB students and take on the challenge of improving the program.

Student leaders face the additional challenge of responding to widespread skepticism about the program. How can students be trusted to motivate themselves? Won't they, like Shor's students, vote to decrease the course's demands? Who will answer questions? Who will serve as guardian of intellectual integrity?

The work done in the GRCD class exceeds the standards found in most honors classes at UMass. The drive for quality within all UACT programs is partly a matter of self-preservation. Because the class threatens the status quo in many ways, students know that they have to prove that a program like this can work. Student leaders therefore promote accountability and document everything. All student papers are archived. The required standard for papers (which are not graded but are marked "acceptable" or "unacceptable") is that they be products "that you would show to another faculty member (or dean) as representative of the good work done in our program." Facilitators, charged with protecting the program's integrity, are often less charitable in assessing acceptability than the faculty adviser would be.

Facilitators set high expectations for themselves and for the students in the class. Students sign a covenant at the beginning of the term, making a collective and individual commitment to be responsible for their own learning and that of their classmates. In the covenant, students agree to requirements expected in any class—to turn in papers on time, to read thoughtfully and come prepared for each class, to attend every class meeting, and so on. But they also agree to hold each other accountable, to endeavor to grow personally and intellectually during the term, to be active and attentive listeners, to try to see the world through the eyes of others, and to work collaboratively. Students who fulfill all the obligations of the covenant receive a grade of A- in the course. Students who do so with flair receive an A. The contract eliminates most of the subjective judgments from grading and helps resolve the dilemma of undergraduates grading other undergraduates, something not usually acceptable at UMass.

Facilitators are not teachers or junior teaching assistants. They model good lesson planning with the hope that the students will assume more of these responsibilities during the term. The facilitators clearly state (and restate) the objectives of the lessons and the course so students can see where their work is taking them. Facilitators manage the discussions and help steer the class toward fulfilling learning objectives, which include mastery of content about community development.

Through academic readings and weekly writings, the facilitators develop a comprehensive, working understanding of grassroots community development and its use in combating cycles of poverty. They examine the roots of poverty, systems of privilege and power, and the difference between grassroots strategies and those of traditional top-down development programs often promoted and implemented by governments and nongovernmental organizations. They explore oral, written, and visual histories of grassroots development organizations and compare the efforts undertaken in different settings. They endeavor to see how the scholarly and non-scholarly accounts measure up to the experience with grassroots organizations during the spring break trip. Finally, they work to connect these topics to their own lives.

Building Community

GRCD differs from most other classes in that it strives to create an intimate learning community, a web of mutual purpose and trust. In a large, atomized, and sometimes alienating campus, community in the classroom enriches students' lives and makes them more effective in their work. Thus, students in GRCD deliberately spend time building trust and mutual support. This requires rejecting the arbitrary separation of the academic from the personal.

Each week, class begins with a check in, an exercise appropriately called a "go around." People share news from their lives and learn to see each other as whole beings. Learning to see each other in this way is essential in order to be effective in exploring racism, privilege, and other cultural baggage.

The weekend off-campus retreat is an important component to help people learn to work in an intimate setting. Some of the retreat is devoted to teambuilding games and lighthearted activities. Some is simply rehearsal for the spring break trip—a chance to practice sharing close quarters, sleeping on the floor, and learning to be patient with the personal quirks of 25 other people. But the bulk of the time is devoted to sharing political biographies, which students write in answer to the question, "Why do I do the work that I do?" Student leaders share their own political biographies the week before the retreat to help other students overcome any reluctance to share and provide models for those who are inexperienced at delving into their own motivations.

The leaders approach classroom work as an active collaboration as well. While they work to accommodate different learning styles, there is no room for passivity. Everyone in the class is responsible for teaching and learning, and for making sure that all voices are heard. Course material is learned through group discussion and participatory group learning activities, often including role-playing or simulation. Chairs are arranged in a circle, and everyone helps move the discussion forward, asks questions, and holds one another accountable. Students who have an easier time with the material are expected to help those who are struggling, and students with complaints are expected to make suggestions and take action toward their resolution.

a**ll the students need to overcome deeply embedded assumptions about learning, power, and difference.**

Spring Break

It's spring break and the students have been working in a small coastal community on Virginia's eastern shore. They are working with an organization trying to sustain the town's remaining African American population, which is being displaced as a result of rapid gentrification. At the end of the day the students gather in the front room of the small old house that has become their home for the week. It's a tight fit with everyone sitting on the floor shoulder to shoulder, among sleeping bags, backpacks, board games, and the occasional Frisbee. Someone volunteers to speak first, and slowly the group moves around the circle, sharing stories from the day, thoughts that have been on their minds, or descriptions of how they are feeling. The stories are punctuated by laughter, frequent nods of agreement, and murmurs of approval, as well as encouragement when the speaker shares disappointment or confusion.

The group becomes animated as someone shares the story of a landlord from Connecticut who stopped to chat with some of the students as they were painting a local church. He had told them, "You know, no one who lives here is really from here." The landlord's comments suggest that the students' hosts, who have lived in the community for generations, are no longer relevant—that this small remaining African American community doesn't register on the radar screen of the town's new wealthy residents.

The energy in the room changes. There is frustration and anger, analysis and hypothesis, camaraderie and solidarity. Everyone is engaged as students take turns speaking and calling on each other. They raise questions, look to each other for clarification, and push and challenge each other. There is an intense and immediate intersection of the theory from the classroom with the problems of the real world and between students' own stories and the stories of others. They wonder aloud what they can do, as they confront the prospects of their own agency. The discussion carries on deep into the night. All present understand that their learning neither begins nor ends at the classroom door.

During spring break, each class spends six days living and working with members of a grassroots community organization in another part of the country. Before the trip, students explore the theory behind and approaches to grassroots development, study the methods and ethics of working in a community not their own, and form their own learning community.

The trip links classroom learning to the real world, and theory to practice. (See Barnhart, 2001, for a description of these trips.) Organizations invite the students into their communities and develop long-standing relationships. Each organization works on mobilizing the community to address specific issues of poverty and political disenfranchisement. While the students' work provides a useful service, the relationship is a partnership. Members of the community serve as guides and teachers. The students frame their work as social justice work rather than as help (Morton, 1995) and find common ground that connects their lives with those of the people in the community. The physical service is less important than the mutual learning and support that the service engenders.

Over the years, students have worked at Boys' and Girls' clubs, painted houses, done construction, picked up trash, helped community members move, and done demolition work. They have attended church services, Bible study groups, and town meetings, met with town councils and local development experts, hosted intercultural dinners, operated summer camps, and jointly applied for funding.

The trip is an opportunity to work with people from different cultural, racial, and socioeconomic backgrounds and, for most students, to experience life in a community very different from their own. They try to connect host communities with the resources of UMass. The goal is a meaningful partnership that allows for financial and emotional support, learning, and sharing.

The Alumni Seminar

Following ASB 2000, two of the student leaders for that year, Comfort Halsey and Meaghan Hamilton, approached faculty advisor Art Keene with a dilemma. They noted that ASB and GRCD had introduced them to an empowered form of learning but that now that the term was over, there was no place else to go with it. It was the end of their sophomore year and they still had a lot of schooling ahead of them. "What do we do next?" they asked. "What is one supposed to do after ASB? Where do we go when so

We know it works because students compete to get into the class even though most regard the workload as "ridiculous."

many courses are hostile to approaches that don't conform to the banking model?" They did not want to go back into a classroom where the professor "drones on and discourages participation."

Keene asked what they wanted to do to address their frustration, and they suggested designing their own course—a seminar designed and run entirely by students that would give them a forum for taking ASB "to the next level." Keene replied, "Make me an offer." A few weeks later they had come up with a draft of a syllabus and the alumni seminar was born.

The seminar is an advanced course on grassroots community development that takes up were GRCD leaves off. The course is now in its fourth iteration and draws 7-14 students per term, all of whom are GRCD alumni. Students meet throughout the fall to plan the curriculum and negotiate a partnership with a local grassroots organization.

Students kick off the spring semester with a weekend retreat that includes a workshop on facilitation. As in ASB, students sign a covenant of mutual commitment. During the term they run the seminar on their own—setting and evaluating weekly learning objectives, sharing facilitation duties, reading and commenting on each other's papers, evaluating each other's work, and holding each other accountable for a high level of intellectual engagement.

Professor Keene receives the weekly digest that the students post on their listserve and is also able to keep tabs on the course informally through frequent (though optional) office hours visits from students in the seminar. Students conduct a spring break project that they design in partnership with a community-based organization of their choosing; the most recent partner was Nuestras Raices, an organization that promotes urban farming in Holyoke, Massachusetts. They also host a one-day campus visitation program for youth from their host community, present a paper evaluating their projects at the annual state-wide honors research conference, and prepare a "how to" binder for the next generation of students in the alumni class.

Praxis and the Radical Classroom

GRCD is an experiment in praxis, the application of theory to practice. The class challenges traditional notions of development and progress through the exploration of grassroots community development. It challenges traditional notions of education through the application of grassroots and participatory strategies in the classroom. It also challenges the ingrained beliefs that knowledge is something possessed by experts and that learning and progress reside in tangible, completed products, such as exams, papers, lab reports, or a newly completed building.

The ASB model centers around the notion of a learning community in which participants rely on their own individual and collective abilities—rather than on the expert advice or interpretation of one instructor—to understand, analyze, and derive knowledge from course material. The approach has been influenced by Freire (1998), Shor (1996), Hooks (1994), Palmer (1998), and Stout (1996), as well as Keene's work with Educators for Community Engagement (see www.e4ce.org). Because there is great value in collective personal experiences, the class devotes time to storytelling. At the same time, the leaders recognize when they need help from professors, members of the host communities, or others. The emphasis is on the process of learning and results. Above all, the class seeks to empower students as learners, community members, and citizens.

To differing degrees, all the students need to overcome deeply embedded assumptions about learning, power, and difference. The course syllabus represents an integrated program designed to help them move through this process. Each lesson builds on the next but also revisits previous learning. Students often complain that the first weeks of class don't make sense, that it's not what they expected, and they have trouble seeing how it all relates. Most students have some kind of epiphany in the weeks after the spring-break trip, noting that they suddenly see the connections among the parts.

Program Evaluation

How We Know It Works

As with any radical or alternative initiative, ASB cannot be evaluated effectively with traditional tools alone. The effectiveness of the ASB program is most visible and best evaluated in the lives of ASB alumni. Students have often said that ASB is a life-changing experience. They alter their majors, rethink their personal approach to education, start new programs, become more involved in UACT, or apply their learning to other kinds of activism both on and off campus.

We know that ASB works because of the large number of students who go on to perform postgraduate national service. We know it works because alumni hold their learning communities together—often through the summer and into subsequent semesters. We know it works because the vast majority of alumni regard themselves as politically engaged. We know it works because students compete to get into the class even though most regard the workload as "ridiculous." One student commented, "ASB is not a class but a lifestyle. It expands to fill all of the free space in your life." Another elaborated:

> I have often considered the rifts between art and societal issues, and the time spent in class in free-writing exercises, informal presentations, and skit-making helped me personally resolve the gap between artistry and social relevance. On our trip, I felt privileged to be able to collaborate on art projects that I felt had a social context, whether it was working at the Boys' and Girls' club to put together the skit in our "drama workshop" or just sitting still and letting the younger girls paint my face and hands.

> I think that until that point, I had seen my pursuits and classwork as an important part of social structure, but not necessarily social justice or even true social service. As a result of a class discussion concerning the power dynamics of expression within a community, I was inspired to propose a workshop to the UMass Writing Center about educating members of the campus community on the basic forms of writing for social change. This was a real turning point for me, since it allowed me to integrate two of the most important issues in my life. Not only were my definitions of social justice being challenged in class, but my exclusive methods of expression were as well. I was finally participating in a program where I was encouraged and inspired to integrate social issues into the areas of focus I had already chosen.

This student went from changing her thoughts about her work and her future to taking tangible actions. By proposing and implementing a writing program for social change, she engaged in praxis. She was able to turn her new understanding of the connections between her major and social justice into an active, successful program.

We also know that ASB works because of the dedication of the students who developed the alumni seminar. These students further explored and effectively demonstrated a radical form of teaching, learning, and praxis. In their writing, they demonstrated that they had built on and moved beyond what they learned in the ASB class. They mastered new content, but more important, they became more adept at group process, became comfortable working in a community initially unfamiliar to them, forged a meaningful alliance across the bounds of race and class, designed and implemented an original project in the community, and increased their understanding of their own agency. Finally, they produced a binder documenting their work, demonstrating what motivated students can do on their own and helping to jumpstart the next group of students who were to undertake this challenge. They left behind a tool to help make the class sustainable, which students continue to adapt and improve.

Seven generations of ASB alumni have actively taken ownership of this program and the learning and growth that comes from it. They have claimed it as their own by engaging its pedagogy and taking on responsibility for probing, analyzing, questioning, reflecting on, revising, and revamping the program year after year.

Traditional Evaluation

The program also uses more traditional modes of assessment and evaluation. The two main methods for in-class evaluation of both the students and the process are a final reflection and a final project—a simulation exercise. At the end of the ASB class, each student writes a final personal reflection of 7–10 pages examining his or her growth and progress throughout the semester. Students take the general reflection process they have used and refined during the course of the semester and apply it to their overall experience.

The final reflection has two components. The first addresses the content of the class and how it has complicated and deepened students' understanding of community development, poverty, and the social, cultural, economic, and political circumstances that frame these issues. The second addresses the personal and educational impact of the course. Students consider how the class has affected their views regarding education, their future plans, and issues of community, civic responsibility, leadership, political consciousness, and spiritual growth. These questions give the leaders a look at how students have grasped the material and grown as individuals as well as a tool for processing the total experience.

Of course, self-reporting has its limits. Most ASB programs, whether they are curricular or not, produce effusive testimonials. Any experiential program that stands in such stark contrast to the traditional classroom should feel transformational for many students. Nonetheless, the testimonials are important windows into how students experienced the course. (See the Sidebar on the next page for a sample of students' comments.)

The second evaluation method is a simulation exercise in which students must put into practice the theory and case studies from the semester. In teams of three to four, students work on issues in a fictional rural Massachusetts community, Earl Gray. Students receive a description outlining a situation that is similar to that of many of the communities they studied in class: the community is dealing with issues of disinvestment, underdevelopment, and poverty. The fictional community members have recently begun organizing and have invited the ASB students to speak to them about possible approaches they might take. Students must prepare and give presentations, during which the rest of the class assumes the role of Earl Gray residents, asking questions from the viewpoints of various community members. Students draw on information and examples from the semester as well as outside research on local resources or programs in order to come up with creative recommendations appropriate for the particular challenges (and assets) of this community.

The simulation identifies how well students can apply what they have learned. They draw on technical knowledge (academic content) of strategies and analyze how it might be applicable in Earl Gray. Do they stand in front of the community and lecture? Do they offer suggestions while looking to the community for direction? Do they see the community as an array of pathologies? Do they help community members recognize their own assets? How conscious are they of their role as outsiders? How well do they understand the implications of this role and the way it affects their relationship with the community and its members?

Although in their final reflections nearly all the students demonstrate a clear understanding of the principles of the course, their practice in the simulation sometimes contradicts what they have written. A common gap between theory and practice occurs when a student asserts the importance of a community setting its own agenda in the reflection and then dictates to the community what it ought to be doing in the simulation (Keene, 2003).

Student Reflections on the ASB Program

"The structure of the course and the discussion that we had taught me that I still had much to learn. In class, I got the opportunity to engage in a dialogue about race with others not of the same race as myself. I got to hear what whites feel about it, and learned that there are whites who care about the issues that minorities face, as well as those who want to abdicate their privileged positions. My role is to talk about being underprivileged and to educate others about what it is like to live as a black person in the United States. It is also my responsibility to learn about what it is like to live like any other group in the United States and the struggles that other groups face, as well as how they deal with issues of power and privilege. Only in an open dialogue such as we engaged in during class, in which we each are responsible for the education and growth of the others, could I have learned the important lesson that we can help one another grow and change for the better."

"The model of community learning that we developed in ASB...is one that I think would be useful in high school education. Students are encouraged to engage in the work. Rather than compete with one another (for grades) as I was taught, they are encouraged to help each other learn. This not only helps students learn better, it also teaches them responsibility for one another, and helps foster community inside the classroom that they can take outside into their larger communities later on in their lives, thus making them better citizens."

"It is easy for me to lose hope in education when I am sitting through lecture after lecture with students who are asleep or doing crossword puzzles. Being able to be a part of such an active community has really given me hope and a new understanding of how I can and should take an active part in my own education."

This gap indicates a failure to overcome a lifetime of school enculturation, as students unconsciously address their reports to instructors rather than to the residents of Earl Gray. They often attempt to demonstrate how much they have learned by enumerating all possible options for the community of Earl Gray, and doing so with the voice of authority. It is easy to see this discrepancy as a failure of our pedagogy. But we are coming to understand that we are pushing the students to change a great deal in the course of 14 weeks. We need to remind ourselves occasionally that the process, once begun, is unlikely to stop at the end of the term.

Conclusion

The UMass Amherst ASB began as most alternative spring break programs begin, as a week-long trip to a distant community to engage in service and learning. After the first year, students were enthusiastic and decided that the academic component should be expanded. Instead of simply reading some books together, they developed an integrated curriculum. As the program grew, it not only made greater academic achievements but also had a more empowering effect on the students involved. Students took on more active roles and pushed for a more extensive program, until in 2002, as Keene puts it, the students effectively kicked him out of the classroom. This was not an act of anarchy, but rather an affirmation that students were indeed coming to feel ownership over the class and the process, absorbing the radical educational pedagogy and engaging in praxis.

As much as he misses being in the classroom, Keene has come to realize that his presence can be an obstacle to student empowerment. When he is not in the classroom, the students have to solve their own problems. There may be greater room for both students and leaders to make mistakes, but they can then learn from their mistakes. Keene is the first to acknowledge that the quality of academic work has continued to improve since his departure from the classroom.

It is important to stress that by emphasizing personal growth and subjective analysis, ASB is expanding our understanding of education to include the subjective factors that affect learning. Students should be able not only to reiterate and demonstrate knowledge of the academic material, but also to connect and explain its meaning and relevance in their own lives and with regard to their understanding of the world. The ability to draw connections, understand texts, and apply concepts is what demonstrates a true understanding of material. The methods of evaluation are not perfect, and the process is often frustrating, but constant questioning, re-evaluating, and experimenting underlie the program. Solving the problems that the approach poses makes the work together challenging, exciting, vibrant, and empowering.

References

Barnhart, B. (2001, Fall). A new road to learning: UMass students choose community service over room service on alternative spring break. *UMass Magazine.* Also located at www.umassmag.com/Fall_2001/A_New_Road_To_LEARNING_80.html.

Freire, P. (1993). *Pedagogy of the oppressed.* (Rev. 20th anniversary ed.). New York: Continuum.

Freire, P. (1998). *Pedagogy of freedom: Ethics, democracy and civic courage.* Lanham, MD: Rowman & Littlefield.

Hooks, B. (1994). *Teaching to transgress: Education as the practice of freedom.* New York, NY: Routledge.

Keene, A. (2003). *Serving Earl Gray: A simulation for assessing learning in a community service learning course.* Paper presented at the Annual Meeting of the Society for Applied Anthropology, Portland, OR.

Kretzman, J., & McKnight, J. (1993). *Building communities from the inside out: A path toward finding and mobilizing community assets.* Chicago: ACTA Publishing.

Medoff, P., & Sklar, H. (1994). *Streets of hope.* Boston, MA: South End Press.

Morton, K. (1995, Fall). The irony of service: Charity, project and social change in service learning. *Michigan Journal of Community Service Learning, 19–32.*

Palmer, P. (1998). *The courage to teach: Exploring the inner landscape of a teacher's life.* San Francisco: Jossey-Bass.

Shor, I. (1996). *When students have power: Negotiating authority in a critical pedagogy.* Chicago: University of Chicago Press.

Stout, L. (1996). *Bridging the class divide and other lessons for grassroots organizing.* Boston: Beacon Press.

Acknowledgments

We warmly acknowledge the contributions of the hundreds of UMass and other Five Colleges students (from Amherst, Hampshire, Mount Holyoke, and Smith Colleges) who have contributed to the evolution of UACT. We especially would like to acknowledge the 2004 leadership team of Sofia Binioris, Nick Demas, Elana Feder, Liz Hartunian, Miriam Mannon, and Natalya Weinstein-Roberts, who impressively raised the bar for the next generation of UACT students. We are most grateful to Marshall Ganz and The Praxis Group at UMass for their wise counsel on matters both pedagogical and spiritual and for their help in developing the political biography exercise.

Service-Politics and Civic Engagement

William Chatwin, Shannon Gillespie,
Anne Looser, and Marshall Welch

I S SALAD DRESSING A CONTROVERSIAL ISSUE? Not usually, unless you consider the question "House, Italian, or Ranch on the side?" to be controversial. But to conscientious young students at the Lowell Bennion Community Service Center of the University of Utah, controversial issues behind a common salad dressing led the way to a discussion that resulted in a new student-directed program—Service-Politics and Civic Engagement (SPACE).

In January 2004, during lunch at an annual retreat in a remote cabin, students were discussing ethical consumerism when one in the group noted the bottle of salad dressing on the table. He pointed out that the dressing was produced by a subsidiary of Altria Corporation, formerly known as Philip Morris, the tobacco giant and multi-industry conglomerate. Students began to discuss the importance of supporting locally owned businesses and progressive companies. As 2004–2005 SPACE coordinator Tara Merrill put it:

> Ultimately, it is our responsibility to decide whether large corporations, such as Philip Morris, or companies that understand the importance of a cleaner and safer environment, such as Newman's Own, are successful. By supporting local merchants, we not only boost our local economy but also foster a greater sense of community.

The students wondered how average people could become conscientious consumers and good citizens when they are unaware of the ethical issues relating to consumerism. Through their discussion, they recognized the role and importance of a continuum of opportunity for civic engagement. They began to explore how to use existing resources at the Bennion Center to promote both awareness and action to bring about change. Sitting at the cabin's kitchen table, they mapped out on scratch paper their ideas for a new program that would integrate three distinct yet related programs within the

> **"S**tudents have energy. SPACE was formed to hone that energy and give students the skills necessary to become the change.**"**

Bennion Center to promote civic engagement through service-politics. The conceptual framework of SPACE was born.

The Journey

A Structure for Change

Throughout its 18-year history, the Bennion Center has been dedicated to service. The students inspired by salad dressing were not the first who wanted to push the boundaries of the center's endeavors. The emphasis of the center has always been on student-led projects that address unmet needs within the community. Yet all along, dedicated students have asked important questions of themselves and others, such as: "Why does this need exist in our community?" "What can we do to eliminate the need for our service?" "How do we make change?" and "How can we make our voices be heard?" Anne Looser, a SPACE coordinator in 2004–2005 and one of this chapter's authors, notes:

> A lot of students want to do their own projects, but they just don't have the skills or the networks to develop them. Many of my classmates, myself included, crave to be change agents. We learn a lot of theory and statistics; we want to use this theory constructively. Until SPACE came along, there was no structure to help students create their own projects in the community that addresses system issues. Students have energy. SPACE was formed to hone that energy and give students the skills necessary to become the change.

The dedicated, mindful students at the center have long called for service and learning opportunities that span a wider range. This issue spurred them to think about how to structure such opportunities. They began holding weekly discussions to explore issues at a systemic level and to act in response. They initiated some attempts to address community issues more holistically—for example, writing letters about issues—but they found it difficult to do more in the way of action or defining avenues for change. Looser comments, "There were some people with ideas about how to create something to address the salad dressing dilemma in the Bennion Center and on campus, but until we put it on paper and created a plan, it was just an idea." At that point, students asked staff to support the establishment of SPACE by providing the additional structure and continuity to help students and the community take action.

Some of the students who developed SPACE were aware of or had participated in Campus Compact's Raise Your Voice campaign after attending Colorado Campus Compact's 2003 Civic and Service-Learning Summit. Inspired by that experience, they proposed establishing another level of civic engagement on campus—to promote systemic change.

Pushing the Boundaries

Students at the Bennion Center work within a continuum of individual involvement that ranges from entry point to acting as an agent of change. This "active citizen continuum" (see Figure 1) reflects the evolution of the Bennion Center in providing a range of opportunities for student service, from volunteer projects that provide direct service and initial awareness of issues to intellectual development through service-learning. In addressing the systemic and political factors at the core of many community issues, SPACE pushes the boundary of the continuum.

FIGURE 1: **The Active Citizen Continuum**

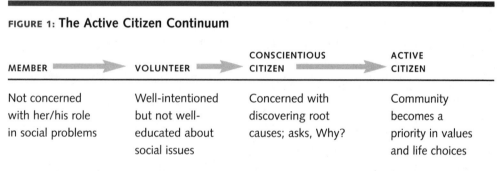

MEMBER	VOLUNTEER	CONSCIENTIOUS CITIZEN	ACTIVE CITIZEN
Not concerned with her/his role in social problems	Well-intentioned but not well-educated about social issues	Concerned with discovering root causes; asks, Why?	Community becomes a priority in values and life choices

Source: Break Away: The Alternative Break Connection. Availale at www.alternativebreaks.org/active_citizen_continuum.asp. Used by permission.

Seeing that they were pushing the edge of the service continuum, students and staff admitted feeling both nervous and excited as they essentially agreed to "make it up as we go along." This spontaneity has brought to light the potential impact and power of SPACE, from initial planning on. For example, one student addressed an early meeting of the Lowell Bennion Center Futures Committee at which faculty and other adults discussed the possibility of providing students with opportunities for change. The group was reluctant to take up the idea at first. The student persisted, saying to the committee, "Let's go to the students and make it grassroots. We have the freedom to do it, the advantage of not having résumés that constrain us. We can do what we want. If we get organized, we can make a splash and really make a change when we all work together."

The students have since adhered to this philosophy of student-centered projects at the Bennion Center by taking on the primary role of conceptualizing SPACE. After brainstorming and generating ideas at a winter retreat, students consulted with staff about how to proceed. A small group of students then met for a half-day retreat to craft a vision and procedures for a program that would most effectively empower students to create change. They developed a description of the program and successfully presented their proposal to staff and board members of the Bennion Center. Finally, students outlined and prepared for a weeklong training to ensure that the program would be effectively implemented in fall 2004.

SPACE and the Bennion Center

Before describing in detail SPACE's development and implementation, a brief history of the Bennion Center and its existing programs will help clarify how this new endeavor will integrate the center's activities. The center was established in 1987 to promote student-directed volunteer projects in the spirit of Dr. Lowell Bennion, a professor at the University of Utah and a theologian at the LDS Institute of Religion. The primary goal of the center is to provide direct service in the community. A second, equally important, goal is to develop the leadership skills of students directing projects. In addition to student-directed projects, the Bennion Center also coordinates service-learning classes and the Service-Learning Scholars program.

Student-Directed Volunteer Programs

On average, the center sponsors about 45 student-directed projects each year, although this number has been as high as 60. Two full-time staff members oversee the student-directed programs. Proposals for projects are submitted by community agencies or students, and are reviewed and selected by a governing cabinet of student coordinators. Each project has a student director who has an operating budget of approximately $300 to recruit and train student volunteers and work with community agency partners. Projects are grouped into four or five issue areas, each led by a student coordinator. Issue areas include environmental, health, education, social welfare, and campus issues. Student coordinators meet regularly with the project directors working on the same topic. Together they develop and run successful volunteer experiences for thousands of students on campus each year.

Students involved in the Bennion Center participate without personal compensation; student leaders and student volunteers receive neither academic credit nor payment for their involvement. This arrangement communicates the ethic of selfless service to others on which the Bennion Center was founded.

Service-Learning Classes

The service-learning program serves as a catalyst for involving faculty in the continuum of civic engagement and is their primary interface with the Bennion Center. The University of Utah offers approximately 130 classes in more than 20 departments that are officially designated as service-learning courses. A review committee composed of faculty with service-learning experience, students who have taken service-learning classes, participating community partners, and Bennion Center staff assists faculty in developing service-learning courses so they meet the necessary criteria. The Bennion Center defines service-learning this way:

> Service-learning is an experience-based form of pedagogy in which students, faculty, and community partners work together to integrate and apply empirically-grounded knowledge in authentic settings to address the needs of the community and meet instructional objectives using action and critical reflection to prepare students to become meaningful members of a just and democratic society.

Service-Learning Scholars

Under the guidance of a supervisory committee, students in the Service-Learning Scholar program complete 400 hours of service with extracurricular reflection, a minimum of 10 credit hours of service-learning courses, and an integrated service project that addresses a community need. The supervisory committee comprises a faculty member, a community agency representative, a student leader, and a staff member from the Bennion Center.

Students implement long-term, self-sustaining projects rather than short-term projects such as food drives. They might, for example, create program training manuals or curricula, assist in evaluation or research, or bring about policy change. Before beginning this capstone experience, students complete a seminar that provides the technical support and skills necessary to complete the project. Students become involved with their peers who are also carrying out service-learning projects, thereby becoming part of an interdisciplinary community of learners. The scholars receive special recognition from the president of the university at commencement, along with written recognition on their transcript and a banquet in their honor.

Integrating the Programs

SPACE was deliberately designed to provide an interface among the diverse programs available within the Bennion Center. Integrating elements of existing programs seemed like a necessary approach to promote service-politics and civic engagement and to connect the new program with the community. William Chatwin, one of the authors and a SPACE coordinator in 2004–2005, notes, "Linkages among Bennion Center entities will facilitate better outreach because we'll know what's going on among ourselves. A unified message within promotes better relations with the outside. The result is coordinated communication both within and without."

SPACE organizers recognized that to be most effective in changing their communities, they needed work with existing systems, cultures, and groups. SPACE facilitates this cooperation. For example, if a student or campus group proposes a project that addresses an environmental issue, SPACE coordinators will identify related student-directed volunteer programs, service-learning courses, service-learning scholar projects, campus group projects, and community projects. They then contact representatives of these entities and urge them to combine resources with enterprising students to engage in various service-politics activities. SPACE coordinators thus serve as liaisons among various university groups as well as between community partners and the university.

SPACE Development

Beyond Brainstorming

After the initial retreat at which the salad dressing issue arose, students met with Bennion staff to discuss how to move beyond brainstorming to implementation. Staff members asked numerous questions to encourage the students to think critically about their idea: What is the vision of SPACE? What does the structure of SPACE look like? Whose approval and support will they need to begin? What will the staff want to know? What will the board members want to know? Students used these questions as a foundation for creating a proposal. The staff acted as consultants without dictating the outcome of the process.

Following the staff consultation, a small group of students and staff met for a half-day working retreat to answer the questions that had been raised and to draft a formal proposal to present to the Bennion Center staff and advisory boards. The proposal outlined not only a vision for SPACE, but also a vision for a new meaning of service-politics and civic engagement. The proposal cites the following definition of service-politics (Long, 2002):

> Service politics is the bridge between community service and conventional politics.... Participation in community service is a form of unconventional political activity that can lead to social change, in which participants primarily work outside of governmental institutions; service politics becomes the means through which students can move from community service to political engagement. Those who develop connections to larger systemic issues building on their roots in community service adopt a framework through which service politics leads to greater social change. (p. 18)

The students also adopted a specific definition of civic engagement from Michael Delli Carpini, Director, Public Policy, The Pew Charitable Trusts:

One useful definition of civic engagement is the following: individual and collective actions designed to identify and address issues of public concern. Civic engagement may take many forms, from individual volunteerism to organizational involvement to electoral participation. It can include efforts to directly address an issue, work with others in a community to solve a problem, or interact with the institutions of representative democracy. Civic engagement encompasses a range of activities, such as working in a soup kitchen, serving on a neighborhood association, writing a letter to an elected official, or voting.

Presenting the Proposal

While Lowell Bennion was involved in advocacy as well as direct action, instilling this value into SPACE was a challenge because, for many, the term *advocacy* conjures up images of violence or illegal activity. Tactics of agitation that include violence or violations of the law are unacceptable to SPACE, so when the students proposed the program to staff and board members, they stressed that its mission included only positive manifestations of advocacy and activism. The members of the staff and the board mostly supported the program, but were concerned about three key questions: 1) How would the student coordinators handle controversial issues? 2) Would involving students in politics and advocacy detract from the center's history of direct service? 3) How would the program be funded?

The students addressed the concern about controversial issues first. One staff member asked Anne Looser what she would do if "a student wishing to promote guns on campus brought an acceptable proposal to SPACE." Looser replied that it would be part of SPACE's mission to provide assistance to that group: "SPACE is about dialogue, not debate. We as a community should be discussing issues, like guns on campus." The staff followed up with a question about what she would do if a project were clearly illegal or otherwise unacceptable. Looser explained:

> Of course, those types of projects would not be approved. But we would refer students to groups who could work with them, or hold a dialogue on campus. Often we learn more from our "failures" than our successes. SPACE is designed to teach students; that doesn't mean that we accept all proposals, but it does mean do have a responsibility to explain why we don't accept a project.

To address the concern that the need for direct, immediate service to the community would be neglected, students made clear that this was not the intention of the SPACE program. When presenting to the Bennion Center's donor board, William Chatwin explained, "The Bennion Center always provided an entry point and numerous opportunities for increasing involvement, up to a certain extent. SPACE merely provides a logical and necessary connection to the next level."

Students argued that student-directed projects would not diminish; rather, the strength of the SPACE program would depend on students' direct service experiences. After gaining firsthand knowledge of community needs through direct service, students become more aware of systemic issues and become passionate about finding ways to effect change. SPACE would give these students the opportunity to integrate and enhance their direct service experiences by focusing their attention on the systemic issues behind the needs their service met.

Finally, students explained their plan for funding SPACE. Because of the unique objective of the program, the development director at the Bennion Center contacted specific donors to ask them to contribute directly to the operation and sustainability of the SPACE program. Bennion Center donors already contributed to specific programs rather than to the center as a whole, so SPACE simply provided them with an additional giving option.

The students presented their proposal professionally and in a way that respected the culture of the Bennion Center. The proposal process itself became an invaluable collective learning experience. When any issue arose, staff and student coordinators solved the problem together through discussion, listening well, and responding creatively. This resulted in the formal structure within the SPACE program that is part of the overall review process. By staying true to this process, the students got approval for SPACE, which was launched on schedule in the fall of 2004.

Program Structure and Leadership

Following the student-centered philosophy of the Bennion Center, student coordinators govern SPACE and have asked advisers to take on the role of "shadow leadership." Student coordinator Timothy Dudley explains:

> Shadow leadership is all about an adviser leading an individual or a group in a way that really forces them to think and act for themselves. A shadow leader guides student coordinators to think through decisions and plans flexibly, analytically, and deductively; and then to act according to vision, goals, and objectives while evaluating performance along the way. Led in this way, we will gain a sense of ownership, responsibility, passion, and creativity while developing the skills of analysis, communication, and leadership.
>
> Ideally, not only will the student coordinators develop these attributes ourselves, but we will also become shadow leaders for others. Individuals from the campus and the local community will come to us for help in leading their own projects and organizations. By being shadow leaders to them, we can help them leave as more fully developed citizen leaders.

The organizational structure of SPACE is nonhierarchical, although there are different roles and responsibilities. SPACE students work as a team to accomplish a common goal. This group solicits, approves, and facilitates project proposals for activities from the general campus and greater community. To maintain the program, SPACE coordinators are responsible for selecting future coordinators through an application and interview process.

Guiding Principles

In developing the proposal for the SPACE program, students created guiding principles intended to honor the history, mission, and culture of the Bennion Center:

1. Attempt to integrate student-directed programs, service scholars, service-learning classes, and other campus organizations.

2. Act within the parameters of the law.

3. Promote dialogue and reflection on different perspectives.

4. Look for consensus—what can we all agree on?

5. Include participation or input from students, community, staff, and faculty.

6. Meet the mission of the Bennion Center.

7. Promote justice through systemic change.

They also generated two guiding mantras: *dialogue, not debate,* and *how, not what.* The first mantra represents SPACE's intent to promote discussion of topics rather than to take a position. Debate in which different parties take firm positions can deter collaborative action, and SPACE wants to foster such action. The second mantra allows SPACE coordinators to help their peers figure out how to bring about the change they envision rather than envisioning for them what to change. This ensures that SPACE avoids taking a position on any issue and instead advocates for all perspectives. As a common SPACE statement notes, "We do not necessarily endorse the views of this event, but we do endorse the ability to express these views."

Operating Budget

Because of the perception on the part of some constituents that SPACE is controversial, with its focus on service-politics, the program focuses on soliciting funding from individuals and organizations that support advocacy and social change. For the program's first year, student coordinators requested $10,000, of which they received $6,000 for bringing speakers to campus, hosting campus and public dialogues, reaching out to the campus and community, and providing mini-grants for individual project proposals.

Initiative Review and Approval

It is the responsibility of the SPACE cabinet to review all initiative proposals developed by students or campus organizations and to distribute mini-grants to support SPACE activities. The initiatives develop, implement, and evaluate service-politics activities and aim to integrate the three existing programs within the Bennion Center. In the process of making the initiatives workable, SPACE coordinators can recommend changing the proposals or refer them to different agencies. Modest grants—up to $300—are awarded to proposals that meet certain guidelines (see the Sidebar opposite).

SPACE proposals challenge social norms and views. Controversial proposals are discussed with the sponsoring student or group, and with Bennion Center staff if necessary. In the event that the Bennion Center is unable to accept a proposal as it is written, staff members and sponsoring students provide constructive feedback. After center staff have held an exploratory meeting to explain why they cannot support the initiative, the proposal's authors may revise the proposal to fit SPACE's criteria for support or work with staff members to refer the proposal to another organization.

Guidelines for SPACE Proposals

1. Initiatives will focus on taking action or raising awareness to promote social and environmental justice through systemic change.

2. If a public or private community agency is currently working with the issue that the initiative addresses, the project will be done in cooperation with or with willing support from that organization. Cooperating agencies should be well committed, effective, and value the efforts of volunteers.

3. Initiatives must include student, community, staff, and faculty perspectives and/or support in planning and implementation.

4. Initiatives must address liability concerns and ensure the safety of all participants.

5. Initiatives must be based on solid, factual information.

6. Initiatives will not discriminate on the basis of race, sex, religion, or sexual orientation, and will be accessible to all.

7. Initiatives that involve political or religious affiliations will be evaluated for compliance with university policy.

8. All initiatives must be within the confines of the law and consistent with the mission of the Bennion Center.

9. Project proposals will be accepted on a rolling basis.

SPACE Activities

Service-politics activities incorporate a variety of strategies, some of which were piloted during the program's first year. SPACE coordinators have served as advisers and consultants to other groups across campus as they explore what social change strategies would be appropriate for their goals. These strategies include awareness and action events, community-based research, alternative weekends, and student-taught classes, among others. All of these strategies are designed to shift charity to include change and to translate awareness into action and advocacy.

Awareness and Action Events

Based on suggestions from Campus Compact staff and other advice, SPACE is committed to helping individual students and groups on campus create awareness and action events. An important guiding principle is that suggestions for action be coupled with awareness. Guest speakers, dialogues, debates, panel discussions, political raves, and information tables known as "Just Say Know" are ways to highlight issues such as those involving the environment, health, education, poverty, and homelessness. Students attending awareness events have an array of options for action to help bring about systemic change, including letter writing, making ethical consumer choices, voting, getting involved in campaigns, and volunteering.

Community-Based Research

Students also promote systemic change through community-based research (CBR), following three overriding principles: the practice is collaborative and driven by community needs; it respects both academic and community-based experiential means of constructing and disseminating knowledge; and it contributes to an ongoing social change process that promotes social justice (Strand et al., 2003). The University of Utah encourages students to engage in undergraduate research and offers modest stipends to conduct investigations under the supervision of a faculty member. Studies can employ either a quantitative or a qualitative methodology.

One CBR project during the 2003–2004 academic year, conducted by William Chatwin, was a waste audit of the student union building. The proposal stated that the project sought to "determine the magnitude and composition of waste." The project, in which students sorted and weighed trash collected at the union, attracted coverage from the student newspaper. Banners on large plastic bags of garbage in the free-speech area of the campus announced: "45% of this garbage could have been recycled." Chatwin notes that the project was successful not only in generating information but also in building momentum for the recycling effort: the waste audit was referenced in student government legislation that provides trial funding for the recycling program. The waste audit project exemplifies service-politics, as a service was provided both directly and indirectly to help influence policy change.

Alternative Weekends

Alternative weekends are an outgrowth of the model used by colleges and universities around the country for Alternative Spring Break trips. These weekend trips combine an intensive service experience with an in-depth examination of the issues underlying the experience. Alternative weekends, a Bennion Center specialty, are more flexible and dynamic than alternative breaks because they can be more easily tailored to local issues. They are planned to coincide with events in the community rather than with fixed academic recesses.

Anne Looser conducted two alternative weekend experiences designed to expose students to the stark realities of homelessness during the 2003–2004 academic year. Students saw the plight of homeless individuals firsthand, listened to their experiences, and worked with people at the shelter to put together hygiene kits. Her experiences leading these trips will guide other trip leaders and help improve projects in the future.

SPACE'S strategies are designed to shift charity to include change and to translate awareness into action and advocacy.

Student-Taught Courses

In this approach, a student identifies a faculty member who specializes in his or her topic of interest and wants to assist with the course. Together, they formulate a syllabus and reading list for approval by the faculty member's department. The university's department of undergraduate studies itself considers such proposals if they do not meet the criteria for a specific department. Student-taught courses are open to enrollment by students from any major. The faculty partner is responsible for assigning grades but participates in the teaching of the course only as much as he or she and the student partner deem appropriate. These courses do not have to include a service-learning component, although they may.

It's About the Journey

With a name like SPACE, puns describing the program's mission abound. Students believe that by providing access to the next level of personal involvement, SPACE is the new frontier of service within the continuum of civic engagement. The metaphorical link to interstellar exploration goes beyond the name, however. Just as a successful NASA mission is linked to the scientists in the control center, successful systemic change depends on strong individuals that make up organizations and institutions.

One unexpected result of the NASA missions was the image of earth from space, which enabled people to see earth's fragile balance between isolation and interdependence. SPACE provides the same vision of a shared future: "SPACE is university and community partners working together to address our societal need for systemic change."

References

Long, S. (2002). *The new student politics: The wingspread statement on student civic engagement.* Providence, RI: Campus Compact.

Strand, K., Marullo, S., Cutforth, N., Stoecker, R., & Donohue, P. (2003). *Community-based research and higher education: Principles and practice.* San Francisco: Jossey-Bass.

Lessons from Building Service-Learning

Ross Meyer

M Y JOURNEY AS A SOCIAL ACTIVIST BEGAN in the ninth grade when a teacher, Steve Elliott, took me to the Over-the-Rhine community of Cincinnati for the first time. Like many alienated, suburban youth, I felt troubled, almost soulless. I was naïve but arrogant, materialistic but desperate. Growing up in a privileged, upper-middle-class home in the suburbs had sheltered me from the realities of the inner city.

When Mr. Elliott took me through the doors of the Drop Inn Homeless Shelter in the winter of 1996, I couldn't handle what I saw. It was a particularly cold evening, and the shelter was more crowded and chaotic than usual. The desperation and destitution of the shelter residents were unlike anything I had ever experienced in my comfortable life. I went through the motions of helping to serve the evening meal, trying hard not to pay attention to the people on the other side of the counter. While I was waiting to leave, an elderly homeless woman started to tell me about the struggles of a woman living on the street. I tried not to listen. Attempting to appear attentive, I casually said, "Yeah, I know what you mean." Suddenly, she moved in front of me to catch my averted eyes and started screaming, *"You have no idea what I mean!* I've seen your kind before, coming down here to try to rescue us poor folk so you feel better about yourselves. How could you possibly know what street life is like? You're just some rich white boy from the suburbs . . ." As she went on for what seemed like hours, I just stood there, terrified, but listening.

Instead of being scared off, I kept returning to the Drop Inn Shelter. This incident in 1996 began my deep relationship with Cincinnati's impoverished Over-the-Rhine community. Something in what the woman had said provoked an acute response within me. It was the first time I felt my privilege. And perhaps due to guilt, it was also the first time I felt a sense of social responsibility. My teacher provided the crucial educational support structure for me to be able to make sense of my experience and understand it within a broader context. He transformed a potentially devastating incident into a powerful learning experience.

On the trips, students can connect faces with academic theories and people with social problems.

Since that experience eight years ago, I have committed myself to service and social justice advocacy work. Because Steve Elliott had set up a structured volunteer program within the school, I was able to continue and deepen my engagement with the community. Throughout high school, I tutored GED classes and after-school programs, mentored youth, led housing construction crews, coordinated service programs, directed a youth summer program, organized advocacy campaigns, and engaged other students in the community. The more I worked, the more I felt a deep sense of commitment and passion.

At Miami University, I was able to apply my prior experience in the community to developing new civic engagement initiatives, including the Over-the-Rhine Weekend Experience, the Empower Program, and the Social Action Center. This chapter describes the development of these initiatives and explores the lessons I have learned while pursuing social change on a college campus.

Over-the-Rhine Weekend

When I entered Miami University in Oxford, Ohio, I wanted to bring the power of my experience working in the community to my peers and create a culture of civic engagement and social justice on campus. As a first-year student, I created a service-learning program entitled "Over-the-Rhine Weekend Experience: An Introduction to Urban America," which I have now coordinated for four years. During the two-day experience, students visit and work in a homeless shelter, work on low-income housing rehabilitation, tour the neighborhood and community agencies, discuss current city issues with community activists and leaders, and reflect on their experiences from an academic and a personal standpoint. Student participants come from relevant courses, such as urban sociology, American minority relations, social welfare policy, and urban planning. Faculty offer the experience to their students in lieu of another course assignment, and students write a reflection paper integrating the experience with course material.

The topics we deal with on the trip include racism, class, power, privilege, and community organizing for change. Although only 45 minutes away from Oxford, Over-the-Rhine is virtually a foreign country to most of the university's students. Whereas 8% of Miami's student body are members of racial minority groups and most students come from an upper-middle-class background, the Over-the-Rhine community is 80% African American, and 95% live below the official poverty level. Historically a home for poor migrants from Appalachia and the rural south, Over-the-Rhine suffers from the traditional problems of impoverished inner-city neighborhoods, including population decline, inadequate public education, homelessness, entrenched segregation, abandoned buildings, high rates of unemployment and underemployment, and lack of access to political power. In April 2001, the neighborhood was the origin of the city's largest incident of racial unrest since Martin Luther King Jr.'s assassination in 1968. Yet despite impoverishment and disenfranchisement, the community is organizing for positive social change and community development.

To date, I have coordinated and led 20 trips involving more than 300 students. On the trips, students can connect faces with academic theories and people with social problems, and gain a sense of empowerment by working on concrete community development projects. Drawing on the lessons I learned from Steve Elliott, I intentionally integrated direct service with lectures from community leaders and group reflections to contextualize the service work. This context helps students understand the structural and political roots of the problems facing the community.

Student participants often report that the Over-the-Rhine Weekend is one of the most powerful learning experiences they have at Miami University. For many, this experience is the first time they have confronted issues of poverty and racism in an inner-city context. On a personal level, experiencing a socioeconomically, racially diverse environment makes students aware of their own privileges. On an academic level, hands-on work in the community gives students a certain practical insight into their coursework that cannot be gleaned from textbooks or classroom lectures. Faculty partners often report that students who participate in the program are more engaged in the course material afterward. Working in the community not only gives students the opportunity to learn from experience, but also allows them to apply their education by working for social change. This experience brings depth and purpose to academia's more detached, analytical approaches.

After each trip, I continue to work with the students to encourage sustained activity and leadership in social action projects in the community. Many remain involved in volunteer work in the community; some have even taken on a more substantive involvement, through internships or research projects with the community agencies.

The Empower Program

Seeking to develop a structure for students to continue and deepen their enagement with the community, during my third and fouth years, I helped coordinate a team of students, faculty, community agencies, and university administrators to develop and run the Empower Program with Miami University's Office of Service Learning & Civic Leadership. The program gives 10–15 student participants an intensive, credit-bearing, year-long service-learning experience in Over-the-Rhine that focuses on issues of social justice. The program integrates community work, academic coursework, and critical reflection to foster development of social responsibility and facilitate personal empowerment. It includes a group-building retreat, regular service trips to Over-the-Rhine, including two weekend trips, and a personal reflection retreat. The program also incorporates meetings with community residents, interaction with community agencies, lectures about community issues, and regular reflection.

The program is integrated directly into the curriculum with academic courses that look specifically at social issues of race, class, and gender. The academic courses give students background understanding and knowledge of the social issues they tackle while working in Over-the-Rhine. To deepen this aspect of the program, we built an interdisciplinary partnership that tapped into existing upper-level courses from several departments that help students analyze the complex social environment from which issues of social justice emerge. In the first year of the program, for instance, we incorporated courses such as "Family Poverty" and "American Minority Relations" in black world studies; "Advanced Social Welfare Policy" in family studies and social work; "Identity: Race, Class, Gender" in anthropology; "Cities of Difference" and "Global Cities, World Economies" in geography; and "The American City Since 1940" in architecture. Such courses encourage students to examine critically issues of race, gender, sexual orientation, age, religion, and socioeconomic status in an urban setting.

The 10–15 students who enroll in these courses must go through an application process to be selected. Student participants can use Miami University's service-learning extra-credit option. To fulfill the academic credit requirement, the students write a weekly reflection on specific topics and a final reflection paper integrating their experience in the program with the academic material in the course.

The service experience in Over-the-Rhine is designed to connect what students are learning and discussing in class with what they find in the environment. Student participants engage in direct service, advocacy, or policy research with various community-based organizations. After the first two weekend trips in Over-the-Rhine, they divide into small groups and choose a particular project with a community partner such as a homeless shelter, a low-income housing cooperative, or a community center.

Some examples of projects include painting a wall mural with neighborhood children and residents in a community garden, developing craft projects and other programming with residents at a homeless shelter, researching affordable housing issues for low-income housing organizations, and rehabilitating low-income housing.

Reflection is incorporated into the program through weekly journal entries, regular group-reflection sessions, and a final group-reflection retreat. This intensive community engagement, coupled with critical personal investigation, has made the program transformative for many student participants. Many participants remain engaged in community work and social activism after their work with the program has ended.

Social Action Center

To help build this form of civic engagement into the fabric of the university, I worked to develop a new Social Action Center (SAC) at Miami University. During my second year, in partnership with various social activist groups on campus, I proposed to the director of the Office of Service Learning & Civic Leadership that we create a center on campus dedicated to fostering student involvement in social change efforts on campus and in the community. An independent research project during the summer of 2003 through Miami University's undergraduate summer scholars program enabled me to visit campuses across the country and learn from the experiences of students, faculty, and administrators with civic engagement and service-learning initiatives.

After intense planning and dialogue with campus administrators, SAC opened its doors in spring 2003 as an initiative of the Office of Service Learning & Civic Leadership. As SAC's coordinator, I worked with a student staff and a newly developed student advisory board to envision, plan, and implement programming initiatives aimed at fostering, supporting, and deepening student involvement in social action.

In the first year, 25 student organizations working to effect change through charity, direct service, advocacy, politics, and community organizing affiliated with SAC. Student organizations as diverse as Amnesty International, Big Brothers Big Sisters, the College Green Party, Circle K, the Black Student Action Association, and Students for Peace & Justice are finding a common space to work together at SAC. During the fall semester of 2003, more than 1,800 students came to SAC for meetings, projects, or programs.

SAC seeks to provide students with resources, programs, and ideas that focus on social change. Students working for change on campus are often polarized into organizations pursuing narrow agendas with isolated approaches. Yet social change requires the sustained work of many hands actively engaged for the greater good. Having been involved in direct service, policy advocacy, and community organizing, I have learned

fragmentation leads to a troubling division between service and politics and a narrow understanding of the causes and solutions to social problems.

that authentic social change depends on multiple organizations employing diverse approaches working collaboratively, purposefully, and strategically. SAC seeks to build community between engaged students and student organizations in the spirit of collaboration in order to increase effective action.

By providing a central physical space for students to find service opportunities and for student organizations to base their work, SAC concentrates campus resources and efforts to effect change. SAC programming encourages new interest in social change on campus and challenges engaged students to develop and deepen their commitment to service and social change.

SAC's three primary programming initiatives are the Change Leaders Forum, Leadership Training Workshops, and Issue Dialogues. The Change Leaders Forum is a monthly meeting in which affiliated student organizations collaborate on joint initiatives and build community among students involved in social change efforts. For example, student organizations as diverse as Habitat for Humanity, the ACLU, and the Association for Women Students recently collaborated to coordinate Hunger & Homeless Awareness Week. The Leadership Training Workshops provide needed advice and skill-based training to help students and student organizations become more effective, purposeful, and strategic in promoting change on campus and in the community. Currently being developed, the Issue Dialogues are a series of community dialogues intended to raise the level of awareness on campus of pressing local and global social issues, foster public debate, and encourage involvement in social action. Finally, SAC undertakes community projects that model purposeful and effective social action initiatives. Examples include coordinating the Over-the-Rhine Weekend Experience Program, an Adopt-an-Apartment Project, and an ESL (English as a second language) program.

Creating and institutionalizing both the Weekend Experience Program and the Social Action Center has taken a great deal of time, patience, and rigor. For both initiatives, I have had to work closely with faculty members and university administrators. The success of the Weekend Experience Program in particular has depended on the close relationships I have developed within both the Over-the-Rhine community and the Miami University community. For this initiative to be sustained, my relationship with leaders and organizations in Over-the-Rhine had to shift from a personal to an institutional level with the university. Moreover, I had to develop policies and procedures to systematize the program and train new student staff of SAC to plan and coordinate the weekend trips. Developing relationships, creating policies and procedures, and training new leaders are all necessary steps to institutionalizing a new program within a university structure. While this work has been frustratingly slow at times, my hope is that it will be sustained for years to come.

Collaboration for Social Justice

While I have learned many lessons from these experiences, I would like to focus on one particularly pressing issue: the increasing fragmentation, isolation, and narrowness confronting those working for social change. Such fragmentation leads to a troubling division between service and politics, a narrow understanding of the causes and solutions to social problems, and an isolated, ineffective approach to solving social issues. Society must begin to foster a vision of social change that transcends the constraining bonds imposed by narrow focus. Building community and making change are evolutionary—involving collaboration, consciousness, and rigor.

Commentators and critics have decried the excessive individualism of contemporary American culture that has created a society increasingly polarized and fragmented. Goals of personal advancement and gratification dominate our culture, often at the expense of broader social, moral, and spiritual meaning. Such individualism rejects community, collective action, and any conception of the common good. This fragmentation undermines many social change efforts on campus as well as elsewhere. Students involved in service work on college campuses often work in isolation from those involved in politics and activism. Having worked with all types of groups, I have become aware of the troubling consequences of this division.

Often service-oriented groups focus solely on volunteer work and neglect to understand or address the root causes of social problems that give rise to the conditions that necessitate direct service. While direct service plays an important role in meeting people's immediate needs, by itself this approach cannot effect lasting change if it fails to address the systemic causes that create those needs.

This isolation may arise from a lack of understanding of the structural and political context for service work, but it may also reflect a conscious rejection of conventional politics. Young people have become increasingly cynical and alienated from conventional politics, turning to volunteer work as a way to make a tangible difference in their communities. Volunteerism allows students to develop meaningful relationships, build community, and make concrete improvements in people's lives. Again, such volunteer work is important and unfortunately necessary, but its impact is limited in the long term if it is not coordinated with approaches that address the underlying structures of oppression and inequality. As Henry David Thoreau said, "There are a thousand hacking at the branches of evil to one who is striking at the root."

Students involved in activism and politics often suffer from a closely related phenomenon of isolationism and narrowness of vision. While student activism is by no means as powerful a social force as it was in the 1960s, students of the current generation are still leading efforts to organize against war, advocate for human rights, promote sound environmental policy, organize workers on their campuses, advance civil rights for minority groups, and support numerous other causes. Activist and political organizing play an important role in drawing attention to the effect of oppressive policies on marginalized groups, both locally and globally. Such approaches channel citizen power to challenge and change government and corporate policies that create oppressive conditions. Often, however, student activists focus on abstract policies, with little connection to or concern for the local reality in their own communities. They are ready to denounce International Monetary Fund policies that further impoverish and disempower the Global South, but they do not connect these policies with the poverty of their own local community.

Activism focusing solely on policy and social structures fails to meet the real, everyday needs of disenfranchised, impoverished, or marginalized people. More troubling, isolated activism that is disconnected from oppressed groups can potentially be counterproductive. For example, student labor activists decry worker exploitation in sweatshops across the globe, but can sometimes fail to notice worker abuses on their own campuses. This isolationism and narrowness of vision fundamentally undermines the scope, sustainability, and effectiveness of social change efforts.

These characterizations are admittedly oversimplified. But in my experience working within such organizations, these generalizations capture a troubling trend toward fragmentation within the social change community. Clearly, when employed alone, service and political-activist approaches are woefully inadequate for effecting lasting, substantive social change. The complexity of the problems facing local and global communities demands complex solutions. Effective social change requires purposeful, strategic coordination between collaborative partners utilizing diverse approaches.

One model that captures this approach to social change is the "Social Change Wheel," developed by the Minnesota Campus Compact. The wheel comprises different approaches toward social change, including direct service, community and economic development, community building, grassroots political activity, formal political activity, and confrontational strategies. Alone, each approach represents one spoke radiating outward in isolation. But together, these approaches form a wheel, which creates movement—or *a* movement.

Combating the rampant individualism within American culture demands a radical revisioning of social change. This shift in consciousness, like the shift in tactics, must embrace inclusiveness, collaboration, and a re-articulation of community. Under the common ideology of social justice, such a broad-based movement can unify issues, approaches, and organizations that have, until now, been fragmented and isolated. Throughout his career, Dr. Martin Luther King, Jr., deepened the definition of *movement* and its goals, coming to the conclusion near his death that only a struggle that fought for economic as well as political rights and that built alliances between blacks and working-class and poor whites could make racial and economic justice a reality. King realized that lasting, substantive social change demands tactical coordination and ideological inclusiveness.

Students, faculty, and service-learning practitioners should employ this approach when developing service-learning and civic engagement initiatives. My experience building service-learning programs between Miami University and the Over-the-Rhine community has shown me that such initiatives must foster collaboration among fragmented groups working toward social justice. The continuing viability of higher education as a public institution demands a similarly radical rethinking of its role within a broad-based effort for social justice and democratic renewal.

Students as Academic Entrepreneurs

The Service-Learning Thesis at Bates College

Bates College, a small liberal arts college located in Lewiston, Maine, was founded in 1855 by Maine abolitionists. From its inception, it has been open to men and women of all races and has been dedicated to the principle of active engagement. Service-learning is one prominent form of teaching used at Bates to integrate, implement, and evaluate student involvement in academic learning and civic engagement.

Service-learning occurs in various venues and in academic courses, independent study, research projects, and senior thesis work. Research focused on community issues is an effective way to build and enhance student engagement because it integrates academic experience, personal interest, and prior service-learning and community service work.

The senior thesis at Bates is designed to serve as a capstone for a student's academic career. The psychology department's thesis requirements illustrate efforts to foster high levels of student engagement. Seniors choose between a community-based service-learning thesis and a laboratory-based empirical thesis. Both options are academically rigorous and require data collection and analysis. Students who choose to do a service-learning thesis are supported by a faculty adviser, Center for Service-Learning staff, and a community supervisor. They also attend a weekly seminar with common readings, discussion, and reflection.

For many students, the service-learning thesis is a logical extension of earlier course-based service-learning. Thus, students' service experiences are developmental, becoming more complex as their skills, knowledge, and interests increase. Examples of recent service-learning theses include:

"ASSESSING INFANT AND TODDLER DEVELOPMENT AT EARLY HEAD START: TWO COMPARATIVE CASES"—The student engaged in extensive classroom work and examined archived assessments to determine if entry into the Early Head Start program facilitated a child's success in reaching federally mandated standards.

"TRANSITIONING TO EMPLOYMENT: A COMPARATIVE CASE STUDY OF TWO JUVENILE OFFENDERS"—The student designed and implemented a program of job-search skills for juvenile offenders and then used record review, observation, and interview to determine what internal and external factors affected participants' ability to utilize program offerings.

"DOWN SYNDROME: THE BEHAVIORAL EFFECTS OF INCREASED CALORIC INTAKE"—The student worked one-on-one with a Down Syndrome child in an integrated preschool program and designed and assessed an intervention to reduce the child's food phobias.

"CULTURAL COMPETENCY IN MEDICAL AND MENTAL HEALTH FIELDS: OUTREACH TO MIGRANT POPULATIONS"—The student partnered with a state migrant-health program, providing direct service and developing and implementing a needs assessment. Data on health needs, access to health care, and satisfaction with services were collected and reported to the agency.

Conducting research requested by the community serves a real need and provides a professional, demanding audience. An analysis of student portfolios, research products, and community feedback indicate that community work may indeed be transformational for the student in his or her future career, educational plans, and understanding of the world. The agency also may transform itself as it analyzes and acts on new information.

Research Collaborations at Macalester College

In December 1997, the W.M. Keck Foundation awarded Macalester College a $500,000 challenge grant in support of joint student-faculty research. Alumni, friends, corporations, and other foundations met this challenge, creating an endowment of more than $1 million to support student-faculty summer research collaborations in any discipline.

The Macalester Student-Faculty Collaborative Summer Research Program enables teams of students and faculty to engage in significant projects over 4–10 weeks during the summer. Projects must be related to the faculty member's curricular, pedagogical, scholarly, or creative interests and are planned and executed by the student and faculty member working together. The projects are designed to permit completion of a substantial portion of the work during the summer; students complete a "creative product" by the end of the subsequent academic year. Examples of a creative product may include a musical score or work of art exhibited for public, critical review; an honors project, poster, or paper for publication or presentation at a professional meeting; or a curriculum module or technology application to be implemented by faculty.

The program operates on the premise that demanding intellectual tasks are best learned through direct experience and shared responsibility for their success. Consistent with Macalester's strong commitment to civic engagement, each summer one or two awards are designated for action research projects. For instance, in 2003, Anne Taft '04 and Professor Laura Smith of the geography department used a Collaborative Research Award to study the proposed Northstar commuter rail line between Minneapolis and St. Cloud, Minnesota. They assessed the effects of the Northstar initiative on community planning by examining both the project's decision-making process and the past and current development trends along the corridor.

Taft made connections with key individuals involved in the Northstar project and in the planning departments of communities along the proposed route, including planners and developers, transit proponents, and state legislators. Taft and Smith also gathered and reviewed all pertinent primary sources on state and national commuter rail policy, as well as comprehensive plans for communities along the corridor. Taft incorporated this research into her honors project in geography, a case study lecture delivered to the Transportation Seminar and presented at the Minnesota Academy of Science Conference.

Service and Social Justice in Georgetown University's Curriculum

Georgetown University offers a wide range of social justice activities through which students can play a leadership role, including direct service and action programs, community-based learning courses, and community-based research. The curriculum basis for integrating service with academic learning has expanded considerably during the past 15 years. The Program on Justice and Peace was the first Georgetown academic minor to include a service-learning component as part of its curricular requirements. The Women's Studies Program also contains a service-learning requirement for majors and minors.

Most recently, the department of sociology and anthropology began offering a major and minor concentration in "Social Justice Analysis" that integrates students' participation in community-based learning elective courses, a required gateway course, and a capstone senior community-based research thesis. This innovative program even allows students who are studying abroad to participate in service-learning courses that have been specially developed to support this program, thereby enabling students to work with nonprofit organizations committed to social justice and social change in the host country.

Georgetown also offers the John Carroll Scholars Program, through which academically gifted students who have exhibited strong leadership abilities actively engage in research, service, and reflection activities that help shape their own experiences as well as the experiences of those around them. The program seeks individuals who want to make a lasting difference in the fields and communities they engage. The program provides models and skills to help these scholars make the most effective use of their undergraduate years, and to assist them in moving from the undergraduate experience to their post-graduate academic and professional lives.

SOCIAL JUSTICE RESEARCH, TEACHING, AND SERVICE

The Center for Social Justice Research, Teaching and Service opened in January 2001 with the purpose of concretely and imaginatively manifesting Georgetown's commitment to "justice and the common good." The center strives to consolidate and develop work in three key areas: service, curriculum, and research. In the first area, the center incorporates and builds on the vibrant student work of direct service and the learning it fosters, whether from tutoring and mentoring or arts education and job development training.

Curriculum work includes promoting and helping to develop curricular offerings that incorporate community-based work, as well as helping students make the connection between service and justice. Georgetown faculty have designed courses that build in opportunities for direct or indirect service in the local community in a way that makes clear, for example, the intellectual context and the policy implications of the service the students render. Courses such as "The Contemporary City" in the sociology department and "Teaching/Literacy/Community Action" in the English department offer students with curricular vehicles for providing service that is explored and deepened in the classroom.

The center also serves as a catalyst to consolidate and advance the exciting community-based research projects. It seeks to provide research opportunities for Georgetown University students and faculty to work in partnership with communities in the district to develop the assets the communities have and to bring needed resources to them in a mutually beneficial way.

For additional information about the Center for Social Justice, see http://socialjustice.georgetown.edu.

STUDENT COMMUNITY RESEARCH

Historically, the Center for Social Justice's Office of Research has worked with community organizations to develop and maintain relationships that lead to the articulation of relevant research projects. Students have typically conducted these projects as part of their coursework. Yet some students want the opportunity to conduct research in collaboration with community organizations without the constraints of a course or the time frame of one semester. To address these interests, the Office of Research has given students opportunities to work as interns within community organizations. These projects are brokered through the Office of Research to assist students in finding projects that meet their interests and/or thesis needs and that match with the skills, knowledge, and interests requested by community organizations.

Research interns have typically worked with the organization for 5–10 hours a week and have engaged in a range of research and development projects. One project included background research on ways to track homeless children in the District of Columbia. Another intern worked with a community organization that was conducting research on Latina women's health. The student volunteer is providing assistance with the advertisement and media relations for this project.

Students either work with organizations on a volunteer basis or are paid through their work-study allotment and/or grant funding. A student may serve as the primary researcher on a particular topic or integrate into an existing team of researchers. If the community organization is conducting the research as part of its core mission, the intern is typically more independent of the Office of Research, which periodically evaluates the success of the match but otherwise takes a hands-off approach. Students who lead projects on behalf of the community organizations meet more regularly with the assistant director of the Office of Research for guidance and consultation on the projects. The Office of Research encourages students to participate in the annual Community Research and Learning (CoRAL) Network local conference on CBR as a means to write up and disseminate their results to the larger community.

Students as Engaged Scholars at Princeton University

More than 200 Princeton University students each year devote their academic work to furthering the mission of local community-based organizations through the Community-Based Learning Initiative (CBLI). Alone or in groups, students collaborate on community-driven research projects in departments such as architecture, engineering, sociology, anthropology, molecular biology, the Woodrow Wilson School of Public and International Affairs, and the writing and teacher preparation programs.

The research must be rigorously academic and meet the legitimate needs of partner organizations. Student course projects—which have included such wide-ranging topics as child-proof handgun technology, the terrorism readiness of New Jersey's nuclear reactors, the demographics of tuberculosis, and immigrant welfare—have had a real impact on the community.

Independent research in a student's major field of study in the junior and senior year is a hallmark of the Princeton academic experience. Each year, students do important research in partnership with local and national organizations. In her sociology thesis research in Philadelphia, for example, Hilary Freudenthal '01 uncovered a significantly greater likelihood of death sentence conviction, controlling for the type of case, if a defendant is represented by a private lawyer rather than a defense association lawyer.

Operations research and financial engineering major Meghan Fehlig '02 documented the long history of traffic congestion and attempts to redress it on Route 1. Her analysis demonstrated the failure of supply-side approaches to reducing traffic and pointed to promising approaches in managing demand. Working with a local environmental organization, she suggested a synthesis of solutions that have worked in other realms (including emissions trading, electronic toll collection, market-equilibrium efficiency theory, value pricing, rationing theory, and game theory) as a realistic, sustainable, and equitable approach to reducing rush-hour congestion.

Jessica Lautin '03 worked with Princeton's local African-American community for her thesis research in history. She examined the relationship between Princeton University and its John-Witherspoon area neighbors. Her work exposed the deep roots of current controversies over the shape of the town's future, such as downtown development and the expansion of the Arts Council building.

CBLI can have a transformative effect on students who find that community-based academic work is meaningful, empowering, and satisfying. Many students who do community-based work get hooked—and want to do more. CBLI now provides opportunities across a full four-year undergraduate career at Princeton: from CBLI projects in first-year writing seminars and freshman seminars, to research opportunities in 200 to 400 level courses in many departments, to junior papers, to summer internship opportunities working with nonprofit organizations, to significant pieces of independent research for the senior thesis.

For more information, see www.princeton.edu/~cbli.

For example, Robin Williams '04 began his CBLI career as a freshman in Professor Kitsi Watterson's writing course, "The Writer in the Community." Later he took Professor Daniel Notterman's course, "Diseases in Children: Causes, Costs, and Choices," and then served as a CBLI summer intern working with TRIAD, an AIDS organization in his native North Carolina. He then completed his senior thesis, "State Policy Making and Syringe Deregulation: The Determinants of Successful Reform," in partnership with the Drug Policy Alliance. He identified the crucial factors in the battle for legalization of needle exchange programs in Connecticut, New Jersey, and Massachusetts and effectively created a strategic map for advocates of such programs in other states.

Finally, CBLI continually works to raise the profile and legitimacy of engaged scholarship locally and nationally through conference presentations, workshops, and the CBLI newsletter and website.

Conclusion:
Beyond Tactical Service-Learning

MUCH OF THE PROGRESS in service-learning during the past decade has been what might be called *tactical.* The service-learning movement has been able to convince an ever-greater number of faculty that community-based work is beneficial to student learning. Faculty can use such work to address issues related to course content and academic skills. For example, a student taking a class in urban studies may be better able to understand issues like immigration, schools, jobs, housing, and economic development when the course includes a community-based component. In other words, service-learning has shown itself to be a useful faculty resource.

However, if the goal is to serve the civic as well as the academic mission of higher education, effective pedagogy of this kind is not enough. Service-learning cannot function simply as a pedagogical tool—a strategy that energizes but does not transform the curriculum. Its deeper potential rests in the fact that it can affect not only *how* students learn but *what* they learn. It can, in fact, change the very meaning of what it means to learn.

The concept of students as colleagues does not, of course, imply that everyone involved in the learning process plays the same role or exercises the same kind of authority. Students—like faculty, staff, and community partners—bring distinctive perspectives, concerns, and strengths to this process. It does, however, imply that students cannot be regarded primarily as consumers of information; they must be allowed to function themselves as knowledge producers. Indeed, the very same decades that brought the service-learning movement to national prominence also saw the widespread dissemination of important research on the teaching-learning process.

For example, in an article entitled "Organizing for Learning: A New Imperative" (1997), Peter Ewell identifies some of what current research tells us about this process. Under the heading "What We Know About Learning," he notes that the difference between "knowledge based on recall and deeper forms of understanding" rests on insights such as "the learner is not a 'receptacle' of knowledge, but rather creates his or her learning actively and uniquely," that "direct experience decisively shapes individual understanding," and that "learning occurs best in the context of a compelling 'presenting problem'" (p. 4). Under the heading "What We Know About Promoting Learning," Ewell's first suggestion for "remaking instruction" calls for approaches that "emphasize application and experience" (p. 5).

Findings and guidelines like these make it very clear why a strategy like service-learning can so powerfully enhance undergraduate education. However, they also suggest that the kind of motivation and participation deep student learning demands closely resembles the kind of motivation and participation effective civic engagement demands: engagement in the classroom and engagement in the community are complementary concepts. Students who have been reduced to knowledge consumers on campus will probably wind up seeing themselves primarily as goods and service consumers in their attitude toward government and society. Harry Boyte (2000), one of the academy's most articulate advocates for civic renewal, captures this mindset when he points to the pitfalls of our legacy of positivism, or reducing "knowledge" to facts:

> Positivism structures our research, it structures our disciplines, our teaching, our institutions long after it had been intellectually discredited. It structures patterns of evaluation, assessment, outcome measures, sustaining patterns of one-way service delivery and the conceptualization of poor and powerless groups as needy "clients," not as competent citizens, as those in need of our assistance. It infuses government spending patterns for "interventions" to fix social problems. It shapes the institutions of the market, the media, health care and political life. (p. 50)

Thus, the failure to see students as colleagues has implications that extend well beyond higher education.

Students as Change Agents

To transform the culture of higher education so that it promotes not only deep learning but also civic values and skills, we must begin to take our understanding and utilization of service-learning to a new level. One cannot reform academic culture without changing traditional practices; this insight has been central to the service-learning movement's appeal. However, it also is not enough to utilize new practices in more or less conventional ways, regarding both students and community members as mere appendages of faculty practice and faculty culture. New thinking and reflective practice require new ways of acting: making the still too often marginalized voices of students (and community partners) a *substantive* part of the curricular design and delivery process represents just such a new way of acting.

Until now, the service-learning movement has emphasized the role of the community far more than that of students in shaping engagement. Without wishing in any way to deny the importance of community voice, we suggest that by themselves successful faculty-community partnerships are not enough to achieve the *civic* goals of service-learning. Student initiative, student responsibility, and student ownership of engagement together constitute a key variable in determining what the social "subtext" of the experience communicates, regardless of its specific academic outcomes or concrete community benefits.

both faculty and community members must remain open to insights and strengths they may never have suspected students possess.

With this in mind, we offer three lessons from the programs and initiatives documented in this book. First, students must be partners from the beginning of the engagement process. Their presence changes the dynamic of all that follows. The more a syllabus is simply handed to students as a *fait accompli*, the less it teaches them about their own potential and their own duties as change agents. Second, like community partners, students should be seen as involved in a genuinely reciprocal undertaking. This means they not only make decisions concerning their own specific spheres of activity, but also help define the shape and the significance of the work as a whole. Third, their potential to contribute should not be artificially limited. This does not mean faculty, students, and community all have the same things to teach and to contribute. But both faculty and community members must deliberately remain open to insights and strengths they may never have suspected students possessed. Genuine respect for all participants leads to maximum advantage for all participants.

The Challenge of Student Engagement

Will the service-learning movement learn from and adopt the kinds of programs and activities documented in the preceding chapters? We believe it will, if for no other reason than that students represent a resource few institutions can afford to do without. Whether the movement will recognize the deeper implications of full student participation remains much less certain, given the many obstacles that lie in the way of such a development. Hence, it is important to temper our hopes for the future with a frank acknowledgement of issues that will need to be addressed.

Most higher education institutions reinforce a power dynamic that leads to exclusion rather than inclusion. The fragmentation so characteristic of colleges and universities is a direct manifestation of this impulse to compartmentalize on the basis of preconceived notions of expertise and responsibility. In such a system, students are most often seen as having little to offer except their tuition money and their respectful attention.

Far from being seen as potential colleagues, new students in particular are socialized into a kind of extended, psychologically disempowering probation in which what they are not yet qualified to do is emphasized far more than their latent strengths. Exacerbating this psychological handicapping is the failure of many faculty to recognize and take into account the full implications of the new information age. Traditional assumptions of structured, linear development—demarcated, of course, by number and type of academic degrees—remain firmly in place. Student initiative may be welcomed in theory but is too often dismissed in practice.

Similarly, demands for greater student voice are often seen as inherently disrespectful, immediately evoking images of the rebellious 1960s and 1970s, when many of today's academic leaders were themselves in college. After all, would students challenge the system if they respected it? And why do they challenge it in the first place? Isn't their hidden agenda simply to make things easier for themselves by dumbing down the curriculum and weakening accountability? Even when those in power are careful not to say so openly, their suspicion of student-led change is profound.

Many structural obstacles also make student leadership and student initiative problematic. For example, most collegiate student bodies turn over every five years, so few mechanisms (and even fewer incentives) are in place for students to pass along information from one class to the next.

Larger institutions and commuter institutions must also factor in the difficulty of establishing any kind of cohesive student community. Although the faculty community is fragmented into departments, programs, and other administrative units, the student community does not even have the binding mechanisms the faculty community has. Granted, there may be a minority of students who would like to play a more substantive role in their own education, but what about all the others who simply "show up" and then disappear again into their purely private concerns? When one adds to all these obstacles the discontinuity caused by breaks and summer vacations, not to mention many students' sense of the fundamental transience of their college experience, one may well conclude that even a genuine desire on the part of faculty and administrators to honor student voice may have difficulty finding any real resonance on the other side.

And yet, are the factors that argue against cultivating student voice on campus any less daunting than those that argue against cultivating the voice of citizens in shaping public life?

Service work should not be seen as self-sacrificing any more than it is seen as punitive.

Student statements like those that punctuate *The New Student Politics* on practically every page suggest that at least some significant portion of what we perceive as student disengagement actually reflects intergenerational misunderstanding and an absence of effective "enabling mechanisms" (Walshok, 1995). How many faculty even realize that the qualities that characterize today's "millennial" generation vary considerably from the "Gen X" stereotypes many still take for granted?

We hope that the examples this volume provides will lead many in higher education to reassess their assumptions about how they and their students can work together for everyone's mutual benefit. In a spirit of cautious optimism, we conclude this text with a set of key recommendations based on what we have learned.

Concluding Recommendations

First, there is no reason why every college and university in the United States that is sincerely committed to education for the public good cannot develop and maintain a service scholarship program. All that is required is a certain percentage of already available scholarship moneys reserved for those students who not only demonstrate academic promise but also social responsibility and initiative.

Ideally, such scholarships would be modeled on athletic scholarships, whereby those selected would be expected to form the nucleus of the institution's service "team," using their skills and experience to interest other students in service and to help faculty and community members build truly reciprocal partnerships. Like students with sports scholarships, students could be recruited for service scholarships on the basis of their ability to excel at a particular "position"; i.e., they have demonstrated excellence in addressing a particular area of social concern in their pre-college years or off-campus life.

Service-learning offices should collaborate closely with work-study programs to ensure not only that additional funds be found to support service leaders but also that student service efforts be "bent back" to add value to institutionalized service initiatives. Students who work in the community are a rich source of community information; with special training, they can become qualified to assist both faculty and fellow students at a particular community site. Furthermore, while many financial aid offices struggle to meet the federal requirements for the percentage of work-study funds that must be used in support of community-related work, other offices, departments, and programs that could partner with community groups find their ability to do so limited primarily by staffing considerations.

Second, students chosen to work as service leaders should be given the highest quality conceptual and practical preparation. Service work should not be seen as self-sacrificing any more than it is seen as punitive. Non-service students should marvel not so much at the commitment of their service peers as at the opportunities those peers have to develop extraordinary personal and professional strengths. Service leaders should be seen as the stars of higher education, students who represent the gold standard for what it means to be an educated person.

Hence, training should never be reduced to a one-time event. Rather, it should be a vehicle for ongoing growth and self-discovery. It should provide multiple opportunities for participating students to acquire special—and in some cases, clearly differentiated—sets of skills. For instance, students facilitating the work of community groups need different skills and strategies from students working primarily with student groups. Students partnering with faculty may well need to expand and deepen their understanding of academic culture to include such topics as tenure and promotion considerations, departmental structures and requirements, and institutional protocols.

Mentoring younger students to sustain program effectiveness and to take over from their older peers is a training area that deserves special attention. The cyclical nature of student collegiate careers can be seen as a serious impediment to program continuity or as an opportunity for student-student relationships of a singularly powerful nature. When students learn to take responsibility for their own legacy, they graduate with strengths usually reserved for much more experienced adults.

The same can be said for students who have learned to succeed as engaged scholars, contributing the kind of high-quality research that forms the bedrock of higher education while at the same time experiencing the challenges and satisfactions of emerging as public intellectuals. Such students may also find that they have entered into relationships with faculty that are transformative in their depth and significance. Encouraging service through engaged research opens up important additional opportunities for students to experience the power of ideas in a democracy.

Still other kinds of faculty-student partnerships can also serve to reinvigorate faculty. The unique insights and energy students can contribute to the curriculum planning process should be tapped whenever appropriate and possible. Since such collaborations in no way challenge faculty expertise or diminish faculty responsibility, they can be said to represent a win-win situation: faculty must ultimately decide on course design but they can do so with the added advantage of a student perspective.

Finally, institutions should understand "students as colleagues" in the context of a broad institutional commitment to civic engagement. Student voice and institutional commitment must not be seen as separate issues. When students see themselves as genuine contributors to core institutional values, their voices become most articulate and compelling. In the end, they can finally knit together the seemingly disparate priorities of faculty affairs and student affairs, of the admissions office and the alumni office, of the institution as a community of scholars and as a citizen.

Perhaps in a decade, the national service-learning movement will be as much enriched by new student voices as it was during the past decade by new faculty and administration voices. Perhaps in a decade, it will hardly seem strange to think of students as knowledge producers in their own right. Perhaps in a decade, students who might not otherwise have gained a confident public voice will have developed one through student service-learning leadership. And perhaps, through them, students who might not otherwise have found a voice at all will have begun to speak out.

References

Boyte, H. (2000, July/August). The struggle against positivism. *Academe: Bulletin of the American Association of University Professors, 86*(4), 46–51.

Ewell, P.T. (1997, December). Organizing for learning: A new imperative. *AAHE Bulletin,* 3–6.

Walshok, M.L. (1995). *Knowledge without boundaries: What America's research universities can do for the economy, the workplace, and the community.* San Francisco: Jossey-Bass.